Ministries
of MERCY

Ministries *of* MERCY

THE CALL OF THE JERICHO ROAD

THIRD EDITION

TIMOTHY KELLER

P&R
PUBLISHING
P.O. BOX 817 • PHILLIPSBURG • NEW JERSEY 08865-0817

© 1989, 1997, 2015 by Timothy Keller
Third edition 2015

Unless otherwise indicated, Scripture quotations are from the HOLY BIBLE, NEW INTERNATIONAL VERSION. Copyright © 1973, 1978, 1984 International Bible Society. Used by permission of Zondervan Bible Publishers.

Scripture quotations marked (RSV) are from the *Revised Standard Version of the Bible*, © 1946, 1952, 1971 by the Division of Christian Education of the National Council of the Churches of Christ in the United States of America. Used by permission.

Scripture quotations marked (KJV) are from the King James Version.

ISBN: 978-1-59638-955-7 (pbk)
ISBN: 978-1-59638-956-4 (ePub)
ISBN: 978-1-59638-957-1 (Mobi)

Printed in the United States of America

Library of Congress Cataloging-in-Publication Data

Keller, Timothy J., 1950-
Ministries of mercy : the call of the Jericho road / Timothy Keller. -- Third Edition.
    pages cm
Includes bibliographical references.
ISBN 978-1-59638-955-7 (pbk.)
1. Corporal works of mercy. 2. Church and social problems. I. Title.
BV4647.M4K45 2015
253--dc23
                            2014047917

To Kathy,
who had a social conscience first

Contents

Editor's Note

Ministries of Mercy was written in 1988 as part of a research project for the Presbyterian Church in America. Many of the statistics and institutions have changed since that time, but the underlying principles—and needs—remain. Our desire is that this book and the principles of mercy ministry it discusses will aid you in the service of your church and city.

Some excellent resources have become available since this book's original publication. Several of these are listed under Recommended Reading at the back of this new edition.

The One Who Showed Mercy

On one occasion an expert in the law stood up to test Jesus. "Teacher," he asked, "what must I do to inherit eternal life?"

"What is written in the Law?" he replied. "How do you read it?"

He answered: " 'Love the Lord your God with all your heart and with all your soul and with all your strength and with all your mind'; and, 'Love your neighbor as yourself.' "

"You have answered correctly," Jesus replied. "Do this and you will live."

But he wanted to justify himself, so he asked Jesus, "And who is my neighbor?"

In reply Jesus said: "A man was going down from Jerusalem to Jericho, when he fell into the hands of robbers. They stripped him of his clothes, beat him and went away, leaving him half dead. A priest happened to be going down the same road, and when he saw the man, he passed by on the other side. So too, a Levite, when he came to the place and saw him, passed by on the other side. But a Samaritan, as he traveled, came where the man was; and when he saw him, he took pity on him. He went to him and bandaged his wounds, pouring on oil and wine. Then he put the man on his own donkey, took him to an inn and took care of him. The next day he took out two silver coins and gave them to the innkeeper. 'Look after him,' he said, 'and when I return, I will reimburse you for any extra expense you may have.'

"Which of these three do you think was a neighbor to the man who fell into the hands of robbers?"

The expert in the law replied, "The one who had mercy on him."

Jesus told him, "Go and do likewise." (Luke 10:25–37)

THE DANGEROUS ROAD

The road to Jericho is steep and dangerous. So dangerous, in fact, that people called it "the bloody way." Jerusalem rests at 3000 feet above sea level, while Jericho, only seventeen miles away, sits on land 1000 feet *below* the level of the Mediterranean. The road between the towns descends sharply through mountainous territory full of crags and caves, allowing thieves to hide, strike, and escape with great ease. Traveling the Jericho road in those days was very much like walking through a dark alley in the worst part of a modern city, except that it was many miles to the nearest streetlight.

In this "dark alley" a man fell victim to a social problem—crime. "He fell into the hands of robbers. They stripped him of his clothes, beat him and went away, leaving him half dead" (v. 30).

THE TWO WHO WALKED BY

A priest and a Levite soon came along in turn, and each passed by on the far side of the road, not wishing to become involved in the man's needs.

We should not be too quick to scorn these men, or we may discover we are convicting ourselves. Consider how you might react if you were anxiously taking a shortcut through a dark alley. Imagine that you see a groaning man on the ground, conclusive evidence that a marauding band of thugs is watching you around the corner! Surely the wisest thing to do is to hurry on to safety and send some official to look after the poor victim. So you run.

There may have been another, very "religious" reason for the priest and Levite to avoid the man. Levitical law declared that anyone touching a dead body was ceremonially "unclean" (Num. 19:11–16), excluding him from worship ceremonies for seven days. What if this man were already dead, or about to die anyway? How easy it would have been for these religious professionals to think, "This will get in the way of my discharging a higher calling!"

So they walked by the man. In the process, however, they also passed by the clear teaching of Scripture—to have mercy on even strangers in need (Lev. 19:34). The irony of this verse is that the priests and Levites were the very officers of God's people who were charged with helping the needy. The priests were public health officials, along with their other duties; the Levites were distributors of alms to the poor. This was a priestly calling, and yet these two pit their *schedule* (full of ceremonies and other valid religious duties) against their *purpose*. Clearly they neglected the principle that to obey is better than sacrifice (1 Sam. 15:22).

THE ONE WHO SHOWED MERCY

Finally a traveling Samaritan arrived, a sworn enemy of the Jewish man lying in his blood. The Samaritan faced the same danger that the priest and Levite had faced. In addition, all of his training and experience should have led him to simply step *on* the victim, not just over him! Samaritans and Jews were the bitterest enemies. (When the Jews were furious with Jesus, they called him a "Samaritan" [John 8:48], because they could not think of a worse name!) Nevertheless, in opposition to all these forces, the Samaritan had "compassion" (v. 33). This compassion was full-bodied, leading him to meet a variety of needs. This compassion provided friendship and advocacy, emergency medical treatment, transportation, a hefty financial subsidy, and even a follow-up visit.

The phrase "ministry of mercy," which we will use throughout this book, comes from verse 37, where Jesus commands us to provide shelter, finances, medical care, and friendship to people who lack them. We have nothing less than an order from our Lord in the most categorical of terms. "Go and do likewise!" Our paradigm is the Samaritan, who risked his safety, destroyed his schedule, and became dirty and bloody through personal involvement with a needy person of another race and social class. Are we as Christians obeying this command *personally*? Are we as a church obeying this command *corporately*?

QUESTIONS RAISED

The parable of the Good Samaritan is nothing if not provocative. To begin with, it is a reverse trap. A law expert sought to trap Jesus into saying something derogatory about the Law, but Jesus showed him that the Jewish leaders are the ones who do not really keep the Law at all. Our Lord attacks the complacency of comfortably religious people who protect themselves from the needs of others. The points he makes are no less shattering to us today, and his teaching instantly raises many questions.

First, there is the question of the *necessity* of mercy to our very existence as Christians. We must not miss the fact that this parable is an answer to the question "What must I do to inherit eternal life?" Jesus responds by pointing the law expert to the example of the Good Samaritan, who cared for the physical and economic needs of the man in the road. Bear in mind that Jesus was posed the very same question in Mark 10:17 by the rich young ruler. There, too, Jesus concludes by saying, "Go, sell everything you have and give to the poor" (v. 21). It appears that Jesus sees care for the poor as part of the *essence* of being a Christian.

How can this be? In Matthew 25:31ff. we see Jesus judging people on the basis of their ministry to the hungry, naked, homeless, sick, and imprisoned. Does he mean that only the social workers are going to heaven? Aren't we saved by faith in Christ alone? Then why does the ministry of mercy appear to be so central to the very definition of a Christian?

Second, there is the question of the *scope* and dimension of the ministry of mercy. Remember that the law expert did not deny the requirement to care for those in need. Virtually no one in the world does! But still he asked, "Who *is* my neighbor?" We can see him as the typical Westerner, saying:

> "Oh come on, now, Lord, let's be reasonable. We know we are to help out the unfortunate, but just how far do we have to go?"

> "You don't mean we should pour ourselves out for anyone! Doesn't charity begin at home?"

> "You don't mean every Christian must get deeply involved with hurting and needy people. I am not very good in that kind of work; it's not my gift."

> "I have a busy schedule and I am extremely active in my evangelical church. Isn't this sort of thing the government's job, anyway?"

"I barely have enough money for myself!"

"Aren't many of the poor simply irresponsible?"

When he shows us the indifferent priest and Levite, Jesus unmasks the many false limits that religious people put on the command to "love your neighbor." In the Samaritan himself, Jesus shows us that the neighbor to whom we must render aid is *anyone* at all in need, even an enemy. Any person reading this parable begins to feel trapped by its logic. But isn't it unrealistic? Aren't the needs of the world's poor too overwhelming? Is Jesus saying that we must all assume a life of voluntary poverty and move in with the downtrodden? Are we ready to make no distinctions between the deserving and the undeserving poor?

Third, there is the question of the *motive* or dynamic of the ministry of mercy. Israel had God's Law, which clearly demanded mercy to one's neighbor, but Jesus shows that the experts in the Law had interpreted it in a way that frustrated its basic purposes. *It is not enough to simply know one's duty.* The priest and the Levite had all the biblical knowledge, all the ethical principles, and all the ethnic affinity with the man in the road. It was not enough. The Samaritan had none of these things, but he had *compassion*. It was enough! What will really make the church merciful? It will not be enough to manipulate American Christians to feel guilty because they are so "rich." Then what *will* make the church powerful to heal the deep hurts, fill the deep needs, and transform the surrounding society?

For decades, evangelicals have avoided the radical nature of the teaching of the parable of the Good Samaritan. At most, we have heard it telling us to prepare a fruit basket for the needy each Christmas, or to give money to relief agencies when there is a famine or earthquake in a distant nation. But it is time to listen more closely, because the world, which never *was* "safe" to live in, is becoming even less so. We are finally beginning to wonder why there are suddenly hundreds of thousands "stripped and lying half dead" in the streets of our own cities.

 Only a small number of people in the history of the world have lived in relatively "safe" conditions. War, injustice, oppression, famine, natural disaster, family breakdown, disease, mental illness, physical disability, racism, crime, scarcity of resources, class struggle—these "social problems" are the results of our alienation from God. They bring deep misery and violence to the lives of most of humanity. The majority of people who read this book, however, probably belong to the relatively small group of folk who, through God's kindness, lead an existence generally free from these forces.

This comparative comfort can isolate us in a fictitious world where suffering is difficult to find. But this isolation is fragile, for suffering surrounds us—even in the suburbs! We need an accurate view of the world in which we live. Perhaps we need to see that, instead of living on islands of ease, we are all living on the Jericho Road.

INTRODUCTION

Who Is My Neighbor?

Someone once said that a "World Christian" needs to read the newspaper along with the Bible. In a sense, this parable of Jesus *directs* us to do so. Though the law expert sought to limit the concept of "neighbor," Jesus expands the concept by showing that *anyone* in need is our neighbor. The priest and the Levite who pass to the other side of the man in the road represent those of us who avoid any close examination of the person in need. Here, our Lord is teaching us to recognize our neighbors lying in the road. Do we middle-class Americans recognize and know our needy neighbors?

Consider Angela, a homeless woman. In the height of the homeless crisis in the mid 1980s, one idealistic seminarian once tried to reach out to Angela; in so doing, he was surprised by what he discovered. His poignant description of their encounter follows:

> A once beautiful woman, Angela, is withering away in front of the library on our urban campus. She wears many layers of clothes. They are plastered on her brittle body like clashing layers of peeling paint. She doesn't have socks on, but it's cold and the weather is growing hostile. I offered her food once, but she rudely rejected it. She turns away abruptly when I try to talk to her. Stung with bitterness I recoil. But then I gradually begin understanding how prejudiced we are with expectations of the poor. My arrogant anticipation of gratitude kills the goodness of the deed. She is hungry, exposed and sick; yet I resist reaching out, because she might not welcome me. Which one

of us is truly sick? Angela, you're a mirror thrust before us, but can we bear the sight?[1]

Have you ever had an experience with someone like Angela? Most likely you have, especially since the poor have become more and more visible throughout the United States in the past few decades. Their presence forces most of us to realize that we do not know or understand the poor at all. Nearly all the hard, cold facts about people in poverty surprise the average middle-class believer.

But Jesus calls us to look, listen, and learn. Let's do that by looking at a "cross section" of needy people. Though we will wade through lots of numbers and statistics in the process, our goal is to look our neighbors in the faces, rather than walking in a wide circle around them.

THE GROWTH OF POVERTY

Kathi was a Jewish homemaker living a normal middle class life. When her son was killed in an accident, her husband took to drinking and withdrew from her. He divorced her and she was left alone at age 43 with no job skills, no job history, and no alimony (her state had a no fault divorce law). Her husband recovered from his alcoholism, remarried and was soon making $65,000 a year. She began working as a waitress for $900 a month. She could not pay the rent on her one bedroom apartment and still eat. She began drinking and sought a psychiatrist, who did little more than prescribe tranquilizers. She began living in welfare hotels, and now is in a rehabilitation center for indigent women.[2]

Kathi is one example of the growing number of those we call "poor." One out of every seven North Americans is poor. Nearly 42 percent of American children grow up in low-income families, and almost one child in four—about 23 percent—grows up in poverty.[3] If we provided no other figures in this chapter, these alone should weigh on a Christian's heart.

1. Mev Puleo, *Christian Century* (24 April 1985): 408.
2. George Grant, *The Dispossessed: Homelessness in America* (Fort Worth: Dominion Press, 1986), 71–72.
3. Colin Greer, "Something Is Robbing Our Children of Their Future," *Parade Magazine*, 4 March 1995, 4.

During the prosperous years of 1950 until the mid 1970s, the percentage of the American population that lived in poverty fell from 30 percent to just over 11 percent. But between 1970 and 1995, the number of poor people in the United States increased from 25.4 million to 36.4 million—nearly 14 percent of the population.[4] (The federal government considers a family of four to be in poverty if its total annual income is $14,800 or less. If the same family earns $27,380, it is considered low-income.)[5]

In addition, (as the song says) the poor really *are* getting poorer. According to the Census Bureau, the real median income in 1995 was 3.8 percent below its 1989 level, this despite the fact that the top 5 percent of all wage earners own a greater and greater proportion of all society's wealth. Thus, for increasing numbers of North Americans, work provided no relief from poverty.[6] And many experts project that the 1996 Welfare Reform Act will remove aid from 2.6 million people, who will need nongovernment agencies to provide relief, job training, and other services. Technically, the bill would increase the "poverty gap" for families with children by more than $4 billion, or 20 percent. Families in which the parents are unemployed (or underemployed) and receive government assistance typically have incomes already below the poverty level. The bill will most likely make these families' needs more acute.[7]

Though the mid-nineties saw a few victories in the "war on poverty," a closer look reveals to us many ominous subtrends that foretell a bleak future. Let's look at those trends.

THE HOMELESS

George is twenty-eight (some surveys find the average homeless person to be thirty-four.) He is a former high school basketball star who once was a construction worker. After losing his job a year ago, his wife

4. Paul Koegel et al. "The Causes of Homelessness" in *Homelessness in America* (Washington DC: Oryx Press, 1996).

5. Greer, "Something Is Robbing Our Children," 4.

6. *Why Are People Homeless? NCH Fact Sheet #1.* (Washington DC: National Coalition for the Homeless, 1997), 1.

7. David A. Super, Sharon Parrott, Susan Steinmetz, and Cindy Mann, *The New Welfare Law—Summary* (Center on Budget and Policy Priorities, 1996), 3.

asked him to leave. He lived on couches of friends until the friend-
ships wore thin. Since then he has been on the street. He rarely drinks
alcohol and keeps his light brown corduroy pants and red-checked
shirt meticulously clean. Last fall he held a job for six weeks at a pizza
joint; no one knew he was homeless. He often worked without sleep
and with no alarm clock to wake him from the subways or abandoned
tenements, he missed several days and was finally fired. "You can't
get a job without a home, and you can't get a home without a job."

Experts agree that it is close to impossible to get an accurate count
of just how many people are homeless in the United States. Some believe
it is well over a half million; others project it is less. They do know that
homelessness has increased considerably in the last decade owing primarily to two trends: a growing shortage of affordable rental housing
and a simultaneous increase in poverty.[8] And two factors account for
the increasing poverty: decreasing labor-market opportunities for large
segments of the work force, and the declining value and availability of
public benefits.[9] In other words, George's sentiments—"You can't get
a job without a home, and you can't get a home without a job"—are
often the case for most of our homeless neighbors.

Who are the homeless? Most of us think of old men with drinking problems, or mental patients forced out of overcrowded institutions
because of budget cuts. While these kinds of people did indeed make
up the majority of the homeless in the 1980s, that is now changing.
An increasing number are the "new poor," former working-class people
currently jobless because of the massive loss of manufacturing/industrial
jobs and the demand for high-tech (translate: high-skilled) jobs. Even
more disturbing is that many more are whole families with children,
displaced by the "gentrification" of inner cities, the conversion of cheap
housing into expensive housing for professionals. The number of homeless families has increased significantly in the past decade; families with
children are currently the fastest growing group of the homeless population, approximately 40 percent.[10] Thirty-five percent of homeless women

8. *Why Are People Homeless?*, 1.
9. Ibid.
10. Ibid., 2.

and children are fleeing abuse, 25 percent of the single adult homeless population suffer from some form of manageable mental illness, and 22 percent of the general homeless population likely suffer from a substance abuse disorder.[11]

These statistics and others suggest that the "new" average homeless person is an unemployed parent in his or her mid thirties looking for work, battling personal challenges as well as those of an entire system that seems to be working against him or her.

> Most of the folks we deal with day in and day out are from the fringe of the middle class. Many owned homes before the big lay-offs. None had ever known real want before. What we're seeing is a change in the structure of American society so fundamental that no one will remain unaffected.[12]—A shelter operator in New Orleans

> Who will hire a twenty year old woman with no high school education and four kids? What are we as a society doing to prepare the kind of work ethic (for these people) to support their children? I have never encountered a client who did not want to work; most just don't have the opportunities or the confidence to pursue change.—Lorraine Minor, director of counseling at City Union Mission in Kansas City, Missouri

THE WORKING POOR

Many of us believe that most of the poor are poor simply because they will not work. But the facts contradict this myth. A significant decline in wages, jobs, and public benefits along with the transformation of the industrialized labor market into a global computerized one all have contributed to increasingly difficult conditions for the working poor. Between 1973 and 1993, the percentage of workers earning wages below the poverty line increased from 23.9 percent to 26.9 percent, while those earning less than 75 percent of the poverty line doubled. Families need to earn at least twice the minimum wage in full-time jobs just to afford a two-bedroom apartment at fair market rent. A look across the country in any number of homeless shelters will show the link between

11. Ibid.
12. Grant, *The Dispossessed*, 34.

impoverished workers and homelessness; most house significant numbers of full-time (minimum) wage earners. In fact, a 1996 survey revealed that one out of five homeless persons is employed in full- or part-time jobs.[13]

Though details differ, the poor in America break down roughly this way: Approximately one-third of the poor are children. Another third are adults who are working, but not making a wage that lifts them out of poverty. A sixth consist of the elderly and the mentally or physically disabled. Only the final sixth consist of the "controversial" people—single parents home with children, and persons who are able-bodied but not working. It is not fair to simply consider all these people "lazy." A great number of them suffer with debilitating social and emotional problems. But even if we did count many in this group as the "shiftless" poor of the popular imagination, we see that it is only a fraction of the massive group of needy North Americans.

THE CHILDREN OF POVERTY

The statistics on poor children in our country reveal a nightmare: Between 1979 and 1994 the number of children under the age of 6 who were living in poverty in the United States grew from 3.5 million to 6.1 million.[14] A study by the National Center for Children in Poverty at the Columbia School of Public Health revealed that the rate of poverty for children under 6 also grew drastically—from 18 percent to 25 percent. The Columbia study, titled *One in Four*, begins as follows: "In the United States, distinguished by its extraordinary wealth, there are six million poor individuals known to few others but their own families. They cannot vote, they cannot work, most do not even go to school. They are America's youngest poor—children under age six."

While African American and Latino children, especially in big cities, are disproportionately poor, the poverty rate for young children grew twice as fast among whites as among blacks during the period studied. The Columbia study also revealed that the poverty rate for young white children in the United States "is substantially higher

13. *Why Are People Homeless?*, 1.
14. Bob Herbert, "One in Four in America," *New York Times*, 16 December 1996.

than that for children in other Western democracies." Most of these children—62 percent—live in working families. Less than a third live in families that rely exclusively on public assistance; 36 percent live in urban areas, 17 percent in suburban areas, 27 percent in rural areas.[15]

As statistics for children in poverty increase, the cohesion of the family has deteriorated. This has led to a major increase in the number of disadvantaged, neglected and abused children. One study revealed a 105 percent increase in the number of neglected and abused children between 1986 and 1993. Those children who were seriously injured quadrupled from 143,000 to more than 572,000.[16]

In 1996, the U.S. Conference of Mayors survey of homelessness in 29 major cities found that children under 18 accounted for 27 percent of the homeless population. Families with children are the fastest growing group in the homeless population.[17] This means they are trudging the streets, waiting in line at welfare agencies (for benefits that have likely been cut) with jobless parents, playing under bridges and on railroad tracks. Nightmares, bedwetting, sleepwalking, violent mood swings, and severe depression—all are commonplace for homeless children. Most of them go to school sporadically, if at all.

> [Homeless children] are either desperate for attention, wildly aggressive or totally withdrawn. They will bite and kick and then hug you, or they won't talk at all. Unless kids like this can be reassured the world is safe, they are likely to be criminals by 12. By 14, they may kill.[18]—A pediatrician who tends homeless families

THE YOUTHFUL POOR

One half of the poverty population consists of the elderly and children.[19] While 35 percent of all elderly people were poor in 1959,

15. Ibid.

16. *New Child Abuse Findings* (Child Welfare League of America, 440 First St., NW, Suite 310, Washington DC, 31 July 1996).

17. *Why Are People Homeless?*, 1.

18. Thomas Ferrick and Stephen Shames, "The Invisible Homeless," *Philadelphia Inquirer Magazine*, 13 December 1987, 16.

19. Bernadette D. Proctor, "Poverty," *Population Profile of the United States, 1995*, U.S. Dept. of Commerce, 43.

just 11.7 percent were in 1994.[20] However, with government assistance being rolled back under the new welfare law, the elderly, low income disabled children, and working poor families will be adversely affected.[21] When welfare recipients start looking for jobs to replace their shrinking welfare benefits, they will most likely be competing with the working poor, who are barely surviving on what they make now. And since more than 35 percent of all families in poverty are run by young single mothers, the future does not appear bright. Why the huge growth in single-female-headed families?

The divorce revolution continues. Reports consistently show that one in two marriages ends in divorce. At least one million households a year will be added to U.S. society each year between now and the year 2000, yet only three of every ten of these new households will consist of a married couple.[22] There are also many more children under 18 living with just one parent than there were a generation ago. In 1970, 12 percent of all children lived with one parent; by 1995, 27 percent did. The Census Bureau cited rising divorce rates and a growing tendency to have children first, then marry. And of the single parents in 1995, 35 percent had never married, 38 percent were divorced, 23 percent were separated, and 4 percent were widowed. Twenty-one percent of white children lived with one parent, 33 percent of Hispanic children did, and 56 percent of black children did, up substantially from 1970, when 8.7 percent of white children lived with one parent and 31.8 percent of black children did. (Such figures for Hispanic children were not kept until 1980, when 20.5 percent lived with one parent.)[23]

Though it was written over ten years ago, I believe Leonore J. Weitzman's book *The Divorce Revolution* still offers a helpful look at the effects of no-fault divorce laws. She began her study assuming no-fault divorce was a breakthrough for women, but she concluded that it had devastating effects. Perhaps her most explosive finding was that men's standard of

20. U.S. Bureau of Census, 1995.

21. Super et al., *The New Welfare Law,* 1.

22. Thomas Exeter, "The Census Bureau's Household Projections," *American Demographics* (October 1986), 46.

23. Katharine Q. Seelye, 'The New U.S.: Grayer and More Hispanic," *New York Times,* 27 March 1997.

living went up 42 percent in the year following divorce, while women's living standard declined 73 percent, even counting alimony and child support payments.

> Sophia is a black single mother with two children, living on $187 per month in addition to her food stamps. She can only afford to live in federally funded housing called the Projects in South Philadelphia. (She is lucky. The average housing project in the U.S. has a 5-year waiting list.) Drug-related violence is common in the Projects. When her son's friend stole her food stamps, she had to get help from a local church. When her 8-year-old daughter wanted to invite friends to celebrate her birthday, Sophia had to borrow money from a friend to buy a cake mix. She spends hours each month walking in and out of businesses looking for a job. No jobs are available, because Sophia cannot read well enough nor add in her head fast enough.[24]

In light of congressional cuts in basic assistance programs, it is likely that these young poor will not be helped as the elderly were. Some experts indicate that between 2.5 million and 3.5 million children could be affected by the bill's five-year time limit when it is fully implemented, even after a 20 percent hardship exemption is taken into account.[25] Unlike the older poor, the new poor are younger, with far more children, and are likely to produce a permanent, hard-core underclass of young people, subjected to crime and addiction with little education.

THE NEW ETHNICS

Many North Americans suffer from two misconceptions about race and social problems.

"Most of the poor are black," many think. In fact, 25.3 million of the poor are white, 10.1 million are black, 8.4 million are Hispanic.[26] Also, many of the new immigrants pouring into the country are falling swiftly into poverty. A new report by the Census Bureau, "The Demographic

24. "Poverty: One View," *ACTS Newsletter* (Tenth Presbyterian Church, Philadelphia, April 1987).

25. Super et al., *The New Welfare Law*, 2.

26. U.S. Bureau of Census, 1995.

State of the Nation," documents explosive growth in the nation's Hispanic population and projects that by the year 2005, Hispanic Americans will surpass blacks as the nation's largest minority. Starting in the year 2020, the report says, more Hispanic Americans will be added to the population each year than blacks, Asian Americans, and American Indians combined. And starting in 2019, the Hispanic American population, relatively youthful, will have the nation's lowest death rate.[27]

"North Americans are typically white" is another common belief. But while that is still true, our demographics are changing much faster than most of the country realizes. In 1995, 46 percent of the 23 million foreign-born people in the United States were of Hispanic origin; nearly 7 million had emigrated from Mexico, the country that exported the largest number of people to America. (The Philippines was second.) About 800,000 people immigrate legally every year.[28]

Although some of the immigrants have good incomes, many of the new ethnics have serious economic problems. The growing ethnic population spells greatly increased demands for assistance, from either the government or the religious community.

THE BLUE-COLLAR POOR

With manufacturing industries declining in the 1980s and corporate downsizing in the 1990s, many of the new poor in the United States are blue collar, that is, the former worker who could once make $25,000+ a year with a high school diploma in a manufacturing job. But the technological revolution has led to the severe shrinkage of these jobs. New industry is high-tech—either oriented to information or service. Such industry has either high-paying jobs for highly skilled technicians or low-paying jobs. The "working class" job, which could once support a family comfortably, is disappearing.

More than 3 million high-paying U.S. manufacturing jobs were shipped abroad between 1979 and 1994 where labor was cheaper.[29] The

27. Seelye, "The New U.S.: Grayer and More Hispanic."
28. Ibid.
29. Gerald Celente, *Trends 2000: How to Prepare for and Profit from the Changes of the Twenty-First Century* (New York: Warner, 1997), 159.

economy has been dropping for more than two decades for low-skilled workers and evidence suggests that most working poor either cannot or will not lift themselves out.[30] And almost a half million workers have been laid off in the past few years, many from the banking and telecommunications industries.

According to the Bureau of Labor Statistics, future jobs will be primarily in the service sector: for example, retail sales clerks, nurses, cashiers, truck drivers, waiters/waitresses, and janitors. All these will see a significant increase.[31] But the salaries in these fields are hardly the rewards of ever more expensive college educations, or even enough to support a family as the cost of living continually increases. Meanwhile, the income gap between the rich and the poor continues to widen. The average income among the wealthiest one-fifth of U.S. households rose 45 percent from 1967 to 1995. By comparison, in the poorest households income only increased by 19 percent.[32] In short, there is no such thing as "job security" anymore for the average worker.

GRAY AMERICA

The proportion of elderly Americans has been growing steadily for decades. The Census Bureau's report, "Demographic State of the Nation," forecasts that people over 85 will become the fastest growing segment of the population by the middle of the next century, carrying sweeping implications for the health care industry and Social Security. In 1995, about 4 million people were over 85 and made up 1.4 percent of the population. By 2050, the report says, there will be 18 million people over 85, who will account for 4.6 percent of the population. By then, people over 65 will be 20 percent of the population.[33]

We have seen that, at the present, the elderly are a "success story" in our culture, most having escaped the low income and poor living conditions that very recently were the lot of many. But the enormous

30. Jason DeParle, "The New Contract with America's Poor," *New York Times*, 28 July, 1996.
31. Celente, *Trends 2000*, 166.
32. "The Working Poor," *Congressional Quarterly Researcher* (5 November 1995), 980.
33. Seelye, "The New U.S.: Grayer and More Hispanic."

increase in the elderly during the next thirty years will make all current social support systems obsolete. Many, many authorities suspect Social Security to collapse or become ineffective. The cost of supporting the enormous elderly population may cause a rebellion and a deadly economic combat with the next generation.

THE SICK

The proportions of the epidemic of AIDS (Acquired Immunological Deficiency Syndrome) have seized the attention of (and frightened) the American public. Claims and projections differ wildly, yet the disease is no longer confined to the homosexual community. Now, AIDS is a disease of the young, the poor, and heterosexuals as well. Whatever the demographic, all agree that the medical cost of treating AIDS sufferers has become massive and devastating.

Even without the specter of AIDS, health care for the needy is at a crisis point. The nonprofit hospital that cares for all, regardless of resources, is quickly disappearing. There are far fewer government dollars for such work, while medical costs and insurance rates keep skyrocketing. Hospitals are having to rely more and more on marketing research and "bottom-line" (profitability) decision making. The hospitals of tomorrow will no longer be social service institutions. Who or what will fill this new gap?

THE PRISONERS

The 1990s has seen a steady increase in crime rates, and many law-abiding citizens do not feel safe as a result. With an increasing negativity of public sentiment ("lock 'em up and throw away the key") and deteriorating government assistance, the poor often find themselves between a rock and a hard place. Some will turn to crime out of desperation. Then, if they are imprisoned for nonviolent crimes (as the public is demanding), they will soon learn a more violent way of life from inside the prison system. Charles Colson tells of Carl, a young inmate he met in a federal prison in Alabama.

> He had been convicted of theft and sentenced to 18 months in prison. The judge wisely put the young first-offender on probation instead of sending him to jail. Carl was a model offender on probation. He

checked in with his probation officer every week, held a job, and kept out of trouble. Then he made a mistake. He left the state without permission—something people on probation are not supposed to do. He thought he had a good reason to travel; he was getting married. But when the judge discovered what Carl had done, he ordered him into prison to serve the full 18 months of his sentence. And there he "sat at the feet" of some tough teachers and learned a lot of tricks of the criminals' trade. . . . Pain and resentment radiated from his eyes. He looked at me and snarled, "I've got only one thing going. I'm going to get even. . . . When I get out of here, they're not going to catch me."[34]

In this one example, it can be seen that prisons are often not part of the solution for crime and poverty, but part of the problem. The number of men and women in the nation's prisons and jails climbed to nearly 1.6 million in 1995, culminating a decade in which the United States' rate of incarceration nearly doubled. Apart from inmates, there were also 4 million people on parole or probation.[35] The United States spent $31 billion on prisons in 1992, an 800 percent increase from 1975.[36] Many experts believe that "the percentage of Americans going in and out of jails is phenomenal . . . as you go down the socioeconomic scale, the percentage gets much higher."[37]

In essence, crime rates (and the prison industry) have produced a crushing financial burden.

CONCLUSIONS

This panoramic view is overwhelming, yet it is this view that Christ advocates when he says that anyone in need is our neighbor. How can we process this? What conclusions can we draw?

1. *We do indeed live on the Jericho Road.* The data show that there are many people in need, their needs are deepening, and the needy

---

34. Charles Colson, *America's Prison Crisis* (Washington: Prison Fellowship Ministries, 1987).
35. Celente, *Trends 2000*, 287.
36. Ibid., 290.
37. Ibid., 289.

are a diverse group. All this is more than most evangelicals are used to seeing.

Our nation is becoming a mosaic of different groups, each with a unique complex of needs. Most churches are surrounded by growing numbers of the unemployed and underemployed, new immigrant populations, singles, divorced persons, unwed mothers, the elderly, prisoners, the dying, sick, and disabled. Poverty is on the rise, the percentage of the elderly in our society is exploding, ethnics are pouring into our country by the millions, and federal money for helping agencies, hospitals, and other such institutions is drying up. Do we want to reach these new neighbors with the gospel? Then we must give our faith active expression through deeds of compassion coupled with evangelism and discipleship.

North American evangelicals once perceived the ministry of mercy as an optional kind of work. But the times are changing, demanding us to respond.

2. *The church of Jesus Christ must squarely face its responsibility for the neighbors lying in the road.* Just the explosion of the elderly population alone could spell a breakdown of the present welfare system. But add the possibility of an AIDS holocaust, the impoverishing of the working class, and the growth of low-income immigrants and female single-parent homes, and we have a virtual certainty that current government programs will be completely inadequate. No institution in society will escape the impact of heavy new social problems, especially with the new welfare reform. Regardless of our political views, it is indisputable that millions of people who once looked to the government will now need service and aid from churches and other agencies. The church will be forced by demographics to see what the Bible has always said. Love cannot be only expressed through talk, but through word *and* deed (1 John 3:17).

While accomplishing that task, Francis Schaeffer said, Christians may be at times, "cobelligerents" with the Left or the Right, but never allies. "If there is social injustice, say there is social injustice. If we need order, say we need order. . . . But do not align yourself as though you are in either of these camps: You are an ally of neither. The church of the Lord Jesus Christ is different from either—totally different."[38]

The ideology of the Left believes big government and social reform will solve social ills, while the Right believes big business and economic growth will do it. The Left expects a citizen to be held legally accountable for the use of his wealth, but totally autonomous in other areas, such as sexual morality. The Right expects a citizen to be held legally accountable in areas of personal morality, but totally autonomous in the use of wealth. The North American "idol"—radical individualism—lies beneath both ideologies. A Christian sees either "solution" as fundamentally humanistic and simplistic.

The causes of our worsening social problems are far more complex than either the secularists of the Right or Left understand. We wrestle not with flesh and blood, but with powers and principalities! We have seen there is great social injustice—racial prejudice, greed, avarice—by those with the greatest wealth in the country (and sadly, within the evangelical church itself). At the same time, there is a general breakdown of order—of the family and the morals of the nation. There is more premarital sex (and thus there are more unwed mothers), more divorce, child neglect and abuse, more crime. Neither a simple redistribution of wealth nor simple economic growth and prosperity can mend broken families; nor can they turn low-skilled mothers into engineers or technicians.

3. *Only the ministry of the church of Jesus Christ, and the millions of "mini-churches" (Christian homes) throughout the country can attack the roots of social problems.* Only the church can minister to the whole person. Only the gospel understands that sin has ruined us both individually and socially. We cannot be viewed individualistically (as the capitalists do) or collectivistically (as the Communists do) but as related to God. Only Christians, armed with the Word and Spirit, planning and working to spread the kingdom and righteousness of Christ, can transform a nation as well as a neighborhood as well as a broken heart. That is what the rest of this book is about.

38. Francis Schaeffer, *The Church at the End of the Twentieth Century* (Downers Grove, IL: InterVarsity Press, 1970), 37.

FOR DISCUSSION

1. The statistics on poverty may have been new to you. What aspect(s) was/were the most surprising? How has your view of poverty in the United States changed after reading the facts?

2. The seminarian's experience with Angela, the homeless woman, speaks of some of the complexities of dealing with the poor. Identify some of these complexities, based on that example.

3. Can you identify a "pocket" of poverty in your community that you or your church might be able to help? Explain.

Part 1

PRINCIPLES

1

The Call to Mercy

But he wanted to justify himself, so he asked Jesus, "And who is my neighbor?" (Luke 10:29)

OVERVIEW: Mercy to the full range of human needs is such an essential mark of being a Christian that it can be used as a test of true faith. Mercy is not optional or an addition to being a Christian. Rather, a life poured out in deeds of mercy is the inevitable sign of true faith.

THE ESSENCE OF LOVE

The expert in the law came "to test" Jesus—to trap him (Luke 10:25). He was probably trying to get Jesus to say something negative about the law or to minimize its role in salvation. Jesus, on the other hand, is laying his own trap for the man, but his trap is a trap of love.

Our Lord asked the man for a summary of the Law, and he replied by articulating what many Jewish scribes and teachers believed, that all the rules of the Law hung on two principles. First, the Law requires a heart and mind totally submitted to and absorbed in God alone (Deut. 6:5). Second, it requires that we must meet the needs of others, with all the speed, the eagerness, the energy, and the *joy* with which we meet our own (Lev. 19:18). How staggering these principles are! They reflect both the holiness of God and the fundamental debt we owe the one who gave us everything. Since he gave us all we have, we must give him all we are.

When the law expert provided this summary of perfect love and righteousness, Jesus replied: "Do this and you will live." What was Jesus' strategy? Why did he not say, "Receive me as your personal Savior" or something to that effect? Was he suggesting to the man that the way of salvation was by the performance of good deeds? No, not at all.

Instead, he had turned the tables on the law expert. When we look at the regulations of the Old Testament individually, we see many that are possible to keep. But if we look at the principles beneath the particulars and at the kind of life that the law is really *after*, then we see how we fail utterly to reach it. Jesus is pointing him to the perfect righteousness the Law demanded so that he could see he is powerless to fulfill it. He was seeking to convict the law expert of sin. Jesus says in effect:

> My friend, I *do* take the law seriously, even more seriously than you do. Yes, you can be accepted by God if you obey the law perfectly, but *look* at the law! See what it is really after. If you can do that, you will live. But if you see clearly, you will realize that the righteous requirement of the Law must be fulfilled in some other way.

Jesus had the same purpose in his confrontation with the rich young ruler (Mark 10:17–22). He was seeking conviction of sin, even as he "looked at him and loved him."

> "You know the commandments: 'Do not murder, do not commit adultery, do not steal, do not give false testimony, do not defraud, honor your father and mother.'"
>
> "Teacher," he declared, "all these I have kept since I was a boy."
>
> Jesus looked at him and loved him. "One thing you lack," he said. "Go, sell everything you have and give to the poor, and you will have treasure in heaven. Then come, follow me."
>
> At this the man's face fell. He went away sad, because he had great wealth. (Mark 10:19–22)

The rich young ruler claimed to have been obedient to the Law, until Jesus called him to give up all his riches and follow him. That was nothing more than an exposition of the first commandment. Jesus was asking: "Are you willing to lose *everything* if it is necessary to gain my fellowship? Will you truly have 'no other gods before me'?" The rich young ruler left in sorrow. Was Jesus being heavy-handed, unnecessarily demanding? No, not at all. The gospel is the gospel of the *kingdom*, and unless we give our hearts to Jesus as king, we have not given them at all. The ministry of mercy is expensive, and our willingness to carry it out is a critical sign of our submission to the lordship of Christ.

THE RICHES AND POVERTY OF GOD

So here too, in Luke 10, we see Jesus is seeking to bring the law expert to despair of any salvation through his own personal efforts. This time, however, he expounds the second great commandment, rather than the first. Why does Jesus find it necessary to do this? Because, to receive the mercy of God, we must all come first to the place where we despair of our own moral efforts. Nathan Cole, a Connecticut farmer converted in the 1740s, put it clearly when describing what happened to him under the preaching of George Whitefield: "My hearing him preach gave me a heart wound. By God's blessing, my old foundation was broken up, and I saw that my righteousness would not save me."[1]

The law expert should have responded in the same way. If he had said, "I see! How then can anyone be righteous before God?" then Jesus could have replied, "Only through the mercy of God." And the mercy of God is simply this. We must see that all of us are spiritually poor and bankrupt before God (Matt. 5:3), and even when we put on our best moral efforts for God, we appear as beggars clothed in filthy rags (Isa. 64:6). Yet in Jesus Christ, God provided a righteousness for us (Rom. 3:21–22), a wealth straight from the account of the Son of God, who impoverished himself through suffering and death that we might receive it (2 Cor. 8:9).

No one understood this more clearly than John Bunyan, who described his conversion in these terms:

> But one day . . . this sentence fell upon my soul, "Thy righteousness is in heaven"; and methought withal, I saw with the eyes of my soul, Jesus Christ at God's right hand; there, I say, as my righteousness; so that wherever I

1. Nathan Cole, "Spiritual Travels," *William and Mary Quarterly* 7 (1950): 591.

was, or whatever I was doing, God could not say to me "He wants my righteousness," for that was just before him. I also saw, moreover, that it was not my good frame of heart that made my righteousness better, nor yet my bad frame that made my righteousness worse; for my righteousness was Jesus Christ himself, "the same yesterday, today, and forever."

Now did my chains fall off my legs indeed. . . . Oh! methought, Christ! Christ! there was nothing but Christ that was before my eyes. . . . Now I could look from myself to him, and would reckon that all those graces of God that now were green on me, were yet but like those cracked groats and four-pence-half-pennies that rich men carry in their purses, when their gold is in their trunks at home: Oh! I saw my gold was in my trunk at home! In Christ my Lord and Saviour. Now Christ was all; all my righteousness, all my sanctification, and all my redemption.[2]

But the law expert resisted our Lord. He did not want to acknowledge that he was poor, spiritually bankrupt. It is clear that he felt the pressure of Jesus' argument, for soon we see him attempting "to justify himself" by asking, "who is my neighbor?"

What was he trying to do? He wanted Jesus to define the second commandment in such a way as to make its requirements reachable. Jesus responds with a parable that expounds the second great commandment. He shows us the extent and the essence of the love God requires.

We must remember this entire context of the parable of the Good Samaritan, or we can fall easily into the trap of moralism. Jesus is not telling us that we can be *saved* by imitating the Good Samaritan, even though he is clearly charging us to follow his pattern. Rather, Jesus is seeking to humble us with the love God *requires*, so we will be willing to receive the love God *offers*.

MERCY IS NOT OPTIONAL

The parable describes a Samaritan who came upon a Jew who had been beaten and robbed. The Samaritan provided physical protection (from a new attack), medical help, transportation, and a financial subsidy. In short, he met his full range of physical and economic needs. The law expert called all of this activity the work of "mercy" (v. 37). This story

2. John Bunyan, *Grace Abounding to the Chief of Sinners,* ed. John P. Gulliver (London: Bradley, 1871), 59.

can only have its fullest impact if we remember its purpose. Jesus' parable has been saved for a description of Christian love to our neighbor. Jesus' reply is to show us a man performing what many today call "social work."

Evangelical Christians today are by no means against helping the needy and hurting. Yet "social relief work" is generally looked at as a secondary duty. It is something we get to if there is time and money in the budget, after we are satisfied with our educational and evangelistic ministries.

This parable shatters that set of priorities. *Jesus uses the work of mercy to show us the essence of the righteousness God requires in our relationships.* By no means is this an isolated example. In James 2:15–16 and 1 John 3:17–18 Christians are charged to meet physical and economic needs among the brethren. This is not optional. If a professing Christian does not do so, "how can the love of God be in him?" The striking truth is that the work of mercy is fundamental to being a Christian.

MERCY IS A TEST

Both James and John also use the ministry of mercy as a test. The apostle John writes his first epistle to set forth the test by which a genuine Christian can be known. One of the tests of Christian love is the ministry of mercy. Christian fellowship must be characterized by the meeting of physical needs.

> If anyone has material possessions and sees his brother in need but has no pity on him, how can the love of God be in him? Dear children, let us not love with words or tongue but with actions and in truth. (1 John 3:17–18)

Real love is expressed in deed as well as in word.

James concludes that a profession of faith unaccompanied by deeds of mercy shows that faith to be "dead," not genuine at all.

> Judgment without mercy will be shown to anyone who has not been merciful. Mercy triumphs over judgment!
>
> What good is it, my brothers, if a man claims to have faith but has no deeds? Can such faith save him? Suppose a brother or sister is without clothes and daily food. If one of you says to him, "Go, I wish you well; keep warm and well fed," but does nothing about his

physical needs, what good is it? In the same way, faith by itself, if it is not accompanied by action, is dead. (James 2:13–17)

In Proverbs 14:31 and 19:17 we are told that to ignore the needs of a poor man is to sin against the Lord. So the poor and needy are a test. Our response to them tests the genuineness of our faith toward God.

No passage is clearer at this point than Matthew 25:31–46. This describes Jesus' examination of mankind on Judgment Day. He distinguishes those who have true faith from those who do not by examining their fruit, namely, their concern for the poor, homeless, sick, and prisoners. How can this be? Jesus, when he says, "Whatever you did for one of the least of these brothers of mine, you did for me," is merely expanding on Proverbs 19:17 ("He who is kind to the poor lends to the LORD"). He is also agreeing with James, John, and Isaiah (cf. Isa. 1:10–17) in saying that a sensitive social conscience and a life poured out in deeds of mercy to the needy is the inevitable outcome and sign of true faith. By such deeds God can judge true love from lip service.

Imagine a wealthy older woman who has no heirs except a nephew who is always kind to her. But how can she know if his kindness is just a façade? How can she know what his heart is really like? Imagine that she dresses up as a homeless street person and sits on the steps of her nephew's townhouse, and when he comes out he curses and threatens her. Now she knows his true character! So too, God is angry when we have one face for him and another for the needy. "When you spread out your hands in prayer, I will hide my eyes from you. . . . Seek justice, encourage the oppressed. Defend the cause of the fatherless, plead the case of the widow" (Isa. 1:15, 17). So too, Jesus can say in effect, "I am the homeless person on your steps—how you treat her tells me what you are really like." A great preacher, Robert Murray M'Cheyne, commented on Matthew 25 to his congregation nearly 150 years ago:

> I fear there are some Christians among you to whom Christ can say no such thing ["Come thou blessed . . . inherit the kingdom" in Matt. 25:34]. Your haughty dwelling rises in the midst of thousands who have scarce a fire to warm themselves at, and have but little clothing to keep out the biting frost; and yet you never darkened their door. You heave a sigh, perhaps, at a distance; but you do not visit

them. Ah! my dear friend! I am concerned for the poor but more for you. I know not what Christ will say to you in the great day. . . . I fear there are many hearing me who may know [now] well that they are not Christians, because they do not love to give. To give largely and liberally, not grudging at all, requires a new heart; an old heart would rather part with its life-blood than its money. Oh my friends! enjoy your money; make the most of it; give none away; enjoy it quickly for I can tell you, you will be beggars throughout eternity.[3]

MERCY IS NOT NEW

The Bible's teaching on the ministry of mercy does not begin with the parable of the Good Samaritan.

Man's first "mission" was to subdue and have dominion over the earth (Gen. 1:28). Genesis 2:15 restates this commission in terms of "tending and keeping" the garden of God. The concept of man as a gardener is highly suggestive: a gardener does not destroy nature, nor leave it as it is. He cultivates and develops it, enhancing its beauty, usefulness, and fruitfulness. So God expects his servants to bring all creation under his lordship. Science, engineering, art, education, government are all part of this responsibility. We are to bring every dimension of life, both spiritual and material, under the rule and law of God.

Obviously, there was no "ministry of mercy" *per se* before the fall of man, since there was no human suffering or need. But it is clear that God's servants at that time were as concerned with the material-physical world as with the spiritual.

After the fall, the effects of sin immediately caused the fragmentation of man's relationships. Man becomes alienated from God (Gen. 3:10). As a result his relationship with other human beings is shattered (vv. 12–13), and so is his relationship with nature itself (vv. 17–18). Now sickness, hunger, natural disaster, social injustice, and death dominate.

The first act of mercy ministry immediately follows the fall: God clothes Adam and Eve with animal skins (Gen. 3:21). Many have pointed out that this action represents the covering of our sins by the work of Christ, but that is surely not the only reason for God's action. Man now

3. *Sermons of M'Cheyne* (Edinburgh: n.p., 1848), 482.

needs protection from a hostile environment. By God's action, Derek Kidner says, "Social action could not have had an earlier or more exalted inauguration."[4]

Even before the giving of the law to Moses, God made his will known concerning the ministry of mercy. Job, who lived in an early pre-Mosaic age, knew that the righteousness God requires includes providing food, shelter, and clothing to the needy (Job 24:1–21; 31:16–23). In fact, Job tells us that he did more than simple social service. "I was a father to the needy; I took up the cause of the stranger. I broke the fangs of the wicked and snatched the victims from their teeth" (29:16–17).

When God gave the law to Moses, he was constructing a believing community in which social righteousness was as required as personal righteousness and morality. Individual Israelites were forbidden to harvest all their produce, so the poor could glean from the fields for free (Ex. 23:10–11). Israelites were told to give to the poor until his need was gone (Deut. 15:8, 10), especially if the poor man was a kinsman or a neighbor (Lev. 25:25, 35–38). The priests gave to the poor out of the tithes to God (Deut. 14:28–29).

God's law required that the poor be given more than just a "handout." When a slave was freed from debt and servitude, he was not to leave empty-handed, but had to be given grain or livestock so that he could become economically self-sufficient (Deut. 15:12–15).

These laws given to Moses were the basis for the thundering of the later prophets, who denounced Israel's insensitivity to the poor as breaking covenant with God. They taught that materialism and the ignoring of the poor's plight are sins as repugnant as idolatry and adultery (Amos 2:6–7). Mercy to the poor is an evidence of true heart commitment to God (Isa. 1:10–17; 58:6–7; Amos 4:1–6; 5:21–24). Finally, the prophets predicted that the Messiah, when he came, would be characterized by mercy to the poor (Isa. 11:1–4; 61:1–2).

THE GOSPEL TO THE POOR

Jesus chose Isaiah 61 as the text for his first sermon. To prove he is the Messiah, he points out that he preaches to the poor (Matt. 11:1–6). Our Lord, in becoming a human, literally "moved in" with the poor

---

4. Derek Kidner, *Genesis: An Introduction and Commentary* (Downers Grove, IL: Inter-Varsity Press, 1973), 161.

(2 Cor. 8:9). He was born into a family that at his circumcision offered pigeons (Luke 2:24; Lev. 12:8), the offering prescribed for the poorest families. Jesus lived with, ate with, and associated with lepers and outcasts, the lowest classes of society. He taught that all humans are spiritually bankrupt (Matt. 5:3) and are spiritually in rags before God (Isa. 64:6). Because he gives his salvation riches to the spiritually poor, so we should do good to the wicked and the ungrateful, even to our enemies.

> But love your enemies, do good to them, and lend to them without expecting to get anything back. Then your reward will be great, and you will be sons of the Most High, because he is kind to the ungrateful and wicked. Be merciful, just as your Father is merciful. (Luke 6:35–36)

We see the words of Jesus and the prophets reflected in the teaching and practice of the early church. Christians are to open their hands to their brother as far as there is need (cf. 1 John 3:16–17 with Deut. 15:7–8). In the church, wealth is to be shared so generously that much of the economic distance between rich and poor diminishes (cf. 2 Cor. 8:13–15 with Lev. 25). James (2:1–23) follows the prophets and the Lord in teaching that true faith will inevitably show itself through deeds of mercy (Isa. 1:10–17).

Christians are charged to remember the poor (Gal. 2:10) and widows and orphans (James 1:27), to practice hospitality to strangers (Heb. 13:2), and to denounce materialism (1 Tim. 6:17–19). Although believers are to give their first and greatest aid to the needy within the church, mercy must also be shown to all people (Gal. 6:10). All of these teachings are direct echoes of the Old Testament revelation.

Not only do all believers have these responsibilities, but a special class of officers—deacons—is established to coordinate the church's ministry of mercy. This shows that mercy is a mandated work of the church, just as are the ministry of the Word and discipline (cf. Rom. 15:23–29).

CHRIST, OUR MODEL

How can we draw into sharp focus all the teaching of the Bible concerning the ministry of mercy? By looking at Jesus Christ! First, he is the true Adam (Rom. 5:14–21) who is subduing all creation to God (Heb. 2:5–8; Eph. 1:10).

Second, he is the true High Priest (Heb. 4:14–16) who can give mercy to all in need. Third, he is the great Deacon (Rom. 15:8) who identifies with the poor (2 Cor. 8:9) and pours himself out in costly service (Mark 10:45).

Because we are united to Christ, every believer is a deacon, who is to wash the feet of others in humble service (Matt. 20:26–28; Gal. 6:10). Every believer is also a royal priest, whose sacrifices to God include deeds of mercy (Heb. 13:13–16). Christians are also now a "new Adam," seeking to bring all creation into subjection to the Lord (Matt. 28:18–20; 2 Cor. 10:5).

CONCLUSION

During the past two decades, Christians have been exposed more and more to the biblical teaching that every believer is a minister. Although most Christians are not polished preachers and apologists, yet every Christian is to be a witness. Although most Christians are not skilled psychologists and counselors, yet every Christian is to be a people-helper. Sermons, seminars, and books have been pounding these concepts into our consciousness for years.

However, in at least one realm, the ministry of mercy, laypeople are still consigning ministry to the "experts." In fact, the church herself has almost completely conceded this work to secular agencies and authorities. Many Christians cannot clearly define this duty, though they may have good understandings of the ministries of evangelism, education, worship, teaching, and fellowship.

Most of us have not come to grips with the clear directive of Scripture that *all* Christians must have their own ministry of mercy. We must each be actively engaged in it ourselves.

FOR DISCUSSION

1. In what ways does our mercy to the needy reflect the love of Christ?
2. Before we are able to give mercy, what needs to happen in our lives? Do you see where change in your own life is needed? Describe that.
3. On what scriptural bases (Old or New Testament) is the necessity of mercy established?
4. Why is it that we tend to think of mercy as an option?
5. In what ways is Christ our model for mercy?

2

The Character of Mercy

He went to him and bandaged his wounds, pouring on oil and wine. Then he put the man on his own donkey, took him to an inn and took care of him. The next day he took out two silver coins and gave them to the innkeeper. (Luke 10:34–35)

OVERVIEW: The ministry of mercy is the meeting of "felt" needs through deeds. As agent of the kingdom, the church seeks to bring substantial healing of the effects of sin in all areas of life, including psychological, social, economic, and physical.

The Good Samaritan met a variety of needs of the beaten man. The first service he rendered was his very physical presence. "He went to him." People in a helpless condition are enormously encouraged by the presence of a friend, an advocate. "Advocacy" is an attitude and a relationship: It mirrors the priestly work of Christ, who stands before the Father as our Advocate (1 John 2:1).

Then the Samaritan supplied other sorts of aid. He provided immediate crisis medical treatment, transportation to a place of shelter, and medical care in the inn overnight. Finally he gave a financial gift to pay the man's rent until he recovered fully or until the Samaritan returned. Knowing the state of medical care (the man was "half dead") and transportation at the time, this must have been a generous offer!

45

The scope of the Samaritan's mercy is broad: the physical, financial, and emotional needs of the victim were met. This prompts us to define the ministry of mercy more concretely. Exactly what needs does it address? What do these needs have in common?

Here is a working definition for the ministry of mercy: it is *the meeting of (1) "felt" needs through (2) deeds.*

HUMAN NEEDS

One of the Puritans wrote, "Grace has to do with man's merits, but *mercy* has to do with man's misery." Theologians have discerned that God's mercy (the Greek word *eleos*) is that aspect of his nature which moves him to relieve suffering and misery.[1] "Mercy" is the impulse that makes us sensitive to hurts and lacks in others and makes us desire to alleviate them. These "hurts or lacks" we call *needs*.

What are human needs? Needs are dependencies. All human beings were created dependent beings. We are not self-sufficient; we are only adequate in God. If we had stayed in perfect fellowship with God, we would nevertheless have had needs. However, we would have known no pain, since all our needs would have been immediately and continuously met in him. But now, separated from him, we are under a curse, and our unfulfilled dependencies bring us emptiness, frustration, and pain in all areas of life. To understand the nature of our needs, we need to look more closely at the fall of man, the root of all our miseries.

The first biblical description of the results of sin is Genesis 3:7–19. From this passage, four different results of Adam's sin, four different "alienations," can be discerned. Let's define alienation as "disintegration which arises from using an object for a purpose other than that for which it was designed." For example, if I use a wristwatch to drive a nail, my watch experiences alienation! Why? Because it is not built for such a purpose. In the same way, man was designed to know and serve his Creator God. When man determined to be his own master, the immediate result was a multidimensional condition of alienation.

1. For example, Herman Bavinck, *The Doctrine of God* (Grand Rapids: Eerdmans, 1951), 206–7.

We can diagram these four alienations as concentric circles. The most basic circle, in the center, is "theological alienation," our separation from God. Next comes "psychological alienation," separation from our true selves. Third is "social alienation," inability to live with one another. Finally, the outermost circle is "physical alienation" which refers to our conflict with the disorder and decay of nature. Let's examine each of these "circles" in turn.

Figure 1

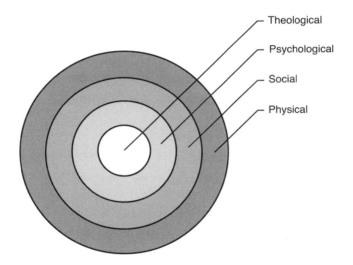

Theological
Psychological
Social
Physical

Alienation from God

First, we became separated or alienated from God. "The man and his wife heard the sound of the LORD God as he was walking in the garden in the cool of the day, and they hid from the LORD God among the trees of the garden" (Gen. 3:8). Evidently it was customary for God to walk in the garden toward evening, when the cool wind blew, and it was just as natural for man to walk with him. What a picture of the fellowship and intimacy we had with God! But now man experienced fear and trauma in the presence of God. He had to hide from God in the trees. "The Hiding Ones" would be a good title for the human race. Adam, who was to protect the garden for God, now must seek to protect himself from God with the garden. Here is the beginning of the great reversal.

The Bible clearly teaches, in both the Old and New Testaments, that sinful people cannot dwell with a holy God.

> The LORD descended to the top of Mount Sinai and called Moses to the top of the mountain. So Moses went up and the LORD said to him, "Go down and warn the people so they do not force their way through to see the LORD and many of them perish. Even the priests, who approach the LORD, must consecrate themselves, or the LORD will break out against them." (Ex. 19:20–22)

> Then Moses said, "Now show me your glory."
> . . . He said, "You cannot see my face, for no one may see me and live." (Ex. 33:18, 20)

One way to understand our alienation from God is to consider the solar system. There is harmony between the planets because they all agree on the center—the sun. But if each planet were to have a different center for its orbit, there would be cataclysmic collisions. God's "center" is his own glory; he does everything because it is consistent with his own righteous, holy, perfect nature. We, however, "center" on our own comfort and happiness; we live for our own glory. Therefore, there is an inevitable collision between God and man. Man is traumatized by and is hostile to the holy presence of God. Yet we were built for fellowship with God. We cannot live with God and we cannot live without God. This is the essence of man's condition. All our problems flow from it, and none can be understood apart from it.

It is only in Christ that we are reconciled to God. Paul teaches that we receive through Christ that safe intimacy that was forbidden to Moses.

> We are not like Moses, who would put a veil over his face. . . . Only in Christ is it taken away. . . . And we, who with unveiled faces all reflect the Lord's glory, are being transformed into his likeness with ever-increasing glory, which comes from the Lord, who is the Spirit. (2 Cor. 3:13–14, 18)

For God, who said, "Let light shine out of darkness," made his light shine in our hearts to give us the light of the knowledge of the glory of God in the face of Christ. (2 Cor. 4:6)

Alienation from Self

Second, we are separated from ourselves. "He answered, 'I heard you in the garden, and I was afraid because I was naked; so I hid'" (Gen. 3:10). Originally the human soul was an integrated, harmonious whole, but now there is disintegration. Where there was peace there is now shame, fear, and a tormenting self-consciousness ("I was naked"). Unhappiness, guilt, fear, loss of personal identity, depression, anxiety, substance abuse, suicide, sexual problems—all stem from our loss of fellowship with God.

This condition occurs because each of us was given a heart, built by nature for worship. We were created to serve God with every dimension of our being. We need to serve God in order to have meaning or purpose; we need to know God in order to have love (our "relational" dimension); we need to be right with God in order to have self-worth (our "conscience").

But sin leads every person to reject God as our only source of meaning, security, and worth. If we reject God, our hearts must constantly manufacture *idols*—persons, relationships, objects, and conditions which we believe will give us fulfillment. We believe that these things, these conditions, will bring us the meaning, security, and worth we desire. The motivation, the drive toward these false goals is dreadfully strong. It is *worship!* We feel we must have these idols or we will die. These drives are called in the Bible the "lusts of the flesh."

They exchanged the truth of God for a lie, and worshiped and served created things rather than the Creator. (Rom. 1:25)

Put to death, therefore, whatever belongs to your earthly nature: sexual immorality, impurity, lust, evil desires and greed, which is idolatry. (Col. 3:5)

But no idol can fill the void in our hearts. All idolatry leads to deep hunger pangs in the soul, because nothing but a relationship with God can fulfill us. Some people choose idols that are more attainable. They feel a relief at first, but then comes boredom, an emptiness, and a feeling of being "stretched thin," like too little butter being spread over too much bread. But many people cannot reach their idolatrous goals at all, and they experience deep, searing pain—loss of meaning, radical insecurity, and profound lack of self-worth. All of this is the registration of the wrath of God in our experience.

In Christ alone can we escape this inevitable psychological disintegration.

> Put on the new self, which is being renewed in knowledge in the image of its Creator. (Col. 3:10)

> Put on the new self, created to be like God in true righteousness and holiness. (Eph. 4:24)

Alienation from Others

Third, we are separated from other people. "Then the eyes of both of them were opened, and they realized they were naked; so they sewed fig leaves together and made coverings for themselves" (Gen. 3:7). Adam and Eve's sudden need for privacy was not a natural thing. Rebels against God do not need to hide only from God, but also from each other. The first marriage squabble, complete with blame-shifting and backbiting, immediately ensues (Gen. 3:12–13)! Now self-centered with their inner passions at war with one another, all sinful humans are on a collision course with others (James 4:1–3).

C. S. Lewis shows clearly how psychological disintegration leads to social disintegration:

> There are two ways in which the human machine goes wrong. One is when human individuals drift apart from one another, or else collide with one another and do one another damage. . . . The other is when things go wrong inside the individual—when the different parts of him (his different faculties and so on) either drift apart or interfere

with one another. . . . As a matter of fact, you cannot have the one without the other.[2]

He then provides an illustration:

> Think of us as a fleet of ships sailing in formation. . . . If the ships keep on having collisions, they will not remain seaworthy very long. On the other hand, if their steering gears are out of order they will not be able to avoid collisions.[3]

So we see, our "social problems" all stem from sin. Those on the Left will blame them on injustice, greed, racism, imperialism, war, oppression. Those on the Right will blame them on family breakdown, crime, personal immorality, selfishness, and a lack of discipline. Both are right! Our social problems are myriad: loneliness, interpersonal conflicts, marital and family problems, poverty, class struggle, constant political confrontation and ineffectiveness. All are the results of sin.

Alienation from Nature

Fourth, God declares to Adam and Eve that they are cut off from nature. Once a "friend," under our dominion, the natural world is now hostile to us. "Cursed is the ground because of you; through painful toil you will eat of it . . . until you return to the ground . . . for dust you are and to dust you will return" (Gen. 3:17, 19).

Paul also refers to the unnatural condition of nature:

> The creation waits in eager expectation for the sons of God to be revealed. For the creation was subjected to frustration, not by its own choice, but by the will of the one who subjected it, in hope that the creation itself will be liberated from its bondage to decay. (Rom. 8:19–21)

We may use chemicals, cosmetics, and refrigeration to hide it temporarily, but nature itself is subject to disintegration and decay. The lovely

2. C. S. Lewis, *Mere Christianity* (New York: Macmillan, 1958), 56.
3. Ibid., 56–57.

flower today is on the manure pile tomorrow. Natural disaster, famine, disease, decay, mental and physical disabilities, aging, and death itself are the results. Our world, with all of its beauty, is only a dim reflection of what it will be like without sin. John Bradford, the English martyr, prayed, "If to thine enemies which love thee not (as the most part in this world be), if to them thou givest so plentifully thy riches here, what shall we think that with thyself thou hast laid up for thy friends!"[4]

Nature is not only in decay, but it is no longer "under us" as before the fall. The point of the curse is that the "dust," the earth, will only very reluctantly yield to us some of its riches. Only with the greatest effort does man learn to get along with the physical world. And even though we may eke out an existence, the earth itself will eventually win, for to it we will return. We will fight the dirt all our lives, and in the end we will be six feet under it. The great preacher George Whitefield, in order to make this point, would ask his audience, "Dost thou know why the wild animals fear and growl and shriek at thee? Because they know thou hast a quarrel with their Master!"

The King's Healing Hands

In Christ, however, even the natural order will be redeemed. Psalm 96 tells us what will happen when Jesus returns to "judge," or *rule* the earth.

> Let the heavens be glad, and let the earth rejoice;
> > let the sea roar, and all that fills it;
> > let the field exult, and everything in it!
> Then shall all the trees of the wood sing for joy
> > before the LORD, for he comes,
> > for he comes to judge the earth.
> He will judge the world with righteousness,
> > and the peoples with his truth. (Ps. 96:11–13 RSV)

This is what Paul referred to when he said "in hope that the creation itself will be liberated from its bondage to decay and brought into the glorious freedom of the children of God" (Rom. 8:20–21). Paul refers

---

4. *The Writings of John Bradford,* vol. 1 (n.p.: Parker Society, 1848), 194–95.

to the final day, when we come finally into the presence of our Lord and know the freedom of being completely submitted to his kingship. At that moment we blossom into our true selves.

> He will make the feeblest and filthiest of us into . . . a dazzling, radiant, immortal creature, pulsating all through with such energy and joy and wisdom and love as we cannot now imagine, a bright stainless mirror which reflects back to God perfectly (though, of course, on a smaller scale) His own boundless power and delight and goodness.[5]

But we shall not be glorified alone. The healing kingship of Christ will extend to all of life and nature. The blessedness of the kingdom is radical and all-embracing (Matt. 5:3–10). All the alienations caused by sin are healed. Each Christmas we sing Isaac Watts' hymn of praise to the blessedness of the kingdom. He paraphrases Psalm 96 in stanza 2.

> Joy to the world! the Saviour reigns:
> Let men their songs employ,
> While fields and floods, rocks, hills, and plains,
> Repeat the sounding joy.

Then, in striking language, he announces that the kingdom of Christ means the complete reversal of all the curse of sin pronounced by the Lord in Genesis 3.

> No more let sins and sorrows grow,
> Nor thorns infest the ground;
> He comes to make his blessings flow
> Far as the curse is found!

The kingdom of God is the means for the renewal of the entire world and all the dimensions of life. From the throne of Jesus Christ flows new life and power such that no disease, decay, poverty, blemish, or pain can stand before it.

---

5. Lewis, *Mere Christianity*, 160.

The Church and the Kingdom

If this is the ministry of the kingdom—to heal all the results of sin in all the areas of life, then the church must intentionally use its resources to minister in every "circle." We are to do not just evangelism but must be a "full-service" body. This becomes clear as we briefly consider the relationship of the church to the kingdom of God. Let us collect what we have seen so far about the kingdom.

1. God created the world to be under his rule and authority. All things were made to be managed by him, and thus they are only what they should be when in his control.
2. Sin disrupted the rule of God, and the universe has fallen into decay and death in every dimension: personal, psychological, social, physical.
3. Christ came to bring the kingdom of God back to earth. The kingdom is *the power of the king.* Thus the kingdom of God is the renewal of the whole world through the entrance of supernatural forces. As things are brought back under Christ's rule and authority, they are restored to health, beauty, and freedom.

The kingdom of God comes in two stages. It will come totally and fully at Christ's second coming, but it has already come partially through the first coming of Jesus.

> Once, having been asked by the Pharisees when the kingdom of God would come, Jesus replied, "The kingdom of God does not come with your careful observation, nor will people say, 'Here it is,' or 'There it is,' because the kingdom of God is within you." (Luke 17:20–21)

The kingdom of God is entered *now* through repentance and faith, the new birth. It is present where the Holy Spirit is present in power.

> Jesus answered, "I tell you the truth, no one can enter the kingdom of God unless he is born of water and the Spirit." (John 3:5)

> For the kingdom of God is not a matter of eating and drinking, but of righteousness, peace and joy in the Holy Spirit. (Rom. 14:17)

The kingdom of God is power, God's ruling power present to heal all the curse of sin. It moves the people of God to meet psychological, social, physical needs, bringing God's kingly blessing far as the curse is found.

> If I drive out demons by the Spirit of God, then the kingdom of God has come upon you. (Matt. 12:28)

> Do not be afraid, little flock, for your Father has been pleased to give you the kingdom. Sell your possessions and give to the poor. Provide purses for yourselves that will not wear out, a treasure in heaven that will not be exhausted. (Luke 12:32–33)

Francis Schaeffer has shown us that, because the kingdom is present partially, but not fully, we must expect "substantial" healing, but not "total" healing in all areas of life.[6] Where God exerts his rule through his Word and Spirit, the effects of sin are healed. Thus the kingdom is like a great banquet (Matt. 22:2) and is a state of total fulfillment or "blessedness" (Matt. 5:3, 10). This healing is always partial, because the kingdom is not fully come, yet this healing is substantial, because the kingdom is already present.[7]

Edmund Clowney writes that "kingdom" evangelism must have a holistic focus:

> The renewal of Christ's salvation ultimately includes a renewed universe. . . . there is no part of our existence that is untouched by His blessing. Christ's miracles were miracles of the kingdom, performed as signs of what the kingdom means. . . . His blessing was pronounced upon the poor, the afflicted, the burdened and heavy-laden who came

---

6. See Francis Schaeffer, *True Spirituality* (Carol Stream, IL: Tyndale, 1971), 134.

7. For the classic statement of the "already but not yet" view of the kingdom of God, see H. Ridderbos, *The Coming of the Kingdom* (Philadelphia: Presbyterian and Reformed, 1962), 36–60.

to Him and believed in Him. . . . The miraculous signs that attested
Jesus' deity and authenticated the witness of those who transmitted the
gospel to the church is not continued, for their purpose was fulfilled.
But the pattern of the kingdom that was revealed through those signs
must continue in the church. . . . Kingdom evangelism is therefore
holistic as it transmits by word and deed the promise of Christ for
body and soul as well as the demand of Christ for body and soul.[8]

What is the relationship of the church to the kingdom? On the
one hand, the church is a "pilot plant" of the kingdom of God. It is not
simply a collection of individuals who are forgiven. It is a "royal nation"
(1 Peter 2:9), in other words, a counterculture. The church is to be a
new society in which the world can see what family dynamics, business practices, race relations, and all of life can be under the kingship
of Jesus Christ. God is out to heal all the effects of sin: psychological,
social, and physical.

On the other hand, the church is to be an agent of the kingdom.
It is not only to model the healing of God's rule but it is to spread it.
"You are . . . a royal priesthood, a holy nation . . . that you may declare
the praises of him who called you out of darkness into his wonderful
light" (1 Peter 2:9). Christians go into the world as witnesses of the
kingdom (Acts 1:6–8). To spread the kingdom of God is more than
simply winning people to Christ. It is also working for the healing
of persons, families, relationships, and nations; it is doing deeds of
mercy and seeking justice. It is ordering lives and relationships and
institutions and communities according to God's authority to bring
in the blessedness of the kingdom.

HUMAN DEEDS

Felt Needs

We see that the church is to be an agent of the kingdom. This means
that the needs toward the outer (social and physical) "circles" of figure 1
are the concern of individual Christians and the corporate church.

8. Edmund Clowney, "Kingdom Evangelism," in *The Pastor-Evangelist,* ed. Roger Greenway
(Phillipsburg, NJ: Presbyterian and Reformed, 1987), 15–32.

As we move toward the outer circles of our diagram we notice that the needs become more visible to everyone. It takes the illumination of the Holy Spirit to understand that the deepest need of the human heart is fellowship with God. But anyone can recognize in themselves and others the need for food, clothing, medical treatment, or human friendship. So we see that the needs on the outer circles of the diagram are perceived or "felt" needs.

It is crucial to understand that these "felt" needs are the door to core needs. In fact, Charles Kraft believes that felt needs are the basis of communication.

> The process of communicational interaction on the basis of felt needs commonly results in two ongoing processes. First, certain of the original felt needs get solved. Then, deeper needs, which were originally not in focus in the interaction because they were not perceived or because the receptor was not open about them, come to the surface.[9]

Let's offer an example. A sermon introduction like this is tedious: "I would now like to provide a survey of the biblical doctrine of the sovereignty of God." The following is more interesting: "Many of you have probably been quite worried about something this week, haven't you? The Bible tells us exactly what the causes of worry are, as well as the proper approach to cope with it." Why the difference in impact? This last example *connects the message to a felt need*. The message sender has earned credibility with the listener.

The unbeliever is not necessarily moved by seeing Christians serving the theological and psychological needs of others. They cannot understand the action because they do not feel the need themselves. But unbelievers do feel physical needs. When they see Christians feeding the hungry, comforting the suffering, supporting the financially and physically weak, unbelievers see our service. Through this, hearts can be softened to Christ.

This is not just a "modern" theory of communication. The incarnation itself is the model for it. When God spoke to the people directly,

9. Charles Kraft, *Communication Theory for Christian Witness* (Nashville: Abingdon, 1983), 203.

they could not bear it (Ex. 20:18–21). God adapted his communication to the capacities and needs of the hearers without compromising it. The glory of God unavailable to Moses (Ex. 33) is now communicated to us through the God-man Jesus Christ (John 1:14). He became one of us.

Deed Ministry

Another characteristic of "outer circle" needs is that they are met more through deeds than words. The Good Samaritan could have carried out his ministry without speaking, if that had been necessary. Needs toward the center of the circles require more a ministry of the word, but needs toward the periphery require more the ministry of deed mentioned in James 2:17 and 1 John 3:18.

A study of the spiritual gifts listed in the New Testament reveals that there are two basic categories. There are "word-gifts" which are exercised primarily through verbal skills, and "deed gifts" which are exercised primarily through active service. Jesus himself was mighty in word and deed (Luke 24:19), and in the same way, the church's ministry is two-pronged.

The key New Testament word for deed ministry is *diakonia*, usually translated "serve" in the Bible. The root meaning is to feed someone by waiting on a table. An example is in Luke 10:40, where Martha is preparing a meal for Jesus. A group of women disciples followed Jesus and the apostles, providing food and other physical needs; this ministry is called *diakonia* (Matt. 27:55; Luke 8:3). The work of providing daily necessities for the widows in the early church is also called *diakonia* (Acts 6:2).

The importance of deed ministry is seen in two passages: Luke 22:24–27 and 1 John 3:17–18. In Luke 22, Jesus asks "Who is greater, the one who is at the table or the one who serves [*diakonia*]?" This question is remarkable because in the value of the Greek culture of the day, it was considered highly demeaning to serve someone else. Plato said, "How can a man be happy when he has to serve someone?" Then Jesus makes the startling statement that Christian greatness is the polar opposite to the concept of the world's. "I am among you as one who serves [*diakonia*]."

A *diakonos!* A busboy! This is the Christian pattern of greatness and the pattern of Christ's work. He came to render the most humble, basic kind of service. How careful we usually are to desire the jobs in the kingdom that entail the Word or speaking in the spotlight! No less crucial to the work of the church is the ministry of deed to the most basic physical needs through the most "menial" service. Do we consider it "menial" service to change bedpans in the name of Jesus? Then we are thinking in a worldly way.

In 1 John 3:17–18, we read:

> If anyone has material possessions and sees his brother in need but has no pity on him, how can the love of God be in him? Dear children, let us not love with words or tongue but with action and in truth.

John is boldly stating that love in word only is not really love at all. "Love" means giving one's neighbor whatever he or she needs. Sometimes we must use words to do that; often we must use deeds. We cannot confine our love to "inner circle" needs only, but to outer circle, felt needs as well. To fail to do so is not just "half love," but rather is *no* love.

CONCLUSION

What does the Bible say about a family or church which says "our job is just to preach the gospel" but does not involve itself in "social concern"? The ministry of mercy is essential to Christian love and lifestyle.

Even though the ministry of mercy aims at physical needs, it is a spiritual ministry to physical needs! It has a spiritual motive in the givers as well as a spiritual impact on the recipients. Both the impact and motive of mercy will be explored next.

FOR DISCUSSION

1. What are the four alienations that result from the fall?
2. How will Christ's second coming change each of those?
3. Describe the relationship of Christ's second coming to the church's job to minister mercy today.
4. What differences exist between a felt need and an inner need?
5. How is ministering to another's physical needs a spiritual act?

3

The Motivation for Mercy

And when he saw him, he took pity on him. (Luke 10:33)

OVERVIEW: The only true and enduring motivation for the ministry of mercy is an experience and a grasp of the grace of God in the gospel. If we know we are sinners saved by grace alone, we will be both open and generous to the outcasts and the unlovely.

In the first chapter we saw that God often uses the ministry of mercy as a test of true faith (Matt. 25:31–46; Isa. 1:10–17; James 2:1–26). But why? How does real faith lead inevitably to a sensitive conscience toward the needy?

This brings us to the question of the core motivation for the Christian's ministry of mercy. What exactly is there about the Christian faith that drives us to care for those in need? Is it a simple sense of duty? Or a load of guilt? What is the real dynamic of mercy?

THE GOSPEL OF GRACE

We have already mentioned that the law expert who confronts Jesus in Luke 10 is a legalist. He believes that his own moral efforts can earn the favor of God. He is a self-justifier (Luke 10:29). Jesus, on the contrary, seeks to show the man his insufficiency by putting before him a picture of the love God's law requires.

The Good Samaritan parable is so familiar that we may easily lose sight of Jesus' point. He was seeking to confound the law expert with a vision of selfless love so lofty as to be impossible!

> As well visualize the Ethiopian changing his skin or the leopard his spots, as imagine a Samaritan helping a Jew. But nothing else will do. "An Irish Republican fell among thieves, and an Ulster Orangeman came and helped him; a white colonist fell among thieves, and a black freedom fighter came to his aid; that is what God's law requires of you."[1]

Jesus' goal was to show the law expert, who believed he was spiritually rich, that he was spiritually bankrupt. To be bankrupt is to declare yourself unable to make good your debts. It means you are out of resources. That sounds desperate! Yet Jesus pronounces as "blessed" anyone who has come to that condition. "Blessed are the poor in spirit, for *theirs* [no one else's] is the kingdom of heaven" (Matt. 5:3). D. M. Lloyd-Jones explains this beatitude clearly.

> It means a complete absence of pride, a complete absence of self-assurance and self-reliance. It means a consciousness that we are nothing in the presence of God. It is nothing, then, that we can produce; it is nothing that we can do in ourselves. It is just this tremendous awareness of our utter nothingness as we come face to face with God. That is to be poor in spirit.[2]

We see, then, that Jesus' true goal was to show the law expert he was *poor*, and to prepare him to seek spiritual riches in the mercy of God. Our most righteous deeds, says Isaiah, are like "filthy rags." More accurately, they are likened to a menstrual cloth, and they make us like "one who is unclean," a street leper, in God's sight (Isa. 64:6). Imagine the most unsightly, smelly, decrepit homeless person, wandering the

---

1. Michael Wilcock, *Savior of the World: The Message of Luke's Gospel* (Downers Grove, IL: InterVarsity Press, 1979), 123.

2. D. Martyn Lloyd-Jones, *Studies in the Sermon on the Mount* (Grand Rapids: Eerdmans, 1971), 50.

city streets in rags. He does not have much of a mind left. He has no resources at all. He has nothing to recommend him. *That* is what all of us are before God, says Isaiah. And perhaps Jesus himself was trying to show the law expert his own helpless condition by depicting him as the half-dead man lying in the road.

What, then, is the gospel that Jesus is preparing the lawyer for? It is this: Though we are all lying in our own blood, spiritually bankrupt and lost, yet God has provided spiritual wealth for us. He impoverished his Son so that his spiritual riches, his righteousness, could be given to those who believe.

Paul talks about this gospel transaction in 2 Corinthians 5:21, when he says, "God made him who had no sin to be sin for us, so that in him we might become the righteousness of God." But later he puts this concept into economic terms. "For you know the grace of our Lord Jesus Christ, that though he was rich, yet for your sakes he became poor, so that you through his poverty might become rich" (2 Cor. 8:9). We were sitting on the dung heap, and by his grace, God has clothed us in kingly robes and made us to sit down at his banqueting table.

What then is the gospel of grace? It means that, though poor, we have been made rich through the mercy of God.

GRACE AND THE OUTCASTS

There are two powerful effects that the gospel of grace has on a person who has been touched by it. First, the person who knows that he received mercy while an undeserving enemy of God will have a heart of love for even (and especially!) the most ungrateful and difficult persons. When a Christian sees prostitutes, alcoholics, prisoners, drug addicts, unwed mothers, the homeless, the refugees, he knows that he is looking in a mirror. Perhaps the Christian spent all of his life as a respectable middle-class person. No matter. He thinks: "Spiritually I was just like these people, though physically and socially I never was where they are now. They are outcasts. I was an outcast."

Many people today are very concerned that relief only go to the "deserving" poor. It is true that we must be sure our aid helps a person to self-sufficiency; this issue will be handled in a later chapter. It is also true that we are not obligated to care for the poor of the world to the same degree that we are bound to help our needy Christian brother. However, we must be very careful about using the word "deserving" when it comes to mercy. Were we ever deserving of God's mercy? If someone is completely deserving, is our aid, then, really mercy?

Years ago, Jonathan Edwards wrote a tract to answer the objections of people to the duty of Christian charity. One objection was, "Why should I help a person who brought himself to his poverty through his own sin?" Edwards responded:

> If they are come [into poverty] by a vicious idleness and prodigality [laziness and self-indulgence]; yet we are not thereby excused from all obligation to relieve them, unless they continue in those vices. . . . If we do otherwise, we shall act in a manner very contrary to the rule of *loving one another as Christ loved us.* Now Christ hath loved us, pitied us, and greatly laid out himself to relieve us from that want and misery which we brought on ourselves by our own folly and wickedness. We foolishly and perversely threw away those riches with which we were provided, upon which we might have lived and been happy to all eternity.[3]

Clearly, Christians who understand grace will not be quick to give up on an "undeserving" needy person. Christ's mercy was not based on worthiness; it was given to make us worthy. So also our mercy must not only be given to those who reach some standard of worthiness.

Nowhere is this principle stated more starkly than in Luke 6:32–36. Jesus speaks here of loving one's enemies. He is very specific that this love should take the form of action: we must lend to them when they are in need (vv. 33–34) and we must "do good" to them (vv. 33, 35). "Then . . . you will be sons of the Most High, because he is kind to the ungrateful and wicked. Be merciful, just as your Father is merciful" (vv. 35b–36). God gives mercy to the ungrateful and the wicked—that is what we were. So shall we be like our Father in heaven if we show mercy even to these.

3. Jonathan Edwards, *Works,* vol. 2 (reprint, Edinburgh: Banner of Truth, 1974), 172.

A parable that makes this principle even more forceful is told by Jesus in Matthew 18:21–35. Jesus speaks of a king who forgave a servant a debt of 10,000 talents. Since a talent represented more than a decade and a half of wages for the ordinary worker, it is obvious that Jesus uses this figure to convey the idea of an infinite sum, a debt impossible to pay. After the servant is forgiven, he comes upon a second servant who owes him a small amount of money. The second servant pleads for leniency as the first man had done with the king, but his pleas fall on deaf ears. When the king finally hears of this, he turns to the servant he forgave and says in a rage: "Shouldn't you have had mercy on your fellow servant just as I had on you?" (Matt. 18:33). Jesus' purpose in the parable is to teach the principle of unconditional forgiveness (vv. 22, 35). The ministry of mercy has the same motivation and rationale—the grace of God.

Now we are in a position to see why Jesus (and Isaiah, James, John, and Paul) can use the ministry of mercy as a way to judge between true and false Christianity. A merely religious person, who believes God will favor him because of his morality and respectability, will ordinarily have contempt for the outcast. "I worked hard to get where I am, and so can anyone else!" That is the language of the moralist's heart. "I am only where I am by the sheer and unmerited mercy of God. I am completely equal with all other people." That is the language of the Christian's heart. A sensitive social conscience and a life poured out in deeds of mercy to the needy is the inevitable sign of a person who has grasped the doctrine of God's grace.

GRACE AND GENEROSITY

The second major effect that the gospel of grace has on a person is that it creates spontaneous generosity. The priest and the Levite did not stop despite many biblical injunctions to help a countryman. But no one expects the Samaritan to give mercy. One of the reasons that Jesus puts a Samaritan in the story is that he, by virtue of his race and history, has no obligations at all to stop and give aid. No law, no social convention, no religious prescription dictates that he render service. Yet he stops. Why? Verse 33 tells us he was moved by his compassion.

What a clear message! As Edmund Clowney has put it, "God requires the love that cannot be required." Mercy is commanded, but it must not be the response to a command, it is an overflowing generosity as a response to the mercy of God which we received.

Often books and speakers tell Christians that they should help the needy because they have so much. That is, of course, quite true. Common sense tells us that, if human beings are to live together on the planet, there should be a constant sharing of resources. So when the statistics are brought out to show Americans how much of the world's resources we use, it creates (rightly) a sense of concern for those with less than ourselves.

But this approach is very limited in its motivating power. Ultimately it produces guilt. It says, "How selfish you are to eat steak and drive two cars when the rest of the world is starving!" This creates great emotional conflicts in the hearts of Christians who hear such arguing. We feel guilty, but all sorts of defense mechanisms are engaged. "Can I help it I was born in this country? How will it really help anyone if I stop driving two cars? Don't I have a right to enjoy the fruits of my labor?" Soon, with an anxious weariness, we turn away from books or speakers who simply make us feel guilty about the needy.

The Bible does not use the guilt-producing motivation, yet it powerfully argues for the ministry of mercy. In 2 Corinthians 8:2–3, Paul tells us that the Macedonian Christians gave generously to the Jerusalem famine victims. He notes that "out of the most severe trial, their overflowing joy and their extreme poverty welled up in rich generosity" (v. 2). The Macedonians were not of a higher social class than the needy in Jerusalem. They apparently were going through terrible trials of their own. What, then, was the dynamic that moved them to give? "Their overflowing joy . . ." (v. 2) and "they gave themselves first to the Lord" (v. 5). It was the Macedonians' response to the self-emptying Lord. Their gifts were a response, not to a ratio of income levels, but to the gift of Christ!

Mercy is spontaneous, superabounding love which comes from an experience of the grace of God. The deeper the experience of the free grace of God, the more generous we must become. This is why Robert

Murray M'Cheyne could say: "There are many hearing me who now know well that they are not Christians because they do not love to give. To give largely and liberally, not grudging at all, requires a new heart."[4]

Put another way, the ministry of mercy is a *sacrifice of praise* to God's grace. The risen Lord of our salvation is not here bodily for us to anoint his feet, but we have the poor to serve as a sacrifice to Christ of love and honor (see John 12:1–8). The offering of the Macedonian believers to the hungry abounds to God in praise (2 Cor. 9:12–15), the Philippians' refreshment of Paul is "an acceptable sacrifice, pleasing to God" (Phil. 4:18), and the writer to the Hebrews teaches that economic sharing is a sacrifice of praise (Heb. 13:15–16).

Why is generosity the mark of being a Christian? Imagine a person who is deathly ill. The doctor announces to him that there is a medicine which can certainly cure him. Without it, he has no hope. "However," says the doctor, "it is extremely expensive. You will have to sell your cars, even your home, to buy it. You may not wish to spend so much." The man turns to his doctor and says, "What do my cars mean to me now? What good will my house be? I must have that medicine; it is *precious* to me. These other things which were so important to me now look pale by comparison to the medicine. They are expendable now. Give me the medicine." The apostle Peter says, "To you who believe . . . [he] is *precious*" (1 Peter 2:7). The grace of God makes Christ precious to us, so that our possessions, our money, our time have all become eternally and utterly expendable. They used to be crucial to our happiness. They are not so now.

THE GOSPEL SELF-IMAGE

Only an experience of grace enables us to live an "incarnational lifestyle." In Philippians 2 Paul exhorts us to have the same "mind" that Jesus had, who left his privileges and comforts and deeply involved himself in our human condition (vv. 6–7), speaking to us and appearing in a form we could comprehend. Jesus was the Word become flesh, truth made *visible* through action and deed ministry. And so, we must imitate him.

4. *Sermons of M'Cheyne* (Edinburgh: n.p., 1848).

Do nothing out of selfish ambition or vain conceit, but in humility consider others better than yourselves. Each of you should look not only to your own interests, but also to the interests of others. (Phil. 2:3–4)

Paul tells us we can only live such a life if we have done with "selfish ambition or vain conceit" (v. 3a), and that is only possible if we receive the gospel. Pride in the form of self-consciousness (the "inferiority complex") *or* in the form of self-confidence (the "superiority complex") will make the incarnational lifestyle impossible. But in the gospel we discover that we are far more wicked than we ever dared believe, yet more loved than we ever dared hope. Not self-conscious nor self-confident, a Christian is liberated to be self-forgetful. Elsewhere Paul exhibits the unique self-image of a believer:

I care very little if I am judged by you or by any human court; indeed, I do not even judge myself. My conscience is clear, but that does not make me innocent. It is the Lord who judges me. (1 Cor. 4:3–4)

Paul is not concerned about the verdicts and standards of others. Yet he does not set up his own standards. He is not "true to himself." He rests on the verdict of God. He knows that he is accepted in the Beloved. True humility is not thinking *less* of yourself, it is thinking of yourself *less*. Real boldness, tender boldness, is possible. The gospel of grace makes it possible.

IMITATING THE INCARNATION

Like Jesus, we must look at the "interests"—the needs of even our enemies. Churches cannot say to the world, "you can come to us; you can learn our language; you can help us meet our needs." Instead, we must go to the people of the world, listen to them, become deeply involved in their needs, doing justice and mercy as we communicate biblical truths.

B. B. Warfield, in a sermon on Philippians 2 entitled "Imitating the Incarnation," explains very clearly what it means to follow Christ's example:

He was led by His love for others into the world, to forget himself in the needs of others. . . . Self-sacrifice means not indifference to our times and our fellows: it means absorption in them. It means forgetfulness of self in others. It means entering into every man's hopes and fears, longings and despairs: it means many sidedness of spirit, multiform activity, multiplicity of sympathies. It means richness of development. It means not that we should live one life, but a thousand lives—binding ourselves to a thousand souls by the filaments of so loving a sympathy that their lives become ours.[5]

PUSHING THE BUTTON

Someone may respond to all this by saying, "It bothers me to hear you saying 'a real Christian will be generous to the needy and the outcast' when I know lots of fine Christians who are not very concerned for the poor."

Of course, many true Christians do not evidence the social concern the Bible says is a mark of real faith. How do we explain that? Though it may not be in evidence, a heart for the poor sleeps in all Christians until someone preaches grace in connection with the ministry of mercy. This "pushes a button" deep in our soul, and we begin to wake up. Let me give you an example of the kind of preaching that "pushes the button."

Now dear Christians, some of you pray night and day to be branches of the true Vine; you pray to be made all over in the image of Christ. If so, you must be like him in giving . . . "though he was rich, yet for our sakes he became poor" . . . Objection 1. "My money is my own." Answer: Christ might have said, "my blood is my own, my life is my own" . . . then where should we have been? Objection 2. "The poor are undeserving." Answer: Christ might have said, "They are wicked rebels . . . shall I lay down my life for these? I will give to the good angels." But no, he left the ninety-nine, and came after the lost. He gave his blood for the undeserving. Objection 3. "The poor may abuse it." Answer: Christ might have said the same; yea, with far greater truth. Christ knew that thousands would trample his blood

5. B. B. Warfield, *The Person and Work of Christ* (Philadelphia: Presbyterian and Reformed, 1950), 574.

under their feet; that most would despise it; that many would make it an excuse for sinning more; yet he gave his own blood. Oh, my dear Christians! If you would be like Christ, give much, give often, give freely, to the vile and poor, the thankless and the undeserving. Christ is glorious and happy and so will you be. It is not your money I want, but your happiness. Remember his own word, "It is more blessed to give than to receive."[6]

Can you feel the Spirit of God "pushing your button" under such preaching?

CONCLUSION

What was the point of Jesus' parable? We could put it this way. He was humbling us with the mercy God *requires* so we can receive the mercy God offers. This is the gospel. All of us lie helpless and bankrupt, dying in the road. Jesus Christ, who is our natural enemy, who owes us nothing, nevertheless stops and gives us of his spiritual riches and saves us.

Yes, it is difficult to prove that Jesus was depicting himself in the parable as the Good Samaritan. But this story depicts the pattern of *God's mercy*, and it is impossible not to see Christ in the pattern.

Anyone who has seen himself as the man lying in the road, as spiritually poor, will then live a life of generosity toward the outcast and the needy.

FOR DISCUSSION

1. What is the scriptural motivation for mercy?
2. What are the internal struggles we have against preaching mercy?
3. What things prevent you from being more merciful?
4. Explain the interplay between self-consciousness and mercy.
5. Do you live as if it's better to give than to receive? What keeps you from doing so?
6. What is humility? How does it impact mercy?

6. Ibid., 480.

4

Giving and Keeping: A Balanced Lifestyle

The next day he took out two silver coins and gave them to the innkeeper. "Look after him," he said, "and when I return, I will reimburse you for any extra expense you may have." (Luke 10:35)

OVERVIEW: Christians must give sacrificially, until their lifestyle is lowered. However, giving must be in accord with calling and ministry opportunities. Also, every believer must be a steward of possessions so as not to become a burden and liability to his or her family.

The service that the Samaritan rendered was very expensive. He obviously set aside his own schedule. Wherever the Samaritan was headed that day, he did not arrive. In addition, the Samaritan risked his own safety to stop on such a dangerous road. The expense of this ministry could have been far higher if the robbers had returned! We are told that the Samaritan took the man to an inn where he cared for him all night. The next day, he offered the innkeeper rent for (probably) a few weeks. But his mercy was, in the final analysis, open-ended. "I will pay you for any expenses he incurs."

The ministry of mercy is costly. The man who says "I gave at the office" has a tokenism mentality that is not the Christian spirit of mercy. The Bible repeatedly tells us that it is not enough simply to give to the poor. We must give *bountifully*. In Deuteronomy 15:7–8 we are told, "If there is a poor man among your brothers in any of the towns of the land that the LORD your God is giving you, do not be hardhearted or tightfisted toward your poor brother. Rather be openhanded." The King James Version says, "Open thine hand *wide* unto him . . . sufficient for his need." Paul suggests that small, ungenerous gifts are not just a form of stinginess, but of covetousness (2 Cor. 9:5).

God requires not only a significant expenditure of our substance on the needy. We are obligated to spend our hearts and minds as well. Psalm 41:1 says, "Blessed is he who considers the poor" (RSV). One commentator notes, "The word *considers* is striking, in that it usually describes the practical wisdom of the man of affairs, and so implies giving careful thought to this person's situation, rather than perfunctory help."[1] We are to ponder the condition of the poor and seek ways to bring them to self-sufficiency. This takes a personal investment of time and of mental and emotional energy. God looks for a willing, generous heart, which freely helps those in need, and what we give with our hands is not acceptable without it (2 Cor. 9:7).

SIMPLE LIVING

Is it possible, then, for middle-class Americans to undertake the ministry of mercy without radically altering our lifestyle?

Modern Proponents

Many today call all Christians to "simple living." Their basic teaching is this: give away to the Lord and the needy everything you make except that which is necessary for the bare essentials of life. Perhaps the most famous proponent of the simple lifestyle is Ron Sider. He advocates a "graduated tithe," in which the percentage of a person's tithe increases

1. Derek Kidner, *Psalms 1–17* (London: InterVarsity Press, 1973), 161.

as his income increases. Thus all income over $14,850 (1977 dollars) for a family of five should be given away.

Sider urges families to live communally, to buy no clothes for two to three years, and to radically lower their lifestyle so that they can give 20–50 percent of their income to the Lord and to the needy.[2] There are churches which have been built on such principles. In a book edited by Sider, several such congregations are profiled. In one group, Reba Place Fellowship, many members live in homes and apartments owned by the church. Cars are shared, and there is a food co-op. In 1980 the average monthly cost of living was just $240 for an adult. About 30 percent of all wage earners gave over 50 percent of their earnings to the church; another 20 percent gave over 30 percent.[3]

Historic Proponents

If anyone were to object that the teaching of "simple lifestyle" is a new fad, we must answer that it is not. Perhaps the most famous model of the past was John Wesley. When he died, his estate consisted of a coat and two silver teaspoons, this despite the fact that he earned as much as 1,400 pounds annually toward the end of his life through the sale of sermons and books.[4] This was possible because he never spent more than about 30 pounds a year for his living, even when his income increased forty-fold. He himself wrote, "If I leave behind 10 pounds, you and all mankind bear witness against me that I lived and died a thief and a robber."[5] Another man who lived in very humble circumstances was the famous George Mueller of Bristol. At death he left $850, but it was estimated that he gave $180,000 dollars to the Lord's work.[6]

The idea of simple lifestyle was not confined to a couple of visible leaders. Rather, it was common teaching in the evangelical churches of the eighteenth and nineteenth centuries. It is intriguing to read a letter

2. Ronald J. Sider, *Rich Christians in an Age of Hunger* (Downers Grove, IL: InterVarsity Press, 1977), 172–88.

3. Ronald J. Sider, *Living More Simply: Biblical Principles and Practical Models* (Downers Grove, IL: InterVarsity Press, 1980).

4. Basil Miller, *George Mueller: The Man of Faith* (Grand Rapids: Zondervan, 1941), 126–27.

5. J. Wesley Bready, *England: Before and after Wesley* (London: Hodder and Stoughton), 238.

6. Miller, *George Mueller: The Man of Faith*.

from the great hymnwriter and pastor John Newton to a young husband who was seeking advice about how much to give to the poor. Newton begins by expressing his displeasure at the worldly way in which most Christians handle their economic affairs.

> For the most part, we take care, first, to be well supplied, if possible, with all the necessaries, conveniences, and not a few of the elegancies of life; then to have a snug fund laid up against a rainy day, as the phrase is . . . that when we look at children and near relatives, we may say to our hearts, "Now they are well provided for." And when we have gotten all this and more, we are perhaps content, for the love of Christ, to bestow a pittance of our superfluities, a tenth or twentieth part of what we spend or hoard up for ourselves, upon the poor. But alas! What do we herein more than others? Multitudes who know nothing of the love of Christ will do thus much.[7]

Then Newton lays out his own two guidelines for the ministry of mercy. First, choose a standard of living which is "barely decent"—the plainest necessities of life, without (what he calls) "conveniences" and "elegancies." Above that, we are to spend a penny on the poor for every penny we spend on ourselves.[8] In other words, we should give away half of our disposable income. In some ways this is a less austere plan than Sider's "graduated tithe," but it is nonetheless a stark challenge to most American lifestyles.

Then, second, Newton discourages the Christian from showing hospitality or entertaining for friends who are *not* poor. "Tell them that you love them," he says, but explain that you cannot entertain them, "no, not for a night." Why? "One would almost think that passage, Luke 14:12–14, was not part of God's word." Newton believed that the Bible commanded us to feed and to house strangers and the poor in our own home. Finally, Newton seems to moderate in his conclusion by saying, "I do not think it unlawful to entertain our friends; but if these words

7. John Newton, *Works* (London: Henry Bohn, 1871), 33.

8. Ibid., 34. "Be very certain that you allow yourselves in nothing superfluous. You cannot, I trust, in conscience think of laying out one penny more than is barely decent, unless you have another penny to help the poor."

[Luke 14:12–14] do not teach us, that it is in some respects our duty to give a preference to the poor, I am at a loss to understand them."[9] In other words, Newton admonished Christians to take the money ordinarily spent on entertainment and recreation with friends to be used for your family's ministry to the poor.

It should also be noted that, when Newton urged a simple lifestyle, he did not envision a lot of income going into savings.

> But it may be asked, would you show no regard to the possibility of leaving your wife or children unprovided for? Quite the reverse: I would have you attend to it very much, and, behold, the Scriptures show you the more excellent way. If you had a little money to spare, would you not lend it to me, if I assured you it would be repaid when wanted? . . . Proverbs 19:17, "He that hath pity upon the poor lendeth to the Lord, and that which he hath given will he pay him again." What think you of this text? Is it the word of God or not? . . . I dare stake all my interest in your friendship . . . that if you act upon this maxim, in a spirit of prayer and faith, and with a single eye to his glory, you shall not be disappointed.[10]

John Newton counseled this young family man to (1) choose a standard of living of the bare necessities, (2) use entertainment funds for a family ministry to the poor, (3) make generosity to the poor a higher priority than your savings and retirement. There is every indication that Newton's views were not unusual for an evangelical minister.

BIBLICAL CONTENTMENT

Christians differ widely over the issues we are discussing. As we have seen, some people see the call everywhere in the Bible. John Wesley, in a sermon on Matthew 6:19–23 ("Do not store up for yourselves treasures on earth") flatly states that any Christian who has more than the "plain necessaries of life lives in an open, habitual denial of the Lord; he has gained riches and hell-fire."[11]

9. Ibid.
10. Ibid., 33.
11. Quoted in Sider, *Rich Christians*, 172.

Others have great difficulty with this perspective. David Chilton writes, "God's simple requirement is that we give ten percent of our income; once we have paid that, we know that no more is demanded."[12] No one, this view states, no matter how rich, can be required to give more than a tithe. This is a complete rejection of the calls to simple lifestyle by Sider, Wesley, and Newton.

What does the Bible say about simple living?

Be Moderate

There is no lack of passages which urge upon Christians a moderate lifestyle. Hebrews 13:5 teaches, "Keep your lives free from the love of money and be content with what you have, because God has said, 'Never will I leave you; never will I forsake you.'" We cannot be happy if we are not free from the love of money and from covetousness, which is here defined as the continual drive to increase our standard of living.

But Hebrews 13:5 is not very explicit about what that standard is. First Timothy 6:6–9 is more specific: "Godliness with contentment is great gain. For we brought nothing into the world, and we can take nothing out of it. But if we have food and clothing, we will be content with that. People who want to get rich fall into temptation and a trap." Some commentators believe a better translation would be "food and shelter."[13] Paul here is saying, then, that we need a lifestyle which is sufficient to preserve our health. With that, we can be satisfied.

Be Content

These texts were John Newton's guide when he challenged believers (1) to establish a barely decent lifestyle ("food and clothing"), and (2) not to invest heavily in savings and retirement ("we can take nothing out"), for God is our retirement ("never will I leave you; never will I forsake you"). In both texts, we are told that we must be *content*, a word that

12. David Chilton, *Productive Christians in an Age of Guilt-Manipulators* (Tyler, Tex.: Institute for Christian Economics, 1981), 80.

13. William Hendricksen, *New Testament Commentary: Exposition of the Pastoral Epistles* (Grand Rapids: Baker, 1957), 199.

means a genuine soul-satisfaction.[14] There is no anxiety, gnawing regret, or resentment toward people who have, as Newton puts it, the "conveniences and elegancies" of life. The difference between the Christian and the non-Christian is a trust in God for material provision. "Whoever sows sparingly will also reap sparingly, and whoever sows generously will also reap generously. . . . And God is able to make all grace abound to you, so that in all things at all times, having all that you need, you will abound in every good work. As it is written: 'He has scattered abroad his gifts to the poor; his righteousness endures forever' " (2 Cor. 9:6, 8–9).

Does this mean that Christians have no motive for making money and increasing their income? Not at all! A Christian's first motive is excellence in work for the glory of God. The Bible calls us to skillful, hard work as a means of glorifying God and serving our neighbor (Prov. 18:9; 22:29; Eccl. 3:22). Hard work tends to increase income (Prov. 10:2–4; 12:1, 24), though that is not the primary aim in a believer's vocation (Prov. 23:4—"Do not toil to acquire wealth" [RSV]; Col. 3:22–25).

A Christian's second motive to increase income is to be fruitful in good works. Paul, speaking of converted thieves says, "He who has been stealing must steal no longer, but must work, doing something useful with his own hands, that he may have something to share with those in need" (Eph. 4:28). Wealth is to be accumulated strictly for doing works of mercy and spreading the kingdom. Wealth is not to be stored up "for yourselves" (Matt. 6:19–21).

WEALTH AND GOD'S CALLING

The texts we have read might lead the reader to the conclusion that (1) the rich should give all their money away immediately, and (2) substantial wealth is a sign of wickedness and a lack of charity. However, these statements cannot be supported from the Scripture. By way of balance, we are told several things about wealth.

Paul, in his first epistle to Timothy, has just said that "people who want to get rich fall into . . . a trap" (6:9). In the same chapter he says:

14. Ibid., 198. See also *TDNT,* 1:464–65. Article on *arkeo, arketos.*

Command those who are rich in this present world not to be arrogant nor to put their hope in wealth, which is so uncertain, but to put their hope in God, who richly provides us with everything for our enjoyment. Command them to do good, to be rich in good deeds, and to be generous and willing to share. In this way they will lay up treasure for themselves as a firm foundation for the coming age, so that they may take hold of the life that is truly life. (1 Tim. 6:17–19)

Notice that Paul does not tell the wealthy to stop being wealthy. His admonition assumes they will stay in this state, but that for Christians, this state becomes a "calling," a kind of "spiritual gift."

First, the rich are directed to develop a sound theology of wealth. God gives wealth, so the rich person must not become arrogant (v. 17). That God gives the riches is exceedingly difficult for people to believe! Their hard work and ingenuity often are the means through which God provided material substance. They may be inclined to believe that their affluence results from their own efforts.

Second, the wealthy must use their money so as to be rich in good deeds (v. 18). The stress is on the word "rich." This is not tokenism. Paul's admonition directly echoes the Lord, who said, "Sell your possessions and give to the poor. Provide purses for yourselves that will not wear out, a treasure in heaven that will not be exhausted, where no thief comes near and no moth destroys" (Luke 12:33). Disposable wealth not put to use in God's work will threaten the very roots of one's spiritual life (Matt. 13:22).

How can we reconcile 1 Timothy 6:6–9 with 6:17–19? How can Paul demand that Christians be content with a simple lifestyle and not seek to be rich, and then tell the rich they have a special calling? We cannot assume that Paul is laying down two different standards for two classes of people. We must conclude that, while there may be *rich* Christians, there should not be *rich-living* Christians. Middle- and upper-income Christians are not required to give away all their capital, but they must invest it in good deeds rather than in their own comfort. Wealth is wrong if spent on "yourselves" (Matt. 6:19 RSV). Wealth should not be laid up in store, if the purpose is to say, "Soul, you have ample goods laid up for many years; take your ease, eat, drink, be merry" (Luke 12:19 RSV). A good steward for the Lord knows that wealth, if held and managed properly, will produce more good deeds over a long period of time than if it is given away for good deeds all at once.

The affluent Christian must remember that the call to be content with a moderate lifestyle is written to them, as well as to those who have little. Paul's appeal in 6:6–8 instructs the poor not to resent their lack of riches, but to be satisfied with a modest economic state. Then his appeal instructs the rich not to be proud, but to voluntarily be satisfied with a more modest standard of living also.

GUIDELINES FOR JUSTICE LIVING

How can we bring these scriptural principles to bear practically on our own lifestyles? What is a "barely decent" lifestyle? Should a minister buy a computer for his writing? Should a Christian family own two cars? Or any cars? *How much should we give away?* Let's extract some guidelines from what we have studied.

Sharing the Burden

First, *we must give so that we feel the burden of the needy ourselves.*

Jonathan Edwards met many people who said to him, "I have nothing to spare; I have just enough for myself and my family." Edwards begins his response by questioning the term "just enough."

> Rich men may say, they have not more than enough for themselves . . . to support their honor and dignity, as is proper for the place and degree in which they stand. Those who are poor . . . will say, *they* have not too much . . . and those who are of the middle sort will say, *they* have not too much . . . thus there will be found none to give to the poor.[15]

In other words, a family adapts their standard of what is "enough" by their expectations of their class. This is not the way to decide a lifestyle!
Edwards proposes an alternative:

15. Jonathan Edwards, *Works,* vol. 2 (reprint, Edinburgh: Banner of Truth, 1974), 171.

In many cases, we may, by the rules of the gospel, be obliged to give to others, when we cannot do it without suffering ourselves. If our neighbor's difficulties and necessities be much greater than our own, and we see that he is not like to be otherwise relieved, we should be willing to suffer with him, and to take part of his burden on ourselves; else how is that rule of bearing one another's burdens fulfilled? If we be never obliged to relieve others' burdens, but when we can do it without burdening ourselves, then how do we bear our neighbor's burdens, when we bear no burden at all?[16]

This is a vivid illustration. A poor man is a man walking with a burden—a burden of discomfort, inconvenience. So when a Christian says, "I can't afford to help the poor," he is really saying, "If I help, it will cut into my style of living." In other words, some of the poor man's burden would slide over onto the helper. The helper would not be able to take the vacation he wants or buy the car he wants. "Well," Edwards is arguing, "isn't that exactly what the Bible demands? If your giving to the needy does not *burden* you or cut into your lifestyle in any way, you must give more!"

This principle has ramifications for us all. What about the upscale family who can tithe its income without any curtailment of its living standard at all? Edwards would say that family needs to give more. Is *any* of the burden of needy people falling on the family? It must!

This also speaks to the people who say that no Christian needs to give more than a tithe of his income to the poor and to the Lord. How can a man who makes a million dollars a year spend $900,000 on his own home, wardrobe, and possessions in light of 1 Timothy 6, Hebrews 13:5, and Galatians 6:2? Appealing to the tithe law as a basis for such behavior is a form of Phariseeism. The tithe was required by the Mosaic Law and it was affirmed by Jesus (Matt. 23:23). But the tithe is only a reminder that God owns all our possessions. The tithe cannot be used as a defense against admonitions to give on the pattern of Christ who became poor for us (2 Cor. 8:8–9—Christ did not just tithe!) or against appeals to live modestly so as to be rich in good deeds.

16. Ibid.

Discerning the Call

Second, *we may only keep whatever wealth we need for our calling and ministry opportunities.* We must keep in view that "mercy," "helps," "service" are listed as spiritual gifts. It is clear that some persons have special gifts and thus a calling to work with the poor, needy, elderly, handicapped, and so on. Others may not be called to as radical a ministry of mercy.

There is a great danger whenever we discuss spiritual gifts. Every Christian must witness; but only some Christians have the gift of evangelism. In the same way, every Christian *must* do deeds of mercy; but only some Christians have special gifts for mercy. There are two opposite errors into which one may fall about this distinction. On the one hand, a Christian may evade the ministry by saying, "I am sorry, I haven't the gift for that! I cannot work with the poor!" At the other extreme, it is possible to feel extremely guilty when reading of Christians who pour their lives out in conspicuous inner city ministries to the needy. So we feel, "I can't be like that! I'm a lousy Christian!"

For example, the *Philadelphia Inquirer* carried a story of a suburban working class Christian family who opened its home to the homeless. In two years, they took into their small home nearly fifty persons. As a result of this ministry, the entire family stays in a state of virtual poverty. Is this the model for *every* Christian family?

Probably not. They are expressing specific gifts and a calling that not every family will share.[17] Yet we may not back out of our obligation by recognizing this distinction. Every Christian family (as Newton reminds us from Luke 14) needs to have the poor into their home for meals. Every Christian family needs to have its own ministry of mercy. We must be careful not to rationalize away our responsibility nor to live in constant guilt before the shining examples of others.

---

17. Some teach that "voluntary poverty" is a gift listed by Paul in 1 Corinthians 13. "Chapter 13 is not a separate sermon on love oddly placed in the middle of Paul's treatment of another subject; it is part of Paul's whole treatment of the subject of this book. Thus the inclusion of poverty and martyrdom in this material suggests that they are gifts in the same sense as all the others" (Donald Bridge and David Phypers, *Spiritual Gifts and the Church* [Downers Grove, IL: InterVarsity Press, 1973], 79).

And if we begin to reach out to the poor, we may discover we have a calling we had not perceived before. The way to determine if God calls you to a special ministry is to find an agreement of three issues. There will be a *desire* to do it, an *ability* to do it, and an *opportunity* to do it. Only when these three elements agree is there a call. All Christians are called to mercy. But explore the possibility that the Lord is calling you to deeper involvement with those in need.

This principle is quite important. A family cannot, in a vacuum, simply adopt the stringent lifestyle-reducing measures urged by Sider. There will be resentment and confusion. The ministry of mercy would be an abstraction to such a family. Only when the family has a specific ministry in view will sacrificial living be fruitful and healthy. Thus Christians who reduce their lifestyle to begin projects to help the needy will find spiritual growth for themselves and their families. The purpose of the sacrifice will be clear. But it would be counterproductive for a family, apart from a specific calling to a ministry, to reduce its living standard suddenly and drastically out of a sense of guilt and conviction, even from a study of the Word.

How difficult it is to tread this line! On the one hand, how easy it would be not to seek ways to do deeds of mercy, so that we can continue a comfortable, noninvolved life! On the other hand, how easy it would be to destroy a family (particularly the children) by forcing them into a sacrificial lifestyle for which they are not prepared and to which they are not called!

Supporting Our Family

Third, *we must not be generous in such a way that we or our families become liabilities to others.*

We have seen how Newton and others discouraged an inordinate investment in savings and retirement funds. Nevertheless, wisdom tells us that we must not give away our income so that we or our children become financial burdens to others in later years. In many ways, this is the most difficult balance of all to strike. Many Christians have taught that money spent on insurance is a lack of trust. On the other hand, Proverbs praises the ant, who "stores its provisions in summer" (6:8). Whoever does not "provide for his relatives . . . he has denied the faith and is worse than an unbeliever" (1 Tim. 5:8). Newton expounded that we were not to save a lot of money, it's true. But Newton could not, in his day, have envisioned the medical expenses of our time. The extent of savings is a matter to be left to a Christian's own conscience.

But let's remind our conscience that we will always have a tendency to rationalize too much investment in our family rather than in the poor. In a sermon on giving to the poor, Thomas Gouge responded to the objection, "If I be so generous in giving, I may be in need myself before I die." Gouge replied:

> "He that giveth to the poor shall not lack" (Prov. 28:27) . . . the poor have a right unto part of thine estate, as well as thy [natural] children, though not unto so great a part. In which respect the Spirit of God calleth that part of the rich man's stock which he can well spare, the poor man's "due," unto whom of right it doth belong; for, saith he, "withhold not good from them to whom it is due, when it is in the power of thine hand to do it" (Prov. 3:27). Whereupon said an ancient father, "It is the bread of the hungry which moulders in thy cupboard; it is the garment of the naked which hangs useless in thy chamber; it is the gold of the poor which lieth rusting in thy chest" [Basil]. So that thy relieving of the poor is not only an act of mercy, left to thy choice to do or not to do, but also of *justice*, to the performance whereof thou standest bound.[18]

Justice! Perhaps, in summary, we must call Christians not to "simple" living but to "justice living." "Simple living" is a helpful term, but it connotes that such a lifestyle is an option. Also it can become an abstract exercise in self-denial, an end in itself, rather than a means to the end of direct ministry. The relief of the poor is not only an act of mercy, but also of justice, "to the performance whereof thou standest bound."

18. Thomas Gouge, "After What Manner Must We Give Alms That They May Be Acceptable to God?" (1 Timothy 6:17–19), *Puritan Sermons (1659–1689) Being the Morning Exercises at Cripplegate.* vol. 1., ed. James Nichols (Wheaton, IL.: Richard Owen Roberts, 1981), 244, 246.

CONCLUSION

The Bible calls Christians to be content with a standard of living which is moderate, based mainly on necessities of life. On the other hand, Scripture does not outlaw the rich nor make it a sin to acquire wealth. God approves hard work and wealth is often the fruit of it. But the rich are not exempt from the call to all Christians to be moderate in their lifestyle, and to give sacrificially to the poor.

How can we determine how much of our income to give away? Be sure that your giving cuts into your own lifestyle so that some of the burden of the needy falls on you. Then, look at your own family's gifts and ministry opportunities and find the calling God has for you. Every person and family must minister in mercy. God calls some people to more extensive ministries by giving them desire, ability, and opportunity. Finally, be sure you provide for your own family so that neither they nor you will be a burden or liability to others. Beyond that, trust in God.

FOR DISCUSSION

1. What is your opinion of the biblical authority for the "simple lifestyle" as outlined by Ron Sider?
2. Discuss Newton's three-pronged view of money management. Is it godly? Is it possible?
3. Explain how the ministry of mercy can be seen as "justice living."
4. Examine your views on the issue of acquiring wealth. Is there anything that needs realignment?
5. What rule of thumb can be used to determine how much to give?

5

Church and World:
A Balanced Focus

But a Samaritan . . . (Luke 10:33)

OVERVIEW: As a priority, we should give to needy Christians both intensively and extensively, until their need is gone. But we must also give generously to nonbelievers as part of our witness to the world.

The purpose of the parable of the Good Samaritan is to answer the law expert's question, "*Who* is my neighbor?" Luke tells us that the man was seeking "to justify himself." He wanted Jesus to circumscribe the commandment of neighbor-love down to a reachable limit. In effect, he was saying to our Lord, "Come on, now. Be reasonable! You don't mean we have to love *everyone* like this, do you? Who *is* my neighbor?"

Jesus responds by making a Samaritan and a Jew the two main characters in his story. They were bitter enemies, yet the Samaritan gives aid. Jesus' answer is clear; it demolishes any limitations put on mercy. Who are we to love in word and deed? The answer is, *anyone* you find in need, anyone you find in the road.

But this raises an immediate question. Does this mean that Christians are to make no discrimination between Christians and non-Christians when giving aid? The answer to this question again is a "balance" that requires careful study and comparison of numerous Scripture passages.

THE PRIORITY OF THE COVENANT

A simple review of all biblical admonitions to help the poor reveals that most texts refer to poor brethren—to poor Christians. As we said earlier, the church is a model of the kingdom. We are a paradigm, a counterculture. We are an exhibit of how all the results of sin—spiritual, psychological, social, physical—can be healed under the lordship of Christ. That is why God says to Israel that if they obey him (i.e. honor his kingship), there will be social harmony, good crops, and a lack of disease and poverty (Deut. 7:12–16).

In Deuteronomy 15, God says to his people: "There should be no poor among you, for in the land the LORD your God is giving you to possess as your inheritance, he will richly bless you, if only you fully obey the LORD your God and are careful to follow all these commands I am giving you today" (vv. 4–5). This is probably a double promise. On the one hand, if the Israelites obeyed all God's social legislation for helping the poor, those who fell into need would not stay there long. On the other hand, God is promising a general providential blessing on agriculture and economics if his people obey him. God is saying, "There will be no *permanent* poverty in your nation if you obey all my laws with all your heart."

We conclude that the ministry of mercy was primarily a *covenantal* blessing. That is, it was a healing ministry for those who entered into God's covenant by promising to live under God's kingship. Along with the ministry of mercy, the ministry of the word and of leadership brings wholeness to the covenant people, the community of the king.

The Family and Church

God puts the first responsibility for a poor man upon those in the very closest covenant relationship with him. For example, the poor Israelite was first of all to be helped by his nearest relative (Lev. 25:25). But notice that this covenantal obligation for mercy extends beyond the immediate family. Paul agrees that the family, the closest covenantal connection we have, has the greatest responsibility for a needy person (1 Tim. 5:8).

Second, the church, the people of God, are repeatedly told to care for their needy members. Most of the Old Testament admonitions say, "do not be hardhearted or tightfisted toward your poor brother" (Deut. 15:7). The ordained ministry of the old covenant community collected tithes out of which the poor of the people were helped (Deut. 14:28–29). The Old Testament social legislation included mercy to strangers, as we shall see, but the laws for giving to the poor favored the fellow Israelite. For example, loans to a needy Israelite could not include interest charges, but loans to foreigners could be with interest (Deut. 23:20). In the Sabbath year, when debts were canceled to other Israelites, payment could still be demanded from non-Israelites (Deut. 15:3).

The New Testament community was just as concerned to care for the poor within it. The famous passages on mercy in Matthew 25:35ff., 1 John 3:17, and James 2:15–17 all make reference to a "brother or sister without food." The poor widows were completely cared for through a formal system of mercy aid (Acts 6:1–7; 1 Tim. 5:3–5). In disaster response, helping needy Christians was a high priority. Paul postponed a missionary journey to western regions so he could take funds to the poor (Rom. 15:23–28). Mercy was indeed an honored ministry of the church!

The State

A third covenantal relationship is that of the citizen to his government. It is remarkable that God held even pagan kings responsible to see to the needs of its poor and weak citizens. For example, Nebuchadnezzar is denounced for not giving "mercy to the poor."[1] Joseph became high-ranking civil magistrate in the pagan state of Egypt. He becomes the first in the line of Abraham to become "a blessing to the nations" by providing a hunger relief program for his own nation and all the surrounding ones (Gen. 41:53–57).

---

1. On Daniel 4:27, E. J. Young observes: "With this exercise of righteousness is coupled the practice of mercy to the poor. In the OT these two virtues are frequently associated, cf. Isa. 11:4; Ps. 72:4; Isa. 41:2. . . . In *Tobit* 12:9; 14:11 righteousness and almsgiving are almost equated" (*Prophecy of Daniel* [Grand Rapids: Eerdmans, 1949], 109).

The Bible tells us very little about the government's role in caring for the needy. It does seem fair to infer that such a lack of information *at least* means that the work of mercy is given by God more primarily to the church and the family than to the state. But it seems just as reasonable, in light of God's judgment on the nations and Joseph's example, that the state has a responsibility to help its poorest members. But as we look at these three social institutions—family, church, and state—we see that the closer the covenantal connection, the greater the responsibility for mercy.

In summary, the Christian's first responsibility for mercy is to other believers, to those with whom he or she is in closest covenant. That covenantal responsibility is heavy. "Be openhanded and freely lend him whatever he needs . . . give generously to him and do so without a grudging heart" (Deut. 15:8, 10). We are to give until the needy brother's need is gone.

MERCY TO THE OUTSIDER

Whereas we recognize that the primary responsibility of Christians is to the poor within the body of Christ, the Bible forbids us to neglect the poor outside of the church. Galatians 6:10 puts it clearly: "Let us do good to all people, especially to those who belong to the family of believers." What is "doing good"? Commentators are nearly unanimous that this phrase refers to deed ministry. The context is on the sharing of burdens (6:2) as well as financial contributions to the support of Christian teachers (6:6). Thus we see Paul saying, "The ministry of deed and mercy must be directed first to our own community, but must be shared also with all people."[2] In other words, the ministry of mercy is not only an expression of the *fellowship* of the church, but also an expression of the *mission* of the church.[3]

2. James M. Boice comments on Galatians 6:10: "Finally, Paul speaks broadly about the obligation to do good to all men, returning, however, primarily to the thought of giving money [v. 6]" ("Galatians" in *Expositor's Bible Commentary*, vol. 10, ed. Frank E. Gaebelein [Grand Rapids: Zondervan, 1976], 504). Luther agrees: "This is the knitting up of his exhortation for the liberal maintaining and nourishing of the ministers of the churches, and *giving of alms to all such as have need*" (*A Commentary on St. Paul's Epistle to the Galatians* [London: James Clarke, 1953], 554, emphasis mine).

3. "*Malista*, 'especially' sometimes defines a class more particularly rather than singling out a subclass. It may then be translated, 'that is,' as in 1 Timothy 4:10; 5:8, and probably

Several general theological principles demand that the Christian extend the ministry of mercy to nonbelievers.

Neighbors

First, there is the biblical concept of loving our "neighbor" as ourselves. Some have said that Luke 10:25–37 only teaches that we should help non-Christians in unusual emergency situations. But that interpretation ignores the context. Our Lord is trying to prevent a Jew from confining the ministry of loving deeds to his own racial/religious community. Why would Jesus choose the extreme example of a bitter enemy, a Samaritan, for the hero of the story? The parable of the Good Samaritan clearly defines our "neighbor" as *anyone* at all—relative, friend, acquaintance, stranger, or enemy—whose need we see. Not all men are my brothers, but every man is my neighbor.

Strangers

Second, the Bible (particularly the Old Testament), tells us to render service to strangers. The "stranger" (Hebrew *ger*), was a non-Jew who lived in the land of Israel. The stranger or sojourner had to observe the basic religious laws of Israel, such as abstaining from work on the Sabbath and refraining from, idol worship (Lev. 20:2; 16:29). But he was allowed to eat unclean meat (Deut. 14:21) and did not have to keep the Passover nor be circumcised unless he wanted to (Ex. 12:48). Thus he was not actually in the covenant community, since he lacked the covenant sign, circumcision. We have seen previously that many laws of mercy ministry gave priority to the needs of fellow Israelites over those of foreigners.

But strangers *were* the recipients of mercy. The sojourner was to take part in gleaning from the harvest fields and vineyards (Lev. 19:10; 23:22). He is classed with the widows and the fatherless as defenseless,

---

Acts 26:3. See T. C. Skeat, 'Especially the Parchments: A Note on II Timothy 4:3,' *Journal of Theological Studies,* Vol. 30, April 1979, pp. 173–177. In view of the Thessalonian passages, however, the translation, 'especially' seems better for Galatians 6:10" ("Biblical Guidelines for Mercy Ministry in the PCA" in *Minutes of the Fifteenth General Assembly of the Presbyterian Church in America* [1987], 507).

and therefore God himself will punish those who oppress him (Ex. 22:21; Lev. 19:33–34). In other words, the stranger, though not of the covenant community, had a right to the deed ministry of the people of God.

What do the Old Testament rules on charity to strangers say to us now? The New Testament assumes them. Jesus says to his servants on Judgment Day, "I was a stranger [*xenos*, a foreigner] and you invited me in" (Matt. 25:35, 43). And the writer to the Hebrews exhorts the readers to continue showing hospitality to strangers (Heb. 13:2; cf. 1 Tim. 5:10).[4]

Enemies

A third reason to give mercy to non-Christians is the pattern of God's "common grace" given even to enemies. Common grace is a term theologians use to describe the general blessings God bestows on all people, regardless of their love for him. For example, Matthew 5:45 tells us that God provides physical health and agricultural prosperity to everyone on earth: "He causes his sun to rise on the evil and the good, and sends rain on the righteous and the unrighteous." How generous he is!

Jesus then tells us to use this as a pattern for our deed ministry. "If you love those who love you, what reward will you get?" (Matt. 5:46). In the parallel passage, Jesus tells us to "do good" and "lend" to the unrighteous, to our enemies, for God gives mercy to both the good and the evil (Luke 6:32–36). Jonathan Edwards, writing on charity to the poor, concludes:

> We are particularly required to be kind to the unthankful and to the evil; and therein to follow the example of our heavenly Father, who causes his sun to rise on the evil and on the good, and sendeth rain on the just and on the unjust. We are obliged, not only to be kind to them that a[5]e so to us, but to them that hate, and that despitefully use us.[5]

4. F. F. Bruce says that the "strangers" in Hebrews 13:2 referred both to strangers in general but also and especially those of the Christian brotherhood (*Commentary on the Epistle to the Hebrews* [Grand Rapids: Eerdmans, 1964], 389).

5. Jonathan Edwards, *Works,* vol. 2 (reprint, Edinburgh: Banner of Truth, 1974), 171.

GOD'S MERCY AND OURS

A fourth reason for extending mercy to the needy of the world is the pattern of God's own saving mercy. His salvation comes to the unworthy, the unexpecting, the enemies of God (Rom. 3:9–18). Paul says that he was shown mercy, as the worst of sinners, to exhibit Christ's unlimited patience. When the New Testament calls ministry to physical needs "mercy" as well, are we to believe that our mercy is to operate on a completely different principle than the mercy of God? Or are we not to offer mercy to unbelievers and enemies?

We must remember that God offers his mercy to rebellious people to make them responsible and whole. So, we should render our aid with that aim in view. But must we only offer it to friends and relatives? That is not God's pattern of mercy. Also, the example of God's grace indicates that we should not passively sit and wait for the needy to beg. Rather, we should study, find, and meet basic human needs. Did Christ sit in heaven and wait for us to beg for his mercy? No, Christ sought us and found us.

A fifth reason encouraging us to extend mercy to the needy of the world is the definition of love. We are commanded to "abound in love . . . toward all men" (1 Thess. 3:12 kjv). We are told that love must always be given with loving deeds (1 John 3:17–19) and not in word only. John is, of course, telling his readers to love Christian brothers in deed and in truth. But are we then to assume we can love unbelievers by telling them the gospel (loving "in truth") but *not* by providing for physical and economic needs? Are we to believe that our love to nonbelievers has an entirely different definition than our love to believers? No. To love all people must mean to love them in deed as well as in word.

The Deed Ministry of Christ

We are told that Jesus Christ was mighty in "word and deed" (Luke 24:19). Peter told Cornelius that Jesus "went around doing good," referring to his healing and demon-exorcism ministry. "The number of His miracles which He wrought may easily be underrated. It has been said that in effect He banished disease and death from Palestine for the three years of His ministry."[6] Jesus carried out a miraculous deed ministry of feeding, healing, and exorcism.

Did Christ minister the word to unbelievers but only confine his healing and miraculous ministry to the community of believers? No. He fed the multitude. Not only did he refuse to confine his deed ministry to the house of Israel. In Matthew 4:24 we read that the news about Jesus "spread all over Syria, and people brought to him all who were ill. . . and he healed them." In Luke 6:17–18 we learn that the people from Tyre and Sidon who came to hear him and to be healed were cured. He also healed the daughter of a Canaanite woman.[7] Jesus went in word and deed to the world outside the house of Israel.

We said before that sin has corrupted all aspects of life—spiritual, psychological, social, and physical. The kingdom of God, however, is the renewal of every one of these areas under the power of God. Jesus' miracles were demonstrations of the coming of the kingdom. Jesus' preaching of the kingdom and his miracles are mentioned in the same breath (Matt. 4:23; 9:35). These supernatural deeds visibly demonstrated the way in which the kingdom of God restores the entire creation, and how all the effects of sin are healed under his rule.[8]

6. B. B. Warfield, *Counterfeit Miracles* (reprint, Edinburgh: Banner of Truth, 1973), 3.

7. Ray Sutton writes of the Canaanite woman who asked Jesus to exorcise the demon from her daughter. He points out that Jesus said, "It is not good to take the children's bread and throw it to the dogs" (Matt. 15:26), and that the woman replied, "Yes, Lord; but even the dogs feed on the crumbs under the table" (v. 27). Sutton concludes: "Jesus would not give the exorcism to her at first. She was a Canaanite, outside the Kingdom. Before He would extend His welfare, she had to come 'under the Table'. . . . Her answer told Jesus that she understood this principle and was in fact a dog 'under' His table. The 'poor' of the Bible . . . were *in* the covenant or dependent *on* the covenant (i.e., the 'stranger in the land')" ("The Theology of the Poor," *Geneva Papers*, no. 37 [March 1985]: 1–2).

A more natural reading is to see her reply as the language of humility and faith in Christ. Does this incident show that God only helps the believing poor? Did all the 5000 Jesus fed profess faith before he fed them? See also Matthew 4:24 and Luke 6:17–18, where droves of non-Israelites came to him and were healed.

8. Some object that Christ's ministry to physical ills and needs cannot be parallel to the church's ministry to the physical needs of people. It is pointed out that Christ's miracles were authentications of his deity and his message. Indeed, they were.

In Acts 2:22, Peter tells us that Jesus Christ was "accredited by God to you by miracles, wonders and signs." So too the message of Paul and the other apostles was accompanied by "signs, wonders, and miracles" as proof of its truthfulness (Heb. 2:4; Gal. 3:5). These data lead Warfield to conclude: "Miracles do not appear on the page of Scripture vagrantly, here, there,

Mercy as a Sign of the Kingdom

So then, our own deeds of mercy also point forward to the promise of the new heaven and the new earth, and they also show that the promise of the kingdom is already being fulfilled in the pouring out of the love of Christ through the Spirit! When we visit the prisoner (Matt. 25:36), we proclaim liberty to the captives that Christ will bring in his kingdom the acceptable year of the Lord (Luke 4:18). While the final day of God's jubilee is yet to come, it is already present in the saving power of Christ, manifest in deeds of mercy through gifts of the Spirit. The church goes into the world as agents of the kingdom (Acts 8:12; 14:22; 28:23). This author believes that the church cannot routinely do *miraculous* deed ministry, but we still are to demonstrate the kingdom by our deeds in the world.

We must remember that, while Jesus' deeds of healing and feeding were miraculous signs of the kingdom, they were motivated by a desire to alleviate basic human needs. When Christ feeds the four thousand, there is no mention of Jesus' motivation to prove anything to the crowd by his miracle. (It is unlikely many of them even knew what happened.) He feeds them because "I have compassion for these people; they have already been with me three days and have nothing to eat. I do not want to send them away hungry, or they may collapse on the way" (Matt. 15:32). He saw the crowd, not all believers, in some danger and he fed them. That is a ministry of mercy.

So too, we must follow our Lord. Our ministry of mercy is not simply a way to validate our preaching. Our deed ministry must be motivated by

---

and elsewhere indifferently, without assignable reason. They belong to revelation periods, and appear only when God is speaking to His people through accredited messengers, declaring his gracious purposes" (*Counterfeit Miracles*, 25–26). Even if one believes that Warfield draws too rigid a conclusion about the cessation of miracles, it is clear that Jesus' miracles were primarily his "accreditation" as the Son of God.

But the meaning of Christ's miracles cannot be exhausted by describing them as proofs of his power and person. Herman Ridderbos writes: " . . . in the *whole* of Jesus' power to work miracles the coming of the kingdom is realized and is evidence of its presence. . . . Jesus preached the kingdom with words and deeds. . . . Jesus' miracles occupy a place that is in every respect organic and 'natural' in the idea of the coming of the kingdom, insofar as they render visible the restoration of the creation, and so the all-embracing and redemptive significance of the kingdom" (*The Coming of the Kingdom* [Philadelphia: Presbyterian and Reformed, 1962], 65; refer to pages 65–70).

compassion. When we move to meet a physical need out of compassion (like the Samaritan—Luke 10:33), though we do it without miraculous power, we demonstrate the renewing power of the kingdom of God.

THE GREAT COMMISSION

Exactly what did Christ commission his church to do, under the government of her officers? Most people turn to the Great Commission in Matthew 28:19–20 which seems to put all the emphasis on preaching and making disciples. However, Jesus not only commissioned his disciples on the mountain. John tells us that in the Upper Room, after his resurrection, Jesus also commissioned his disciples saying, "As the Father has sent me, I am sending you" (John 20:21; cf. 17:18).

This is surely a more encompassing statement than Matthew 28:19–20. As we have seen above, Jesus was "powerful in word and deed" (Luke 24:19). He preached the good news of the kingdom, but he also healed the sick, comforted the afflicted, and raised the dead. We have seen that we do not expect ordinarily to follow Christ in a miraculous deed ministry, but we also are to go "into the world" with both words and deeds.[9]

Jesus commissioning the apostles in this way has ramifications for the whole church. The apostles were given the "keys of the kingdom" (Matt. 16:19). "The keys represent stewardship, and this is government," writes John Murray.[10] The apostles not only had unique authority, but they represent the government and leadership of the church in all ages. For the apostles to be sent into the world to minister in word and deed certainly means that the church is being sent as well. We go not just as individual Christians, but as an organized institution.[11]

9. For more on this interpretation, see John R. W. Stott, *Christian Mission in the Modern World* (Downers Grove, IL: InterVarsity Press, 1975), 22–25.

10. John Murray, *Collected Writings*, vol. 2 (Edinburgh: Banner of Truth, 1977), 338.

11. Murray sees the certification of the apostles as governors in all the "sending forth" commissions of Christ (Matt. 16:18, 19; John 20:21–23; John 14–17 as a whole). (See *Collected Writings*, 2:341.)

HISTORICAL MODELS

We learn from history that the early Christians were remarkably generous with economic aid to non-Christians.

Julian became emperor of Rome in A.D. 361. He tried to revive paganism, but found to his disgust that the older religions were falling to the rising popularity of the Christian faith. In a letter to a pagan priest he mentions the characteristics of Christianity that (to his mind) had made it so successful. "It is disgraceful that. . . while the impious Galileans [Christians] support both their own poor and ours as well, all men see that our people lack aid from us!"[12] Interestingly, Julian elsewhere distinguishes the diaconal aid of Christians from that of the Jewish community, which confined its aid to its own members.[13]

The ministry of mercy Julian so ruefully observed was not a new development. In the century preceding, during the great plagues, the church provided financial aid and help to all members of the city. In obedience to the command "love your enemies" many Christians gave their lives in caring for the diseased. This was such a contrast with the selfish conduct of many of the heathen that Christians won great respect for their faith.[14]

There are many modern examples of mercy ministry to the world, but let us choose one that deserves to be better known. That is the work of Thomas Chalmers in Scotland.

The Reformed (Protestant) Church in Scotland was established by John Knox in the sixteenth century. The country was divided into parishes. Each church consisted of two classes of officers: elders and deacons. The deacons were given the responsibility to care for the poor in each parish out of the funds of the congregation. The responsibility of the parish minister included both the temporal and spiritual welfare of all parish inhabitants. He supervised the deacons in the collection and distribution of the parish poor-relief fund.[15] However, both the

---

12. G. W. H. Lampe, "*Diakonia* in the Early Church," in *Service in Christ*, ed. J. I. McCord (Grand Rapids: Eerdmans, 1960), 50.

13. Ibid.

14. Ibid., 52.

15. Stewart J. Brown, *Thomas Chalmers and the Godly Commonwealth in Scotland* (New York: Oxford University Press, 1982), 70.

parochial system and the office of deacon began to vanish by the eighteenth century.

Under Rev. Thomas Chalmers, however, this system was restored in the church of St. John's, Glasgow, during the early 1800s. His parish included 11,513 residents, of which 2,633 were members of his church. Four thousand of the residents were completely unchurched. The entire area was divided into "quarters," each with a deacon over it. Each deacon's job was to keep the Session (the elders) informed about the economic conditions in his quarter. He was to help the unemployed get work and help uneducated children get schooling. When a family was found in need, he was to seek out resources within the neighborhood. If there were no other options, the family was admitted to the poor roll. The statistics from one year show 97 families on the relief rolls of the church, from an approximate total of 3500 families in the parish.[16]

The deacons did not work alone. Each "quarter" was cared for by a ministry team consisting of an elder, a deacon, a Sunday school teacher, and often a lay "evangelist." The gospel was shared and children enrolled in church school as diaconal aid was offered. Chalmers called this program his "moral machinery."[17] At one point, his ministry was criticized as being in competition with the government welfare system. Chalmers readily agreed! He went on to say that the church could do what the government could not. He saw that it could deal with the moral and spiritual roots of poverty.[18]

16. John S. Lorimer, *The Eldership of the Church of Scotland, as it was—is—and may be again: also the Office of Deacons* (Glasgow: William Collins, 1834), 25–26.

17. John G. Lorimer, "Model of A Home Missionary Enterprise, of pastors, missionaries, elders, deacons, week-day and sabbath school teachers, in connection and growing out of a parochial church" in *The Eldership of the Church of Scotland*, 32–34.

18. Thomas Chalmers, "The Influence of Bible Societies on the Temporal Necessities of the Poor," in *Works*, vol. 3 (Bridgeport: M. Sherman, 1829), 67ff. As "radical" as this sounds to us today, Chalmers was actually proposing nothing new. Rather, he was applying the principles and system of the days of the Reformation. Lorimer writes, "Nor is this a new system, but only the old parochial system of Scotland applied to a new state of society, and with such additions as that new state of society demands" (*The Eldership of the Church of Scotland*, 32). Chalmers was a pioneer in "holistic" ministry to the world.

Why did Presbyterians not carry this holistic concept of ministry to the New World? Very illuminating are the minutes of the General Assembly of the Presbyterian Church (USA) in 1892: "The government of Scotland wisely assigns the care of the poor to the Church officials; but this arrangement seems impracticable in an American theory of the relations of Church

CONCLUSION

The Christian's first responsibility for mercy is to those with whom he or she is in covenant. We must give priority to needy believers. Such aid is then one of the healing blessings of Christ to his own.

However, the Christian must go into the world with the gospel in word and deed. It is dangerous even to ask whether we should give aid to nonbelievers, as it shows the spirit of the Pharisee. Jesus has already given us, in the parable of the Good Samaritan, our answer. He provides the most staggering exposition of Leviticus 19:18 imaginable. Who is my neighbor? Any brother, any neighbor, any stranger, any enemy. Our job is nothing less than seeking out and meeting their basic human needs.

FOR DISCUSSION

1. Identify the three social units that have a responsibility to the needy. How is the degree of responsibility dispensed among them?
2. What three biblical principles generally imply that aid to nonbelievers is necessary?
3. How did Christ offer mercy to unbelievers while he was on the earth (other than giving salvation)?
4. How does the ministry of mercy reflect the kingdom of God coming on Judgment Day?
5. Why is the use of a Samaritan an extreme example of a neighbor. Who is a "Samaritan" in your life?
6. Is there anything preventing you from praying for God to use you in a mercy ministry? Explain.

---

and State, and our present denominational divisions" (167). In other words, the Church of Scotland had official recognition by the government and the general weight of support of the culture. It was *the* church. In America, Presbyterian churches were overwhelmed by the size of the country and their comparative smallness. The "parochial" system was never adopted there. Yet this same General Assembly (1892) proceeds to say: "In the meantime, our usages have taught the poor that the State and not the Church is their almoner, but it is high time that it be rescued from this neglect, and restored to its proper dignity as the most ancient and one of the most significant of ecclesiastical functions. . . . The municipal overseer can never be a substitute for the deacon. . . . The Church must prove herself the friend of the workingman. She can and should answer and conquer the communist by the deacon."

6

Conditional and Unconditional: A Balanced Judgment

When he saw him, he took pity on him. He went to him and
bandaged his wounds. (Luke 10:33–35)

OVERVIEW: God's mercy comes to us without conditions,
but does not proceed without our cooperation. So too our
aid must begin freely, regardless of the recipient's merits.
But our mercy must increasingly demand change or it is
not really love.

The Samaritan did not look into the background of the man lying in
the road. Nor did the Samaritan make him fill out an application. He
simply went to the needy man to render mercy as soon as he saw him.
Is this a complete picture of how unconditional our service should be?
Are we to help anyone, regardless of his or her circumstances?

The previous chapter showed us that we are to extend our mercy
to nonbelievers. But are we then not to make any distinctions among
the needy at all? If so, what are they? *Under which, if any, conditions
shall we give aid to the needy?*

WHO DESERVES MERCY?

Many people divide the poor into two categories: there are the "deserving" poor, whose poverty is not their responsibility, and the "undeserving poor" whose poverty is due to their own sin and foolishness.[1] Some think we should only aid the deserving poor. Others believe that our mercy should be indiscriminate and unconditional, except in the most extreme cases (such as aiding and abetting criminals). Our responsibility extends to all the hungry people of the world—everyone is therefore "deserving" of our mercy. Our obligation to them is limited only by our opportunity and resources.[2] These two views clash within the evangelical community.[3] But both views are emphasizing certain sound biblical principles. Again we are confronted with the need to strike a balance.

THE CASE AGAINST "CONDITIONS"

In many ways, we have already examined the scriptural basis for "conditionless" mercy. We have seen that the Good Samaritan parable teaches that we should give aid to our enemies. We have seen that Jesus ministered in both word and deed to the multitude. Though he declared a priority for the House of Israel (Matt. 15:26ff.), he went preaching and healing the sick, inside and outside of Israel.

1. "No theory of helping the poor may be said to be Christian if it does not discriminate among the poor. The old distinction, now despised among social workers, between the deserving and the undeserving poor is a reflection of a biblical theme" (Herbert Schlossberg, *Idols for Destruction: Christian Faith and Its Confrontation With American Society* [Nashville: Thomas Nelson, 1983], 314).

2. See *And He Had Compassion on Them: The Christian and World Hunger* (Grand Rapids: CRC Board of Publications, 1979), 38–40.

3. For an example of the "discriminate" view, see David Chilton, *Productive Christians in an Age of Guilt Manipulators* (Tyler, Tex.: ICE, 1981), especially pages 73–110: "Jesus declares that God's concern for the poor is discriminatory. It is not just 'the poor' in some abstract, general, universal sense who are the objects of God's care. Here they are on the same level with the rich: if they reject Christ, they are themselves, rejected by Him. They wanted benefits, but were ready to murder Him when they discovered he practiced discrimination in His welfare plan" (107). For the "indiscriminate" view, see Ron Sider, *Rich Christians in an Age of Hunger* (Downers Grove, IL: InterVarsity Press, 1977), especially chapter 3. Almost everywhere Sider assumes the "indiscriminate" view. For example, he writes: "The United States and Russia have a bountiful supply of natural resources within their national boundaries. Do they have an absolute right to use these resources as they please solely for the advantage of their own citizens? Not according to the Bible! . . . We must conclude the human right of all persons to earn a just living clearly supersedes the right of the U.S. to use its natural resources for itself" (209–10).

We have seen that Jesus even tells us to do good to the "wicked and ungrateful" and to give without expecting anything in return (Luke 6:32–35).[4] Finally, we saw that our mercy ministry should imitate the saving mercy of God. God did not come to us because we were working for him nor even because we were willing to work for him (Rom. 3:1–18). We were enemies (Rom. 5:10). Is our mercy to operate on a wholly different principle than God's? The ministry of deed should extend to all, regardless of their condition, just as the ministry of the word does.

What conclusions do we reach? First, it is quite difficult to speak biblically about the "deserving" poor. Our aid is called *mercy*, not a reward. How can someone deserve mercy? If it is deserved, is it really mercy? Second, mercy or deed ministry must be done for a particular purpose: to spread the kingdom of God. That means we seek to open hearts to God and bring rebellious wills under his lordship with our deeds, just as we do with our words. Are we to wait until a heart is somewhat righteous before we minister? We *are* ministers of reconciliation (2 Cor. 5:20).

Our mercy ministry, then, must follow the pattern of God's mercy. It comes without conditions.

THE CASE FOR "CONDITIONS"

Despite all we have just seen, there are also very important scriptural bases for having "conditions" attached to our aid.

The Scripture teaches that all people must work. The fourth command says, "Six days you shall labor" (Ex. 34:21). We were built for work, and thus we cannot be fulfilled without it (Eccl. 3:22; 5:12). One modern philosopher said rightly that work is the only thing people can take in any but the smallest doses!

Therefore Paul makes his famous declaration: "If a man will not work, he shall not eat" (2 Thess. 3:10). Paul's term "will not" in a continuous tense probably means a habitual attitude.[5] This is not simply a prediction of poverty for the lazy. Rather, it appears to be an admonition

---

4. Although some want to read this passage as simply a teaching against revenge, a comparison with the parallel text in Matthew 5:45 reveals that it refers to deed ministry as well, based on God's mercy ministry to all men through his common grace.

5. Leon Morris, *The First and Second Epistle to the Thessalonians* (Grand Rapids: Eerdmans, 1959), 255.

to the congregation to allow the lazy brother to experience the consequences of his own behavior. "Don't keep giving food and support to people who then will have no incentive to find a living," Paul is saying.

Another relevant passage is 1 Timothy 5:3–10.

> Give proper recognition to those widows who are really in need. But if a widow has children or grandchildren, these should learn first of all to put their religion into practice by caring for their own family. (vv. 3–4)

It is important to notice that the economic support given to destitute widows is called "honor" or "recognition" (*timaō*). Poverty was not something to scorn! The poor need respect as well as resources. But Paul also tells Timothy to be careful only to support widows who are truly without resources.

Then he continues:

> But the widow who lives for pleasure is dead even while she lives. . . .
> No widow may be put on the list of widows unless she is over sixty, has been faithful to her husband, and is well known for her good deeds. (vv. 6, 9–10)

Here Paul lays down conditions for the widow's admission to the poor roll. She shall not "live in pleasure." The word used here usually refers to immoral living. It could be that single women were then (as now) tempted into sexual sin for emotional and even financial support.[6] Especially important is Paul's insistence that the widow be active in "good deeds." He fully expects the widows on the permanent role to be "working," if not for a financial livelihood, then full of diligence for good deeds. The object of mercy shall be merciful herself!

Let's summarize the scriptural conditions for aid. First, our mercy must *not* make it easier for someone to disobey God. Second, our mercy to the poor must be such as to make the poor merciful themselves. *We must serve them with such wisdom and love that they become, not more selfish, but less!* They must become "well known for their good deeds."

6. Donald Guthrie, *The Pastoral Epistles* (Grand Rapids: Eerdmans, 1972), 101.

One writer puts it perfectly. " 'Serving the poor' is a euphemism for destroying the poor unless it includes with it the intention of seeing the poor begin to serve others, and thereby validate the words of Jesus that it is better to give than to receive (Acts 20:35)."[7]

THE TWO SIDES OF GOD'S MERCY

How, then, can we reconcile these two sets of scriptural teaching? How can we give our mercy freely even to the wicked and the ungrateful, yet still honor the precept "he who does not work shall not eat"? Again we discover that we can only understand our own duty when we look at the grace and mercy of God.

When God's grace first comes to us, it comes unconditionally, regardless of our merits. His mercy is "unconditional" in that God calls us with the gospel before we show any interest or desire for him (Rom. 3:9–18), while we are still enemies.[8] But though God's mercy *comes* without conditions, it does not *proceed* without conditions! God demands our cooperation in sanctification. Why? Because he loves us, and we can only be happy if we are holy. God cannot leave us in the condition in which he originally found us. He therefore demands cooperation with his mercy. We must give ourselves to Bible study, to fellowship with God, to the practice of the truth. If we do not, we will not grow.[9]

7. Schlossberg, *Idols for Destruction,* 315.

8. Ray Sutton writes: "Are churches obligated to give to every drunken and drug addicted poor person that comes to their door? No. A person who has no family or friends to turn to indicates that he has consistently violated the trust of everyone around him. He is a chronic repeater of some offense. He's unrepentant! To give to him unconditionally, sight unseen, is a waste of God's money. . . . Christ had to meet the conditions of the law. In the end, He suffered the full wrath of God the Father. He paid a price. Salvation was not unconditional. Furthermore, anyone who wants his salvation and the offer is to everyone, must repent and believe. Are not these conditions? So, the practice of 'unconditional' welfare is a denial of the gospel!" ("The Theology of the Poor," *Geneva Papers,* no. 37 [March 1985]: 4).

Both theologically and pastorally, these remarks are off-center, I fear. Though the procurement of our salvation was conditional for Christ, of course, Sutton as a Reformed believer should acknowledge that the reception of saving grace is totally unconditional. Regeneration is completely by grace. Man contributes nothing to it at all; God justifies the *wicked* (Rom. 4:5). But in addition to this, it is quite unfair to conclude that anyone without family or friends must have "consistently violated the trust of everyone around."

9. "When it is said that man takes part in the work of sanctification, this does not mean that man is an independent agent in the work, so as to make it partly the work of God and

THE TWO SIDES OF OUR MERCY

So too, *at first*, we should show mercy to anyone in need, as we have opportunity and resources. We should not turn them away by analyzing them as "undeserving," even if sin is part of the complex of their poverty. Of course we should be on the lookout for fraud, and we must not give aid naively, in such a way that it is immediately abused. We must give as a witness to the free grace of Christ and as an effort to turn rebellious hearts to the Lord.

But we cannot stop there. The goal of mercy is not simply to provide spot relief or to stop the suffering. Our real purpose must be to *restore* the poor person. We must carefully build up the individual until he or she is self-sufficient, and that means we must, in love, demand more and more cooperation. Mercy must have the purpose of seeing God's lordship realized in the lives of those we help. We must give aid so that people grow in righteousness. We must not give aid so as to support rebellion against God.

This principle is everywhere supported by the Scripture. When a slave's debt was erased in Israel, the master was required to send him out with the grain, tools, and resources necessary for a new life (Deut. 15:12–15). Counseling, encouragement, education, job training, grants of capital—all these and more may be necessary to develop the poor. Also, Psalm 41:1 (RSV) pronounces a blessing on the one who "considers" the poor. This word means to give careful thought and to propose a design, rather than to provide perfunctory help.[10] So our mercy must have as its goal the rehabilitation of the whole person.

And though we must be extremely patient, *eventually* aid must be withdrawn if it is abused.

We see then that mercy ministry operates on the same basis as evangelism. *Initially*, we offer the gospel to anyone and everyone, as we

---

partly the work of man; but merely, that God effects the work in part through the instrumentality of man as a rational being, by requiring of him prayerful and intelligent co-operation with the Spirit. . . . [Sanctification] differs from regeneration in that man can, and is in duty bound to, strive for ever-increasing sanctification by using the means which God has placed at his disposal" (Louis Berkhof, *Systematic Theology* [Grand Rapids: Eerdmans, 1972], 534).

10. Derek Kidner, *Psalms 1–72* (London: Inter-Varsity Press, 1973), 161.

have opportunity and resources to reach them. "Whosoever will"! We do not wait for them to come to us. But, if *eventually* a person or a group evidences a rebellious and disrespectful attitude toward the gospel, we withdraw. Continued pressure only hardens them and dishonors the message.

"LET US INTO YOUR LIFE"

A man came to the pastor's study asking for money. He strongly smelled of alcohol. The pastor asked him where he lived and what the money was for. "For food!" the man said. He explained he lived in a room nearby and had not been able to find work. The pastor said he would not give him cash, but would take the man out to eat. The man was not too pleased, but accepted the offer. Taking cash from the mercy fund, the pastor took the man out and as they ate, explored his background and shared the gospel with him. He was neither hostile nor interested.

A week later, he came to the church again, asking for money. The pastor said, "Jim, I will buy food for you again, but if you want us to continue to help you, *you will have to let us into your life.*" The man asked what he meant. "I mean that there may be habits and patterns in your life that are involved in why you can't keep a job. If we as a church are to truly help you, we need to look at your *whole* life. You may need help in managing finances; you may have some personal problems (you told me you can't control your temper, remember?). So you see, it would not be truly loving for us simply to give you money unless you let us minister to you more extensively." The man balked and said his life was his business. After that last meal, he has not returned.

Here we see the balance. At first, we must witness to the free love of Christ in our mercy. But at some point, we must call the *whole* person to Christ. Very, very often, it is the needy person himself who then removes himself from your aid. We must strive to maintain this balance. The problem with "conservatives" is that they tend to establish conditions immediately, denying mercy to people who are living unrighteously. By contrast, "liberals" may never attach conditions to further aid.

LET MERCY LIMIT MERCY

At what point, then, do we begin to set conditions? What is the guideline? It is this: We must *let mercy limit mercy.* Sometimes we let revenge limit mercy. "Look at all I've done for that person," we say, "and what thanks do I get?" Perhaps you have looked foolish to others for your involvement with a needy person, and his lack of response has embarrassed you. In other cases, we may let selfishness limit mercy. "That family is bleeding me dry. I quit!" But in the final analysis, only mercy can limit mercy. We may cut off our aid only *if it is unmerciful to continue it.* It is unmerciful to bail out a person who needs to feel the full consequences of his own irresponsible behavior.

Sometimes we may have to say: "Friend, we are not *withdrawing* our mercy, just changing its form. We will continue to pray for you and visit you, and the minute you are willing to cooperate with us and make the changes that we believe are needed, we will resume our aid. Please realize that it is only out of love that we are doing this!" Let mercy limit mercy.

SOME FALSE LIMITATIONS

It is quite difficult to draw fair limitations to our aid. We are always ready to put up too many barriers and conditions.

For example, some of us are opposed to aiding people economically unless they are quite destitute. But Jonathan Edwards, writing two centuries ago, warns that this condition

> is not agreeable to the rule of loving our neighbor as ourselves. That rule implies that our love toward our neighbor should work in the same manner, and express itself in the same ways, as our love towards ourselves.[11]

Edwards asks whether we wait until *we* are destitute before we try to improve our own condition. "So . . . we should in like manner lay out ourselves to obtain relief for him [our neighbor], though his difficulties be not extreme."

11. Jonathan Edwards, *Works,* vol. 2 (reprint, Edinburgh: Banner of Truth, 1974), 170.

We have seen that many are opposed to helping a person if that person was responsible for bringing on his poverty through his own fault. Edwards again subjects this condition to biblical analysis. He first asks what "fault" may mean.

> If you mean a lack of a natural faculty to manage [financial] affairs . . . that is to be considered his calamity. Such a faculty is a gift that God bestows on some, and not on others.[12]

But what if the poverty is not caused by weakness, but rather by outright unrighteous living?

> If they are come to want by a vicious idleness and prodigality; yet we are not thereby excused from all obligation to relieve them, unless they continue in those vices. If they continue not . . . and if their fault be forgiven, then it will not remain to be a bar in the way of our charitably relieving them. . . . Now Christ hath loved us, pitied us, and greatly laid out himself to relieve us from that want and misery which we brought on ourselves.[13]

We see here that Edwards uses the approach we have been advocating. The aid is extended with a call to the person to submit to Christ's ministry to the whole person. But Edwards then asks, What if the person will not change his course of living?

> If they continue in the same courses still, yet that doth not excuse us from charity to their families that are innocent. If we cannot relieve those families without their having something of it, yet that ought not to be a bar in the way of our charity.[14]

Edwards's approach is balanced! There is no room for self-righteous suspicion and condescension. Yet it is full of loving limits and firmness. How much more "modern" was our forefather than we are!

12. Ibid., 172.
13. Ibid.
14. Ibid.

THREE CAUSES OF POVERTY

It is critical to our whole discussion to distinguish among the biblical causes of poverty. What does the Bible say are the causes of poverty? Biblically, there are three answers to that question. One cause is "oppression" or injustice. One of the key Hebrew words most often translated "poor" in the Old Testament is *ani*, meaning "the wrongfully dispossessed." Oppression is any social condition or unfair treatment that brings or keeps a person in poverty (see Ps. 82:1–8; Prov. 14:31; Ex. 22:21–27). Delayed (Deut. 24:15) or unjustly low wages (Eph. 6:8–9), court and government systems weighted in favor of the great and wealthy (Lev. 19:15), and high-interest loans (Ex. 22:25–27) are examples of oppression.[15]

A second cause of poverty is natural disaster or calamity. Examples abound in the Scripture, including crop failures, disabling injury, victimization by criminals, floods, storms, and fires. Joseph's hunger relief program (Gen. 47) helped those in poverty because of famine. God's social legislation assumes that there would be a steady stream of Israelites who would "wax poor" (Lev. 25:25, 39, 47). Such passages seem to have in view this kind of poverty, caused by circumstances.

Third, poverty is caused by personal sin. A life of laziness (Prov. 6:6–7) and problems of self-discipline (Prov. 23:21) can bring about poverty. Expensive tastes and luxury-seeking can be a reason for economic trouble (Prov. 21:17).

Do we see now how crucial it is to distinguish these three causes? These distinctions are essential if we are to avoid uncritically adopting either the "liberal" or the "conservative" ideology toward the poor. The "liberal" tends to see all the poor as oppressed, and thus does not see the importance of conditions in mercy ministry.[16] But the "conservative"

---

15. John Murray concludes that under God's law, even slaveholders were bound to pay just and fair wages. "And this means that bond-servants are to be compensated for their labor in proportion to the service rendered. The principle 'The laborer is worthy of his hire' is not suspended [in bond service]. This places the slavery which the New Testament recognizes in an entirely different perspective from what the word 'slavery' is liable to connote to us" (*Principles of Conduct* [Grand Rapids: Eerdmans, 1957], 99).

16. Liberals tend to see the poor almost strictly as oppressed people—victims of injustice. Thus the *main* component in the social program of liberals is *legislation*.

Consider for example the naive statement by the author of an introductory textbook to tends to see all the poor as irresponsible, and thus overemphasizes conditions in mercy.[17] Both sides oversimplify the complex causes of poverty.

We also must distinguish these three causes if we are to give appropriate kinds of help. We must beware of becoming one-dimensional in our analysis. We should recognize that the roots of much poverty will not only be dealt with by an exhortation to "work," but also with counseling, education, various sorts of aid, and with a display of respect and loving concern.

CAUSES OR CATEGORIES?

It is a mistake to conclude that the three causes of poverty are always separate categories. Many would conclude that the poor victimized by oppression or calamity are "deserving," and those poor through sinful living are "undeserving." It is true that often we can look at a family or individual in need and trace the root to one simple cause. However, those who work with needy families will recognize that very often, all three causes of poverty are present—interrelating and interlocking.

Consider the following three cases:

Shortly after the purchase of their first house, the wife found herself with a surprise pregnancy. The husband then developed a kidney

---

social work: "Although not politically viable, poverty could be totally eliminated in our society by further taxing the rich, and redistributing this tax money to the poor in such a way to raise everyone above the official poverty line" (Charles Zastrow, *Introduction to Social Welfare Institutions* [Homewood, IL: Dorsey Press, 1978], 42).

17. Conservatives, by contrast, tend to see the poor as people who have not "pulled themselves up by the bootstraps." They believe that poverty has increased largely because government welfare has trained people not to work. Thus the main component in conservatives' poverty plan is work programs.

George Grant, in his very helpful book on helping the poor, *Bringing in the Sheaves,* nonetheless limits the scope of his work when he takes this approach. "What is the Scriptural blueprint for poverty relief? Work. Actually, it is not quite as simple as that, but almost" (74). Though he acknowledges the fact that "it is not quite as simple as that," the author stresses programs that provide no aid except as an exchange for some labor (see, for example, 185–89.) He dislikes the "handout" programs of the government, including the School Lunch and Breakfast Program, the Elderly Nutrition Programs, and the Meals on Wheels Program (p. 185). Such an approach displays little thought for the other causes of poverty besides personal sin and laziness. It certainly does not acknowledge how often these causes are intertwined (George Grant, *Bringing in the Sheaves* [Atlanta: American Vision Press, 1985]).

problem and was out of work for nearly a year. He is now back working, but they are saddled with unpaid medical bills, they have gotten months behind on the house payments. They are trying desperately to sell the house, but the market is terrible in their town. They have gotten to the place where they are not eating properly.

A young woman, age twenty-eight, had recently separated from her husband, who fled to a state where he cannot be forced to support his family. The woman has few job skills and must work at minimum wage while trying to support three children, ages six, three, and one.

A man, age thirty-four, comes to the church in need of funds for food. He has a long pattern of not holding jobs because of irresponsibility (being late, calling in "sick" constantly, etc.). His wife left him in frustration with his inability to provide financially for the family with any consistency. He has in the past three years become an alcoholic.

In each of these cases, one of our three causes is dominant and easy to discern. The first family has been victimized by the calamity of illness and physical disability. In the second case, the single mother has been the victim of oppression, the unjust action of her husband; she was sinned against. In the third example, the man has lost control of himself and is in the grips of his own sinful life patterns. In the first two cases, the families did little to bring on the poverty themselves. In the last case, the poor man is clearly responsible for his problem.

Now let's look at another situation:

Two laypeople from your church are visiting in the home of children who attended Vacation Bible School. They find a mother, Mrs. C., age thirty-two, with five children. The oldest girl is sixteen, single, and has one-year-old twins of her own. Mrs. C. has only a third-grade education. Her husband left her five years ago, and she can barely provide for her family. She has been unable to work for a couple of years because of chronic back problems. Oldest daughter Joan shows positive signs of interest in the gospel. But she admits to you that her mother is a drug addict, and that she gets Joan to supplement their income through occasional prostitution. "That's how I got the twins," she adds sadly, "and maybe I've got another coming."

In this situation, the family has been the victim of unjust treatment (by Mrs. C.'s husband and by her parents, who kept her in school only until she was eight). Also, she cannot work because of a physical disability (the back problem, which may have been brought on by stress). Finally, the drug addiction and selling of sex are sins that have already had consequences that are economically and personally devastating. The three causes of poverty are completely intertwined and aggravating to one another.

What do we conclude? Experience reveals that the three causes of poverty often exist simultaneously in a case of need. The person may have sinned, *and* have been sinned against, *and* have been the victim of natural calamity. Thus in many, many, instances of economic need (who can say what the proportions are?) families cannot be clearly categorized as deserving or undeserving, responsible or irresponsible. In such cases, the family is *both*.

CONCLUSION

The adage "grace is free, but it is not cheap" applies to the ministry of mercy. Grace comes to the undeserving, but its goal is to intercept self-destructive behavior. A truly evangelistic church will dispense diaconal aid to non-Christians with boldness, as freely as it spreads the gospel itself.[18] But our love is not mere sentiment. It is active, and it longs to bring about healing and change in the lives of the recipient under the kingship of Jesus. Nothing less will satisfy it.

FOR DISCUSSION

1. Describe the biblical basis for giving mercy initially without conditions.

18. See "The Theology of Diaconal Involvement," Report of the General Assembly Advisory Committee on Diaconal Ministry, in *Minutes of the 45th General Assembly of the Orthodox Presbyterian Church,* 20.

2. What is the biblical basis for changing unconditional mercy? What are your feelings about conditional mercy?
3. What is the overriding goal of mercy?
4. What guidelines can we use to set conditions for mercy? Explain.
5. What are the three causes of poverty, as written in the Bible?
6. Give an example of giving mercy that could encourage rebellion against God. Give an example of giving mercy that could encourage faith in God.

7

Word and Deed:
A Balanced Testimony

"Which of these three do you think was a neighbor to the
man who fell into the hands of robbers?"

The expert in the law replied, "The one who had mercy
on him." (Luke 10:36–37)

OVERVIEW: The ministry of mercy is not just a means
to the end of evangelism. Word and deed are equally necessary, mutually interdependent and inseparable ministries,
each carried out with the single purpose of the spread of the
kingdom of God.

THE GREAT REVERSAL

Most commentaries on the gospel of Luke note that Jesus *reverses*
the lawyer's original question. He had asked, "Who is my neighbor?"
Now Jesus tells a story and asks, "Who *was* the neighbor?"

What was Jesus trying to do? One of the older commentators writes,
"[Jesus is] compelling the lawyer to give a reply very different from what
he would like, . . . making him commend one of a deeply-hated race.
And he does so, but it is almost extorted."[1]

1. David Brown, *The Four Gospels: A Commentary, Critical, Experimental, and Practical*
(reprint, Edinburgh: Banner of Truth, 1969), 267.

How is Jesus able to "compel" the lawyer to acknowledge the hated Samaritan as the hero of the story? *Even a fictional* description of a real act of mercy is by its very nature attractive and compelling. Even an unwilling bigot must bow begrudgingly in honor.

Had we confronted this lawyer, most of us would have concocted a story like this: A Jew (with whom the lawyer could identify) comes down a road and finds a man lying in the road, dying in his own blood, robbed of all his possessions. Upon closer look, he sees it is a Samaritan. Nonetheless, he alights from his animal, bandages up his wounds, and takes him to safety. "Now," we would have said to the law expert, "there is your answer! 'Who is my neighbor?' you asked. Why, even an enemy like a Samaritan is your neighbor if he is in need!"

I doubt the lawyer would have been moved. He would have said, "Ha! If I came upon a dying Samaritan, I would ride over him and finish him off! What a ridiculous story! What Jew with any integrity would act in such a foolish way?"

But Jesus is a far wiser counselor than any of us. He reverses the expected roles of the characters. He puts a Jew (with whom the lawyer could identify) dying in the road. Along comes a hated Samaritan. What does the Jew want from the Samaritan? Why, help of course! And to everyone's surprise, the Samaritan stops and shows mercy.

Now we see how Jesus deftly cornered the law expert. Of course, if the law expert had been dying in the road, he would have wanted aid from the traveler, even if he was a Samaritan. In a sense, Jesus is asking, finally, "Now friend, who was a neighbor *to you*?" The only answer is: "My enemy, the Samaritan!" And the final word? "Well, then, go and give as you would receive! How can you really insist on acting differently yourself?"

THE GRAND APOLOGETIC

Mercy has an impact. It melts hearts. It removes objections. It forces respect out of even those hostile to the gospel. Our good deeds glorify God in the eyes of the world (Matt. 5:16). Our concrete deeds of love for one another are an apologetic for the validity of the Christian faith. "By this all men will know that you are my disciples, if you love one another" (John 13:35).

The ministry of mercy within the Christian community is perhaps the most startling and visible display of our love for one another. This is probably the dynamic behind Acts 4:32–33:

> All the believers were one in heart and mind. No one claimed that any of his possessions was his own, but they shared everything they had. With great power the apostles continued to testify to the resurrection of the Lord Jesus, and much grace was upon them all.

Many have pointed out that this was not a form of communism. Rather, verse 32 is telling us that when any Christian was in need, the other brothers responded with great speed and generosity. In a sense, no Christian acted as if any of his possessions were his own for the using. This economic sharing had to be conspicuous and amazing to outsiders. Apparently it helped give the preaching of the apostles even more power. All the world could see how different the Christians were.

This same pattern is seen in the early church. We have seen how the Roman emperor Julian tried in the fourth century to revive a paganism that was dying before the spread of Christianity. As part of his plan he ordered that hospices must be established in every town for poor relief. "It is disgraceful that. . . while the impious Galileans [Christians] support both their own poor and ours as well, all men see that our people lack aid from us!"[2] Can we avoid hearing an echo of Jesus' words? "And if you do good to those who are good to you, what credit is that to you? Even 'sinners' do that" (Luke 6:33). The Christians were "promiscuous" with their charity, and the world paid attention!

THE PROBLEM OF PRECEDENCE

So we see that the ministry of mercy goes hand in hand with the ministry of the word in spreading the kingdom of Jesus Christ. That sounds like a simple truth! But how that is practiced can be complicated.

2. G. W. H. Lampe, "*Diakonia* in the Early Church," in *Service in Christ,* ed. J. I. McCord (Grand Rapids: Eerdmans, 1960), 50.

How do word and deed actually relate? Must they always go together? Does one have to precede the other? Is one more important than the other? There are several views, and again, we see a need for a balanced approach.

Peter Wagner discerns five views concerning the relationship of word to deed, or of evangelism and social concern. He calls them Positions A, B, C, D, and E. "A" teaches that the ministry of mercy and social justice is the only legitimate function of the church in its mission to the world. "B" holds that social concern is the most important function, but evangelism is part of our mission. The "C" position is that social concern and evangelism, deed and word are absolutely equal in importance. "D" believes that evangelism is the primary function of the church, and the ministry of deed is necessary, but secondary. "E" states flatly that social concern is not the job of the church at all in the world. We carry on only the ministry of word.[3]

Which *is* more important—word or deed? Let's propose the possibility that differences arise on this issue because the very question of "importance" is misguided. For example, which commandment is more important: "repent" or "be baptized"? From one perspective we could say that the consequences of disobedience to the first command would be more disastrous than to the second. But would we be comfortable determining which of God's commands were more important to obey? Doesn't the very question create an unbiblical distinction within God's Word? So, too, it is inappropriate to ask whether evangelism or social concern is more important. They constitute a whole that should not be divided.

Let's study some biblical principles that give us a more biblical picture of how word and deed relate to one another.

NECESSARY MINISTRIES

The first principle is that the ministry of word and the ministry of deed are equally *necessary* ministries. In previous chapters, we have seen that the ministry of deed is not optional. It is a mandate given to all of the people of God and to the church through its officers. In the

3. C. P. Wagner, *Church Growth and the Whole Gospel* (New York: Harper & Row, 1981), 101–4.

Old Testament, there were not only the prophetic and kingly offices, but there was also the priestly office. In the New Testament, there were not only the minister and the elder, but there was also the deacon. Jesus himself went everywhere teaching *and* healing (Matt. 4:23). As Christ came both to speak and to serve, so the church is gifted both to speak and to serve (1 Peter 4:11).

If both word and deed are commands, how can we decide which commands of God are more important? Is it really possible to decide, for example, that some of the Ten Commandments are less important than others? And if this was determined, would that not lead us into the danger of assuming that we can put less energy into our obedience to some of God's laws? If word and deed are both imperative, then they are equally necessary for Christians and the church to do.

Means to an End?

Some teach that evangelism has primacy over mercy, meaning that *mercy is a means to the end of evangelism.* That is, we minister to people in deed as a way of bringing them to Christ. We conduct a social relief program simply to get names for our evangelism visitation team to approach. But deed ministry, like grace itself, is unmerited favor. Luke 6:35 and context warn us not to lend or to do good so as to expect anything in return. God sends down the rain on the just and the unjust, the grateful and the wicked (Matt. 5:45). First John 3:17 tells us that the motive of any ministry is love. If we see a need, we meet it, if we can. This puts evangelism and mercy on an equal footing motivationally. Does a person need an understanding of the way of salvation? Then we share it. Does the individual need medical help, a better education, or legal advocacy? Out of love we give those as well.

On a personal (not abstract) level, it is unthinkable that we could truly love an individual and *not* want both to share the gospel as well as to meet the person's basic human needs. Word and deed are the pro-verbial "two wings of the airplane." Which wing is more important? If you love a person, you recognize your friend's most fundamental need is reconciliation to God. But you do not care for his illness or feed him *just* as a means to that end. You tend to your friend, because you love him.

An Option?

Some teach that evangelism has primacy over mercy, meaning that *mercy needs only to be done in certain circumstances*. "The average church cannot afford to help the poor," is a common response. The attitude is that mercy ministry is a great idea, if we can find the time or the money for it. But to fail to provide for the ministry of word *and* the ministry of mercy is sin, since both are commands of God! To cry that you can't "afford" to be merciful is just a lame excuse. Can the local church actually "afford" to fulfill the evangelistic mandate to take the gospel to every creature? Neither can it "afford" to feed all the hungry. But we must use the resources we do have to obey all the mandates of God to his people.

Next on the Schedule?

Still others teach that evangelism has the primacy over mercy, meaning that *there is a biblically ordained time sequence of word and deed*. There are those who fear mercy will create "rice Christians," people who make a profession of faith to continue receiving food or money or other benefits from Christians. So they counsel against helping a poor man until he has accepted or at least shown interest in the gospel. However, that is an approach far *more* likely to produce nominal Christians.

If we look at Jesus' ministry, however, we see there is no set pattern of sequence between word and deed. Jesus healed a man born blind (John 9:1–7), but not until some time later (days perhaps) did he call the man to himself (vv. 35–41). At other times, he challenges or calls to discipleship before or immediately after he heals (cf. Matt. 15:21–28; Mark 5:21–43).

We see that the status of both the ministries of word and deed is *an imperative*, and the motive of both ministries is *love*. Thus they are equally necessary for the church to carry out.

INSEPARABLE MINISTRIES

A second principle is that word and deed, mercy and evangelism are inseparable, existing in a "symbiotic," interdependent relationship.

If there is one thing we must conclude from all that we have explored up to this point, it is that word and deed are inextricably united and inseparable.

We must not make the error of those who *confuse* word and deed. The World Council of Churches, especially in its statements on evangelism from Bangkok in 1973, holds that social concern *is* evangelism. This group claims that when we feed the hungry, we are evangelizing.[4] Biblically the ministry of word and deed are distinct, but never separate.

The Two-Ends Model

John Stott comes close to separating the two when he says:

> Social action is *a partner of evangelism.* As partners the two belong to each other and yet are independent of each other. Each stands on its own feet in its own right alongside the other. Neither is a means to the other, or even a manifestation of the other. For each is an end in itself.[5]

This seems to be inappropriate language. We can recognize that Stott is seeking to avoid what we also argued against—calling social concern a means to an end. But to say in turn that the ministry of mercy can stand on its own and is an end in itself may pave the way for social concern that is divorced from the preaching of the gospel. This must never happen. Such deed ministry, even with a Christian motivation, cannot spread the kingdom of God. In no way can we say evangelism and social concern are "independent." They are interdependent equals.[6]

4. Quoted in Wagner, *Church Growth and the Whole Gospel*, 102–3.

5. John R. W. Stott, *Christian Mission in the Modern World* (Downers Grove, IL: Inter-Varsity Press, 1975), 27.

6. Though John Stott certainly does not envision our social concern as being completely divorced from evangelism, his statement opens up the possibility. He could be placed by Peter Wagner as a "C" on his spectrum, for Stott seems to indicate that word and deed are equal partners. But at this point the limitation of Wagner's own spectrum is revealed. Stott has set up a "dualism," just like those (at position "B") who say mercy is a means to the end of evangelism! That is, he does not see word and deed as an inseparable, interdependent whole. He sees each as an end in itself. However, Stott gives conflicting signals in his book *Christian Mission in the Modern World* (see page 35: "Yet I think we should agree with the statement of the Lausanne Covenant that 'in the church's mission of sacrificial service evangelism is primary' ").

The Single-End Model

The proper model is not (1) to see mercy as the means to evangelism, or (2) to see mercy and evangelism as independent ends, but (3) to see both word and deed, evangelism and mercy, as means to the single end of the spread of the kingdom of God. To say that social concern could be done independently of evangelism is to cut mercy loose from kingdom endeavor. It must then wither. To say that evangelism can be done without also doing social concern is to forget that our goal is not individual "decisions," but the bringing of all life and creation under the lordship of Christ, the kingdom of God.

Any less comprehensive view will make it impossible to understand Jesus when he says, "Blessed are you who are poor, for yours is the kingdom of God" (Luke 6:20), or when he says he is come to bring the good news of the kingdom to the poor (Luke 4:18ff.; Matt. 5:3). Some (who elevate social concern) simply interpret this as a call to revolution. They say that God wants all the poor of the world to receive a redistribution of wealth. Some (who stress mercy as a means to the end of evangelism) spiritualize the term "poor" completely. They say that it refers only to those who are repentant and humble in heart.

But Herman Ridderbos, a great New Testament scholar, writes, "It may be said that the concept of 'poor' is determined both socially and in a religious-ethical sense."[7] That means we can neither "spiritualize" nor "materialize" the exegesis. The kingdom means bringing the kingship of Christ in both word and deed to broken lives. We have seen that poverty, sickness, injustice, emotional problems, and social problems are all the fruit of sin. We must minister to the whole person. We must reconcile people to God, counsel them to emotional wholeness, free them from structures of injustice, and meet physical needs. But we participate in these ministries all in conjunction with each other. We proclaim the gospel of the kingdom through word and deed.

---

7. Herman Ridderbos, *The Coming of the Kingdom* (Philadelphia: Presbyterian and Reformed, 1962), 189.

INTERDEPENDENT MINISTRIES

We said in our second principle that word and deed are "interdependent" and exist in a "symbiotic" ministry. Now it is time to explain this latter term.

Although we mentioned that mercy and evangelism do not need to be offered at the exact same time, yet they must be coupled, because they are interrelated. The preaching of the Word produces faith (Rom. 10:16–18) and faith always produces good works in general and deeds of mercy in particular (James 2:1–23). On the other hand, we have seen that deeds of mercy have an impact. God often uses them as a means to open hearts to the gospel (Acts 4:32–33; cf. John 13:35; 1 John 3:17–18).

Vain Offerings

Tetsunao Yamamori has expressed this interdependent relationship vividly by referring to the biological phenomenon of "symbiosis." Symbiosis is a condition in nature in which two functionally dissimilar living organisms live harmoniously in interdependence, with each organism being at least heavily dependent on the other, or even not being able to live without the other. Symbiosis is different from "parasitism." A parasite is an organism that feeds off another one to the parasite's gain and to the host's harm. An example of this is a flea on a dog.[8]

Yamamori sees both the ministry of the word and of deed as relating symbiotically.

> From the perspective of the prophets, to have an intimate, personal, loving relationship vertically with Yahweh . . . was one facet of Israel's covenant responsibility; and to "let justice roll down like waters and righteousness like an everflowing stream" in one's horizontal relationships was another. To the prophets, the two were neither identical nor exclusive. They viewed the two relationships as involving two distinctly separate objects but at the same time as mutually inseparable and essential for the full realization of God's kingdom. . . . one

---

8. Tetsunao Yamamori, "Toward the Symbiotic Ministry: God's Mandate for the Church Today," *Missiology, An International Review* 5, no. 3 (July 1977): 267, 271.

could not live without the other; one without the other was a "vain offering" in the words of Isaiah.[9]

Word without deed, a "vain offering"!

Bring no more vain offerings;
  incense is an abomination to me.
New moon and sabbath and the calling of assemblies—
  I cannot endure iniquity and solemn assembly.
Your new moons and your appointed feasts
  my soul hates;

. . . .

When you spread forth your hands,
  I will hide my eyes from you

. . . .

  Learn to do good;
seek justice,
  correct oppression;
defend the fatherless,
  plead for the widow. (Isa. 1:13–15, 17 RSV)

God is saying through Isaiah: "Orthodoxy without social concern is *not* orthodoxy!" So, too, social concern without the ministry of word would be a vain offering. The sharing of our money and material resources with those in need is a pleasing sacrifice (Heb. 13:16), but it must ascend to God also with the sacrifice of praise from lips that acknowledge his name (v. 15). Deed without word, word without deed—either is a vain sacrifice.

Parasitic Possibilities

Yamamori warns, "Where a constant care and self-examination are not exercised, the Church's ministry, instead of becoming symbiotic, may degenerate into a parasitism."[10] This important caution alerts us to the constant tendency for churches either to engage in

9. Ibid., 268.
10. Ibid., 271–72.

mercy at the expense of evangelism or to evangelize at the expense of social concern.

This is clearly borne out by an examination of church models. Many vigorously evangelistic churches become involved in relatively small mercy ministries only when they become very large, if at all. By contrast, many churches who are very committed to extensive programs of mercy and social concern tend to stay small and exclusive. This is true even of evangelical works.

It is this latter phenomenon which has led missiologists like Donald MacGavran and Peter Wagner to give social relief work a "back seat" and to discourage "social action," specifically, efforts to change unjust social structures and institutions. Wagner teaches that churches involved in social action do not grow.[11] But this effort to separate word or deed is not supported by either the Bible or experience. For instance, when the Taiwan Presbyterian Church began to speak out against human rights violations of the minority-controlled Mandarin government, the church discovered that many of the majority of Taiwanese, the Minna Chinese, became receptive to its ministry. The gospel spread among a burdened people when the church moved to help them in their need.[12]

RADICAL MINISTRIES

A third principle is that the ministry of the word, though it does not function properly apart from deed ministry, addresses the most radical and foundational roots of human need.

Many people who say that evangelism and the Word are more important than mercy and deed base this on a belief that the "spiritual" (ministry of the word) is more important than the "physical" (ministry of deed). It is common to speak of "the priority of the spiritual," but is that a biblical idea? God created both the material and the immaterial halves of reality (Gen. 2:4–7). Both the material and immaterial came under the disorder and decay of sin (Gen. 3:14–19). Moreover, God plans to redeem both our spirits (Heb. 12:23) and our bodies (1 Cor. 15)—

11. Wagner, *Church Growth and the Whole Gospel*, 37.
12. Harvie M. Conn, "Taiwan: Church Growth, Ethnicity, and Politics," in *Exploring Church Growth*, ed. Wilbert Shenk (Grand Rapids: Eerdmans, 1983), 60–76.

both the material and the immaterial. How, then, can we speak about the "physical" as being less important than the "spiritual"?[13] Does God give one priority over the other?

> To be interested in things spiritual is not to be interested in things nonmaterial/supernatural/invisible/sacred as opposed to things material/natural/visible/secular. To be interested in things spiritual is to be interested in all of life, now touched by the healing hand of the Holy Spirit. . . . The heavens and the earth, what we call "the natural half of reality," are dignified by God as covenant witnesses (Ps. 19:1ff., Rom. 1:20f.). They are witnesses to what the earth really is designed to be, the garden of God (Ezekiel 28:13) where the Creator meets the creature in fellowship. Adam's fellowship with God is to be shown in his earthly, material activity, his subduing rule over the natural (Gen. 1:28). That is true spirituality.[14]

Having said this, we must nonetheless recognize that, from one perspective, the ministry of the word is the most *radical* ministry. What do we mean by that? "Radical" often is used to mean "extremist," but that is not the fundamental meaning of the word. The *radix* is "the root"; to be radical means to go to the root of a thing. We said in an earlier chapter that our alienation from God, our condition of being in a state of "condemnation" (Rom. 8:1–2), is the root from which all our miseries flow. Psychological brokenness, social injustice, and even physical disintegration are due to and flow out of our warfare with God. Thus, the more radical ministry to the condition of man is to proclaim the word of faith (Rom. 10:8–13). There is no more fundamental means to cut the root of sin and death than with the verbal message of the gospel.

13. When Paul speaks in 2 Corinthians 4:16–18 about "outwardly wasting" and "inwardly being renewed," he is not speaking of the priority of the "spiritual" over the "physical." See Phillip E. Hughes, *Commentary on the Second Epistle to the Corinthians* (Grand Rapids: Eerdmans, 1962): "But the 'outward man' would not be understood in a merely material sense, for it indicates the human constitution with all its faculties and energies, mental as well as muscular, perceptive as well as practical. Indeed, there is no doubt that the significance of the expression is to be found most simply and adequately in terms of that aspect of Paul's being which, being outwardly manifested, is visible to his fellow-men: it is what they see of him" (153).

14. Harvie M. Conn, *Evangelism: Doing Justice and Preaching Grace* (Grand Rapids: Zondervan, 1982), 64.

CONCLUSION

We have seen that (1) both word and deed are equally commanded and necessary for the church because, (2) word and deed exist as interdependent ministries, both as means to the end of spreading God's kingdom. Nevertheless, (3) the ministry of the word is the more radical and basic of the two ministries, in that it goes to the root or the fount from which all human brokenness flows.

What does this mean in practical terms? Experience shows that, no matter how much we acknowledge the theological necessity of both ministries, it can be extremely difficult for a group of Christians to focus on the two equally at the same time. And that may not be inappropriate.

In his article on symbiosis, Yamamori says that either word or deed may be the priority in a given setting. He calls this the principle of *contextual* symbiosis. In other words, "the nature of needs, problems, opportunities, and available resources within a given context of the church's ministry must determine which aspect of the ministry be underscored at any given time."[15]

Let's use an obvious example. There is a tornado in your town. The home of an unbeliever near your church has a tree on it. Do you send an evangelism team there first? Of course not! You go and pull off the tree. You offer the family shelter and encouragement. In this extreme example, we see that mercy clearly has the priority.

Most situations are not so easy. New mission churches may need to concentrate on evangelism, simply to grow into a self-supporting, self-propagating congregation. A church in South Africa may need to display the kingdom with deeds of racial reconciliation which will bring persecution, and make church growth difficult or impossible. Some neighborhoods have obviously more poor in them than others, and so on. Then, too, churches may have *phases* of ministry. There may be a period of several years in which one ministry has the priority over the other, even as both are maintained.

In practice, it will take very careful planning and constant evaluation to be sure that the ministries of word and deed are intertwined in

15. Yamamori, "Toward the Symbiotic Ministry," 272.

the life of the church as in the theology of the Bible. It will not happen naturally. In chapter 12 we will discuss in detail ways to keep the two interdependent.

Mercy and evangelism are like smoke and fire—where one is, the other must be near. If we fail to provide for both the ministry of mercy and the ministry of the word, we may still have an active and successful-appearing church. But actual growth of the kingdom of God will not be occurring. Some of our most famous churches may themselves be "vain offerings"!

FOR DISCUSSION

Read the following case study and the responses of the members of the board. Each one represents a lack of biblical understanding. Write a brief response, based on the Word of God, to each objection.

> A member family of an evangelical church consists of a married couple and two teenage children from the wife's first marriage (she was widowed), as well as two additional teenage children from the husband's first marriage (he was divorced) who live with the family approximately half of the time. While the wife Cheryl has been raised in the church, the husband Max became a Christian and joined the congregation three years ago. Neither could be considered "strong Christians" but they attend regularly.
>
> The husband is legally blind and holds a modest job which was sufficient until Cheryl's children lost their survivors' benefits check. The family knew this was going to occur, but they did not prepare for it, having even taken out some unwise loans which were now outstanding debts. Now they are in severe financial straits.

The pastor discovered the need and brought it to the church board. They very reluctantly approved a small loan, and the following statements were recorded:

1. "If we help this family it will exhaust our resources and we will not be able to help anyone else who may need aid."
2. "This is *God's* money; we can't just throw it away."

3. "If we give them a free gift it would set a precedent, and then we would have to give to anyone who asks. Make it a loan, so we won't have a run of requests."

4. "I don't think we should give to those who have been irresponsible in their planning. People should have to learn to stand on their own two feet. Besides, they'd probably pay the wrong bills."

5. "We once lent to someone else in the church but they never paid it back. I don't think the church should get into such sticky business."

6. "Who is to say who is needy? Lots of people get pinched financially. Why single these out?"

7. "What if someone else made a bad business mistake and had liens on his property? Would we have to help him?"

8. "It's that child support that is his problem, and I won't pay for that. His divorce was not really biblical."

9. "If people in the church knew we were spending money like this they would stop giving. If we give them any more, I will stop giving."

10. "There had better be no pets there—I am not paying for dog food."

Part 2

PRACTICE

8

Getting Started

OVERVIEW: Every Christian family must develop its own ministry of mercy by looking at the needs closest to it and meeting them through loving deeds and a spirit of encouragement.

You are a Christian who is moved by the biblical teaching on the ministry of mercy. Where do you begin? The principles we have been looking at seem to be so all-encompassing, but our resources are limited and our skills are so undeveloped! Where do we begin? How can we even get an overview of what there is to do? Let's start by discerning the Christian's four basic channels for discharging his duty before God to be a minister of mercy.

THE CHANNELS OF MERCY

The first "channel" is the family itself. All individuals and families have a responsibility to develop their own ministries of mercy. We will explore that later in this chapter. The second channel is the local church. Each congregation should develop programs and ministries of mercy that mobilize the gifts and resources of the congregation to aid the needy. We will discuss this in chapters 9 and 10.

Christian service can also be carried out through voluntary associations or "mission societies." These are individuals and families who band together to form parachurch organizations that perform needed services.

131

Historically these societies have been good ways to establish institutions of mercy such as hospitals, orphanages, homes for the elderly, and so on. They are also, perhaps, the best way for Christians to discharge their responsibility to work for justice in society. Some examples of such parachurch organizations will be referred to in chapters 11 and 12.

A fourth channel for the Christian's ministry of mercy is the state. Many argue strenuously that the state has no biblical warrant for helping the needy.[1] But we see that both pagan kings (Dan. 4:26–27) and Hebrew kings (Ps. 72:1–2; Prov. 29:14; 31:9) were called by God to render justice and mercy to the poor. Joseph, a believer who served as a civil officer in a pagan government, saved thousands through a hunger relief program (Gen. 47:13–17). Therefore, Christians can sometimes fulfill God's call to mercy through their function as civil servants. Of course, such a course is often fraught with difficulties. Our ministry to the needy should go hand in hand with the ministry of the word, and many modern governments put obstacles in the way of our doing so.

THE FAMILY AS MINISTRY BASE

The first organization for the ministry of mercy is the Christian family. When God sees a person in need, he puts primary responsibility for aid on that person's family. He who does not care for his own family is worse than an unbeliever (1 Tim. 5:8; cf. Lev. 25:25). But even beyond that, the Bible instructs each family to have a diaconal ministry to the community around it.

In Israel, families were to take care to leave grain in their fields so as to provide for the poor through gleaning. "Do not reap to the very edges of your field or gather the gleanings of your harvest. Leave them for the poor and the alien" (Lev. 23:22). Boaz made provision for Ruth to glean behind his harvesters, to protect and give refreshment to her as she gathered food (Ruth 2:9).

Also, each year, each family celebrated the Feast of Weeks (Harvest), by offering the firstfruits of its farming to God (Ex. 23:16; Lev. 23:15–21). This was celebrated in a family meal before the Lord, including all

---

1. See David Chilton, *Productive Christians in an Age of Guilt Manipulators* (Tyler, Tex.: ICE, 1981), 94, 187–201.

the sons and daughters, manservants and maidservants. But the Lord commanded that each family include the Levites from the town, the aliens, the fatherless and the widows (Deut. 16:11). Heads of families were apparently given the responsibility to see to it that the family's material blessings were shared with the servants of God (the Levites) and the local poor.

In all of these references, we see how important it is for the believing family to establish its own ministry of mercy. The Bible gives directives to take in the hungry and homeless poor for hospitality (e.g., Isa. 58:7). Hospitality is, of course, preeminently the work of the family. This is not to say that a single, unmarried person is without responsibility! What we do mean is that the individual Christian home is the first "building block" in the ministry of mercy of the people of God.

THE FRONTLINE OF MERCY

Newspapers (though not history books) abound with examples of families who were willing to see themselves as God's "frontline" in mercy. The *Philadelphia Inquirer* recently told the story of Al and Laura Miller in Pemberton Township, New Jersey. On just Al's salary as an equipment operator at a local steel plant, the Millers have taken some four-dozen homeless into their modest home during the past two years. Some are victims of fire, or have been evicted from their homes; some are recovering alcoholics or drug addicts, some are teenagers who at eighteen were thrown out of their homes by parents. The Millers allow no one to stay over ninety days. All guests must abide by house rules (no drinking, drugs, beds left unmade, curfews violated, etc.) and must fill out a statement of goals through which they can move to financial self-sufficiency.[2]

In another story the same newspaper tells about Ada Alexander, a resident of West Philadelphia. Five years ago, Cambodian, Laotian, Vietnamese, Thai, and Chinese families began pouring into the neighborhood. Ada saw scores of their children picking through garbage for food. Also, most of the children are left at home alone all day during

2. "Giving Freely: N.J. Family Opens Up Home to the Needy," *Philadelphia Inquirer, 27* August 1985.

the summer, while parents go to work picking the New Jersey summer crops. By slowly working to get the confidence of the children, Ada was able to begin giving free box breakfasts and lunches on her front porch each day during the summer. She procured funds from local Catholic charities and government agencies. Today she daily distributes food to over 300 children.[3]

BEGINNING WHERE YOU ARE

These examples are certainly inspiring, but we are still left with a fundamental question. How does a family begin its own mercy ministry? To answer this, refer to the diagram below and look at the concentric "circles of concern." Each family can explore their specific roles in each of these circles.

Figure 2

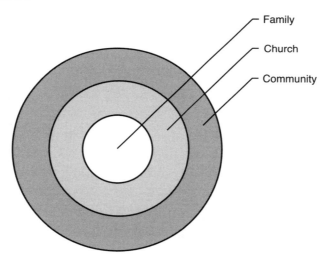

Let's look first at the inner circles.

The inmost circle is in the immediate family itself. Many a Christian family has found its primary mercy ministry in the care of disabled or elderly or chronically ill members. If a family has elderly or infirm

3. "A Clash of Culture and Hunger: Rule May Block Lunches 'to Go' for Refugee Children," *Philadelphia Inquirer,* 16 March 1986.

parents, uncles and aunts, cousins, and other relatives in need, it must not look elsewhere! *Far too many evangelical Christians today hide behind the high mobility and privatization of our society to screen themselves from duties of mercy to their kin.*

The second circle is within the church. In the best churches, most of the mercy ministry is not done through official programs or by the officers. Rather, sensitive individuals watch for needs and meet them out of their own schedules, out of their own pockets, and out of their own hearts. In one modest-sized church, the officers gave away over $10,000 annually through their fund for those in need in the congregation and community. But the pastor estimated that individuals within the church gave twice or three times that much to meet needs in informal, non-programmed ways.

The third circle is your neighborhood or nearby community. Families generally do not need to take a full-scale survey of the community as a church does (see chapter 9). However, we do need to keep our eyes open. The Good Samaritan gave mercy to the man he found in his path. Are there perhaps needs in your vicinity that you may be "passing by on the other side" to avoid, like the priest and the Levite in the parable?

To begin, you can watch the immediate neighborhood the way you should watch your church. Do you see neighbors struggling with grief, loss, sickness, divorce, age, disability, personal problems? Beyond your block, do you see needs in the community? Ada Alexander saw the Southeast Asian families pouring in. The Millers saw the homeless sleeping in the woods and in cars out in the country.

What is the principle here? The family needs to "look in close" before it "looks afar." You must be sure that there is no bleeding man right under your nose, in your family, church, or neighborhood. "Who is my neighbor?" asked the law expert. Anyone you find on your road! So look down at the roads you are walking now. A family's mercy ministry should develop naturally, not according to a formal program. It should be comprised of the needs God has led you to.

The number of needs near us, in our own personal "circles of concern" are actually quite numerous, if we but open our eyes to see them.

STOP, LOOK, AND LISTEN

Perhaps now we are beginning to see that we need to develop a whole new way of looking at our world, if we are to become ministers of mercy.

Do you really stop, look, and listen in the middle of your church and neighborhood? If you do, you will notice a multitude of needs. There is a college student who has had to drop out of school for lack of funds. Over here there are numbers of elderly folk without sufficient support from children, who need transportation, friendship, and other aid. Turn in another direction and listen hard. You will hear single parents, divorced and widowed people, struggling financially and emotionally to be "both mother and father" to children. They often don't seem all that poor and threadbare to the eye, but a sensitive ear will hear the anguish.

Now see the families temporarily in need because a mother or father is sick or injured. Other families struggle under more permanent disabilities; one has a mentally retarded child, another has a father forced to retire early due to a severe back ailment, another family has a mother with Alzheimer's disease. Then there are the terminally ill—families struck by cancer, leukemia, and other such maladies.

Many personal problems that are more obvious in urban areas remain hidden in the suburbs. There are the alcoholics or drug addicts, unwed mothers, abused children, juvenile delinquents, and ex-convicts trying to reenter society.

BUILDING BRIDGES

One of the reasons we do not "stop, look, and listen" is because we *do* know how many needs there are out there, and we are *afraid*. Afraid of what? There appear to be two major fears. First, we do not know how to make contact; we are afraid of "breaking the ice." Second, we do not think we have the resources to help; we are afraid of failure.

Dealing with Fears

Let's look at the first fear. Many of us do not know how to approach another person who is suffering. We know how difficult it is to ask for help or to admit weakness, and we do not wish to embarrass or hurt the person further. So we become passive, fearing to help anyone in our road unless they call to us.

But there is a better strategy to take. We can make it easier for a hurting person to express his or her need and weakness. Your job is to initiate contact. You must turn strangers into contacts, contacts into acquaintances, and acquaintances into friends. A minister of mercy looks around his church and community and makes deliberate efforts to develop relationships in order to find needs to be met through word and deed. Or, if you can already identify someone who appears to have a need, you develop relationships to create a "safe climate" for sharing needs.

Neighboring

Can you actually create these contacts? Absolutely. Here are some simple suggestions. On the most basic level, you must have a general demeanor of "neighborliness." Smiles, waves, facial expressions must be open and warm, even (especially!) in chance meetings.

Or, if you hardly know a person, develop your relationship through social gestures. By "social gestures" we mean efforts simply to demonstrate a desire to know the person better. For example, if you are seeking to meet your neighbors, your newest neighbors will be the most receptive to you. Think up your own "welcome wagon" ideas. Invite them into your home very soon after they arrive. Provide help for them while they are moving in.

The most basic social gesture is hospitality. Invite neighbors and church members into your home. Make friendly phone calls, invite people to eat breakfast with you. If you have children, especially young ones, use your children as bridges for relationships. At church or in your neighborhood, you will find that the presence of your children lowers barriers. Put a child in a stroller and take a walking tour of your neighborhood to invite people to a backyard cookout. You will find people much quicker to talk to you than if you were alone!

Loving

You can also develop relationships through loving deeds. Little loving deeds for more obvious needs may help open people's hearts to let you know of more extensive and deeper needs. Do you have a tool that others often do not have? Offer it to others. Go to the elderly couple on the corner and offer to till their garden this spring. Is there some kind of neighborhood social action you could render? For example, try taking an opinion poll about the heavy traffic on your street, and discuss what the neighbors could do about it together. Can you find some natural way to give gifts? Buy too many bedding plants or too many tickets to the big game. Make too much bread, or plant too many tomatoes in the garden. Then take the extras to your neighbors, to the folks at work, or to people in the church with whom you are trying to cultivate a friendship.

Is there some specific service you could render? You could offer the elderly lady on your block transportation to the market. You could offer free baby-sitting to a single parent. You could notice a neighbor starting to build a shed or doing some painting, and offer to help. Watch especially for crisis situations and be there to offer help.

Perhaps all of the above suggestions seem rather obvious. We do these things naturally to make friends. But keep in mind, most people only work to cultivate relationships with people they *like*, with people they enjoy being with. Christian ministers of mercy are unique in that they intentionally and systematically seek to build bridges with all the people around them at home, at work, and at church. They do this to discover needs and to create a climate in which others can share their weaknesses.

THE SPIRIT OF ENCOURAGEMENT

But besides the contact, you will need to adopt a caring, encouraging, listening stance. It will not do any good to have persons in your home or to spend time with them if you are not an approachable person yourself.

There are many helpful little books for laypeople on how to be a good listener and encourager.[4] Perhaps the most insightful one is Larry Crabb's *Encouragement: The Key to Caring*.[5] The following principles are based heavily on this valuable volume.

---

4. See Gary Collins, *How to Be a People Helper* (Santa Ana, CA: Vision House, 1977); Paul Welter, *How to Help a Friend* (Wheaton, IL: Tyndale, 1978); Alan Loy McGinnis, *The Friendship Factor* (Minneapolis: Augsburg, 1979).

5. Larry Crabb and Dan B. Allender, *Encouragement: The Key to Caring* (Grand Rapids: Zondervan, 1984).

1. *All people hide out of a fear of rejection.*[6] All sinners, like Adam (Gen. 3:10), know that they are fundamentally unacceptable to God. This translates into a general fear we all have to let others see our real thoughts and feelings. We feel that, if we were truly exposed, we are sure to be rejected. Therefore, we all have developed "layers," patterns of behavior that make us comfortable because they hide us from people. Layers are ways of avoiding real confrontation or real exposure of ourselves. For example, some people use talkativeness as a layer, while others use shyness or nontalkativeness.

2. *Encouragement occurs when we help out of love, not out of fear.*[7] It is very possible that our efforts to listen and to help another person are controlled by fear rather than love. For example, some of us may be very hesitant to approach a person straightforwardly about a problem we see in his life. Why? Because we fear the person will reject us, that we will lose a satisfying relationship. If we are controlled by this fear, our encouragement will be quite superficial. On the other hand, some of us are all too willing to tell another person what is wrong with him or her. We tend to "take control," to give lots of advice. Why? Because we fear making mistakes, and we feel self-imposed pressure to solve the problem. Thus our take-charge approach is based on fear as well. And our "mercy" will help no one.

Our mercy is truly *love* only if our efforts are a response to a desire to obey God and to help the person. But our mercy is really *fear*, if our efforts are responses to a desire to stay safe, to look good, and so on. A real minister risks anything—social awkwardness, a tongue-lashing, looking foolish—to respond in love.

3. *Encouragement occurs when we speak to a person's fear without rejecting him.*[8] Some books seem to say that a Christian encourages others by simply affirming and accepting them regardless of what they say or do. But real encouragement seeks to expose and to speak to the fears that

6. Ibid., 27–37.
7. Ibid., 71–77.
8. Ibid., 77–81, 103–9, 125–28.

are driving a person even as we communicate acceptance and warmth. All persons' fears arise because we are pursuing love and meaning apart from God. We deeply fear the loss of status, popularity, love of family or friends, and so on because we do not see that they can meet their deepest needs for self-worth and security in the love and service of God.

People hide because they believe that exposure will mean rejection. We can only help them if we expose them without rejection. We can only do it in stages, with gentle, loving exposure that in turn encourages the person to greater openness. This means, on the one hand, that too quick advice and answers will communicate that we do not take the person seriously. On the other hand, we must be willing to expose, gently and firmly, people's distorted ideas about how they can find love and purpose apart from God.

To accomplish this, we must slow our own responses, and listen carefully with gentle, probing questions. Next, we should constantly check with the person whether we are getting an accurate picture of what he is saying. We must demonstrate that we understand. As we do all of this, the person will find it easier to talk about his fears and troubles. Last, we need to give the person the truth! Encouragement will consist of careful advice, compassionate rebuke, support and assurance, or all of these together.

4. *Encouragement occurs as we communicate our encouragement nonverbally.*[9] Our heart may be motivated by love for a person, but the person cannot see our heart! Outsiders see our eyes and face and body and hear our voice. We must use these things to express love. Squarely face the other person. Lean forward and try to keep hands and arms open. Keep eye contact and relax. Try to smile with your eyes, as well as with your mouth.

CONCLUSION

Dying persons on the road might moan audibly, but they do not have the energy to grab us and tell us all their troubles. Nor would we expect them to. Yet we in effect demand this from those around us.

9. Ibid., 124–25.

Our biggest problem is that we are not willing to consider the bleeding man on our road until he bites us on the ankle! You can easily see the absurdity of the notion.

Are you an active, full-time Christian minister or only a reactive, part-time one? Stop. Look. Listen. Give. Act.

FOR DISCUSSION

1. Identify the four channels of mercy.
2. What are the "circles of concern"?
3. What needs do you see in your particular circle of concern? Are those needs being met? Is there anything else that can be done?
4. What keeps you from attending to the needs you see around you?
5. What kind of encourager are you?
6. In what areas of encouragement do you see a need for the Lord to do a greater work?

9

Preparing the Church

OVERVIEW: "Fertilize" the church for mercy by motivating the whole church. Then do the "spade work" of meeting some basic needs within the church and of surveying the community for felt needs.

THE CHURCH AS GARDEN

We have seen that every Christian individual and family unit is to have a ministry of mercy. In the last chapter we described two families that had extensive ministries to their neighbors. But ordinarily, a Christian should seek to express mercy ministry through his or her local congregation. There our work is enhanced and complemented by all the varied gifts of the body of Christ.

If you are a Christian convinced of the importance of mercy ministry, you may be quite unhappy with your own congregation! Very few evangelical churches do much in the way of deed ministry outside of the annual donation of food at Christmas or Thanksgiving. But there is no "quick fix" for this situation. Many conscientious Christians, whether laypersons or pastors, have tried to rush their local churches into beginning programs for the needy. The result is usually failure, frustration, and anger. Why?

Let's think of the church as a garden (as does Paul in 1 Corinthians 3). How do we get tomatoes from the garden? By rushing out on the first day of spring and throwing seeds out onto the ground? No, we must prepare the garden carefully for the seeds. We may fertilize the soil. We have to break up the ground and prepare the earth for the seeds. In the same way, ministries of mercy will only spring up if the church is prepared for them. We cannot emphasize this too much. Fertilize and "dig up" until the congregation is ready!

FERTILIZING THE GARDEN

"Grass-Roots" Motivation

As soon as we exhort a lay Christian to work through the local church, we are immediately confronted with a round of objections. "My church hardly knows what the ministry of mercy is! Do I have to convince the officers and leaders of my church about their responsibilities before I can do anything here? Whenever I bring these matters up, half the folks look at me like I'm a little 'liberal', and the other half complain that 'all this would take too much money!' And besides, who am I to instruct my own pastor in such things?"

There is no doubt that the ministry of mercy can be carried out on a costly, grand scale. For instance, there is a black evangelical church in a poor, inner-city area of northern Philadelphia that is currently building high-rise housing for the elderly, a Christian medical center, and a whole shopping center to generate jobs and income for that region. Obviously the leadership is spearheading this operation. The bill for the project is over $20 million.

On the other hand, it is possible for churches to carry out significant ministries of mercy without taxing the church budget for even one cent. In one church, five laypeople began to pray and study about ways to minister to prisoners. They began to visit prisoners and write some of them weekly. Soon they made arrangements to bring prisoners (accompanied by a prison guard) monthly to a Sunday morning worship service. After the service forty to fifty church members provided a covered-dish supper for the inmates and befriended them. When some of the men began to finish their prison terms and be released, several member families agreed to help them find jobs and places to live.

The real key to mercy ministry is *motivated lay volunteers*. When a group of people begins to learn how to minister to a particular need, and when they are willing to commit significant time and emotion to the ministry, then you have all the resources you need.

It is a great mistake to believe that mercy ministry can be imposed from "the top down" on a congregation by the leadership. It is most effective when it "bubbles up" out of the lives of people who are burdened for ministry to a particular need. Officers cannot simply begin to say, "All right! We are going to reach out to this neighborhood and to the needy! The sign-up sheet is on the bulletin board." Mercy *is* a command of God, yet it cannot simply be a response to a demand. It must arise out of hearts made generous and gracious by an understanding and experience of God's mercy. It is the hearts of the congregation that must be melted until they ask, "Where is my neighbor?"

Motivation for mercy ministry, then, must begin at the grass roots. Any layperson can begin the process. The Bible says we are to "consider [ponder, plan] how to stir up one another [each layperson speaking to others] to love and good works" (Heb. 10:24 RSV).

Motivating the Congregation

The major way to do this is by exposing the people to what the Word of God says about the ministry of mercy.

Of course, the main way to motivate and move a congregation is through the pulpit. If you are a preacher, you must take the responsibility to preach the gospel of grace in such a way that it motivates people to deeds of mercy to the poor. Chapters 1–3 of this book isolate important themes and lines of argumentation that a preacher can use. By no means will one or two super sermons do the job. Rather, the preacher must preach mercy periodically, routinely.

If you are not a preacher, there are many other ways to spread biblical teaching on mercy around the congregation. If you are an officer, and your church's worship format allows it, you may ask to occasionally give brief addresses to the congregation on stewardship of our gifts and substance.

Let Bible study groups look at the reasonable provisions in Israel for the lifting up of the poor (Deut. 15:1–11). Explore the prophets' and Jesus' teaching that mercy toward the poor is a necessary sign of true religion (Isa. 58:6–7; Amos 4:1–6; 5:21–24; Matt. 25:34ff.; Luke 6:29–34; 14:13–14). Consider the ministry of mercy of the early church (Acts 2:44–47; 4:32ff.; Rom. 15:1–28; 2 Cor. 8:13–14; Gal. 2:10; 6:9–10; James 1:27–2:16; 1 John 3:16–17).

Another important way to generate motivation for the ministry of mercy is through classes, study groups, or just the informal circulation of books on the subject. The importance of study groups cannot be overestimated. Countless plans and programs tor mercy ministry have arisen out of classes of people who learned these biblical principles together. If your church has an elective system, there should be *at least* an annual class exploring the ministry of compassion and caring.

The volume you are reading now is explicitly designed to be used as a basis for such study. An excellent volume also designed for such study groups is *Good Samaritan Faith* by Bernard Thompson (Regal). Other recommended books that can serve the same purpose include *Unleashing the Church* and *Unleashing Your Potential* by Frank Tillapaugh (Regal), *The Second Greatest Commandment* by William Fletcher (NavPress), *Evangelism: Doing Justice and Preaching Grace* by Harvie Conn (Zondervan), and *With Justice for All* by John Perkins (Regal).

Another way to "stir up" people to deeds of mercy is through direct observation of actual churches which effectively minister through word and deed. These may be few and far between in your vicinity! However, if you know of an evangelical church with a particularly effective ministry of mercy, arrange a field trip. Take a group of people to visit the site of the ministry and talk to the volunteers who work with it. If this is not feasible, get someone from the church or ministry to come to your congregation to speak and to share about the work.

Perhaps the greatest way for an individual Christian to "stir up" others to deeds of mercy is with the attractiveness of his or her own life. Peter exhorts elders to lead "by example"; they are to earn their persuasiveness through the moral beauty of their own godly lifestyle. One aspect of this would be our own willingness to pay the cost of mercy. In one congregation, a family adopted a number of Ethiopian orphans. Later, the head of that family found it easier than anyone else to recruit others for service ministries. His call to others had the power of authenticity!

Modeling a Servant Heart

Do you have the spirit and heart of a servant? Unless you do, you will not be able to incite others to love and good works. Many Christians who wish to motivate their congregation to deeds of mercy are completely ineffective because of their own impatience and self-righteousness. As we have seen in chapter 3, self-righteousness destroys any impulses to mercy.

Once there were two young men who began to help the poor through their church. They soon discovered that many members were unhappy that they were bringing to church some of these folks of another race. The young men were furious, and they took every opportunity to castigate the church for its lack of mercy. But their resentment and anger exhibited their own bigotry: they looked down their nose at people who looked down their nose at people! They did not recognize that they were saved from racial prejudice by grace alone, and therefore they could not correct others trapped in the sin with patience and gentleness (Gal. 6:1). When they did try to motivate people to mercy, they appealed to guilt instead of to grace. They were not patient with the people or with God's sovereign timing. In the end, they were ineffective as pacesetters for their congregation.

Jesus, the Servant

It is important to develop the mindset and spirit of Jesus. Look at Jesus washing the feet of the disciples in John 13:1–14. Foot washing was pleasant for the hot and tired guests at a dinner, but it was menial work, fit only for slaves.

Why did he do such a thing? In Luke 22:24–27 we are told that immediately after the first Lord's Supper, a dispute arose among the disciples over who would be the greatest. Jesus asked them "Who is greater, the one who is at the table or the one who serves? . . . I am among you as one who serves." The word he uses for "serve" is *diakoneo*, to deacon. Again, let us remember that this word originally referred to a table waiter or a busboy—one who humbly meets the most basic needs of people. That is the pattern Jesus chose to describe his own ministry. It is safe to assume that John 13 had reference to the discussion in Luke 22. In a sense, the foot washing was an exposition of

Luke 22:24–27 and thus a pattern for the ministry of service that all Christians must have.

A deacon, then, is someone with both a special task *and* a special attitude. The task of deaconing is to meet basic human needs for food, shelter, and so on. Thus the daily distribution of funds for the support of poor widows was called the *diakonia* (Acts 6:1–6). But a deacon must also be characterized by an attitude, the servant heart.

Three aspects or characteristics of that attitude can be seen in the example of our Lord that night. First of all, Jesus washed feet despite his impending death. Jesus was to have the wrath of God poured out on him. He was feeling the tremendous weight of that even at the supper. When we are hurting, with a load of care on our backs, do we look around and notice that people's feet need to be washed? Do we look for little ways to serve? No! We are usually absorbed in our troubles, and we want people to take care of us. But Jesus loved *without self-pity*.

A real servant does not say, "When I get my life together, when I get over my blues, when I get my schedule in order, then I will start to minister." Perhaps you are hurting, and you may even be angry because no one is noticing. But where would you be if Jesus had your attitude? Serving others is one of the best ways to overcome depression. (Isa. 58:10—"If you spend yourselves in behalf of the hungry . . . then your light will rise in the darkness, and your night will become like the noonday.")

Second, Jesus served despite the unworthiness of the disciples. Notice John's reminder that Jesus knew the betrayer was present (13:2, 10). Jesus saw them all—one betrayer, one denier, all forsakers! When he needed them most, they would leave him. One of those sets of feet was dirty and sore from an errand that arranged for his torture and death. What did Jesus do? He washed those feet. Jesus loved *without discrimination*, without looking at our worthiness.

Jesus tells us that when servants have worked hard at *diakonia*, they must avoid expecting lots of recognition and thanks. After the Lord has asked for *diakonia* (Luke 17:8), and we have rendered it, we must say, "we are unworthy servants; we have only done our duty" (17:10).

A real deacon, then, can serve those who are not kind and grateful in return (Luke 6:35). Why? A Christian is no man's creditor, and every man's debtor. A Christian, when he is in his right mind, says, "Look who I am in Christ! I have come to fullness of life in him. I will rule and reign with Christ forever. I am accepted in the Beloved. God will meet all my needs according to his riches in glory. Oh, world, you owe me nothing! I deserved hell, and now, by God's mercy, I am rich beyond the wildest dreams of an earthly billionaire. Do I need recognition, awards, pats on the back, expressions of gratitude? Does a billionaire mind when a thief steals a quarter from his pocket? How then shall I ever be shaken by an insult, a cold shoulder, or a thankless person."

The Mind of a Servant

Are you in your right mind? Aren't there unattractive, thankless people in your life whom you should be loving and serving, but whom you are about to give up on? Maybe it is a spouse? Your parents? Others in the church? Pastors often hear: "I work my fingers to the bone in this church and what thanks do I get?" Is that the way it is? Your service was for thanks? Are you in your right mind? Servanthood begins where gratitude and applause end. Do you only serve people whom you like or whom you find attractive or who are like you? Even sinners do that (Luke 6:32–34). Christians, like Peter's mother-in-law, give *diakonia* because they have been healed and given *diakonia* by Christ (Matt. 8:15).

Third, Jesus served despite his stature. He was the King of the universe, and he was about to take his place again at the right hand of the Father. Most people who get promotions find it difficult to run errands, meet basic needs, and take a humble servant attitude. But Jesus served despite his position. He served without pride.

How often Christians who are committed to the ministry of mercy become self-righteous and proud toward those who appear less committed. We can begin to look down our noses at those who look down *their* noses at the poor. How then are we any different than they? If we are proud toward those who seem complacent toward the needy, we will soon discover that no one is following us, and for good reason. We have not the spirit of a servant, so we cannot attract people to service. We will be seen (often unfairly) as "agitators" and "rabble-rousers." Without Christ's spirit, we will not be able to disarm such objections.

A servant serves without pride. The spirit of a deacon is that nothing is too *small* to do to serve another. Remember, waiters spend a lot of time getting catsup, taking away dirty plates. And nothing is too *great* to do to serve another. It may mean the sacrifice of time, plans, goals, resources, money. *Whatever* it takes to build a person up, to bring them toward God, the servant does. Those of us without the spirit of a deacon are too proud to do little things and too lazy to do big things. Our service is mediocre; it transforms no one. But a deacon will do it all.

Ultimately, the most persuasive "apologetic" for the ministry of mercy is the attractive servant-heart of ministers of mercy.

Identifying Friends of Mercy

We have said that the entire congregation needs to be "fertilized." As you use the methods mentioned above, you will discover that God leads certain people to catch the vision for the ministry of compassion. Identify them and get them together for more action-oriented reflection and prayer. Ask: "What can we do to stimulate the congregation to the ministry of mercy? What can we do ourselves to model the ministry of compassion to others?"

Where will you find these individuals? Some of them will rise out of the electives and classes; they are the ones who really want to "do something" now that the talking is over. Others you can identify just as you talk about mercy ministry—some people will express similar ideas and goals. Also look in your church for people who may be doing deeds of mercy with other organizations or groups. Or share your hopes with the officers and pastors, and they often can direct you to like-minded people.

This group of "friends" can organize themselves into a mission task force or a standing committee of the church so that they can begin to act. To do that, they must set up a relationship with their leaders.

In identifying and making friends for mercy ministry, do not neglect the leadership of the church! If the first circle of "friends" mainly consists of church officers, this is a simple matter. But if the "friends" are all laypeople, then there must be a balance in the approach to the leadership. On the one hand, mercy ministries do not need to be initiated or conducted by the pastor and officers. It is a great mistake for you, if you are a layperson, to try to start mercy ministries by nagging the pastor to make time for it. The pastor is already swamped with worthy demands on his time. Often pastors will postpone or oppose new ministries that take their time *if they did not originally conceive the idea*. If, however, you share your dreams and offer to carry the ball, you may find that you are the answer to your pastor's prayers! If you cannot procure the support of the officers, seek their permission. If you cannot procure the permission of the officers, seek nonopposition. You do not need solid support to have a ministry.

On the other hand, your leaders are over you in the Lord, and you are responsible to let them watch over you (Heb. 13:17). It is important to keep the leadership informed, to constantly invite pastors and officers to take part in the ministry, and to submit to supervision. To involve the leadership, be sure to encourage them strongly to attend electives and study groups that examine the ministry of mercy.

DIGGING UP THE GARDEN

Now we move to the second stage. Has the garden been fertilized? Have you identified friends of mercy ministry? Is the leadership aboard? Are the people beginning to show some interest? You are now ready to begin digging up the garden!

Organizing the Leadership for Mercy

You need to determine who will be responsible for the ministry of mercy. It could be a group of "friends" that asks to be recognized as a standing committee of the church. Bernard Thompson describes how this can be done in his account of "the Barnabas Group." This group grew out of a class, and organized itself for this purpose:

> To stimulate the implementation of caring ministries at Pulpit Rock Church through: identifying and communicating needs; personal example; coordinated group efforts; coordinated church-wide efforts.[1]

1. Bernard Thompson, *Good Samaritan Faith* (Glendale, CA: Regal, 1984), 70.

In other churches, boards of officers may wish to organize a "mercy subcommittee." For such a subcommittee to work, the appointed officers must be freed from other duties so that the ministry of mercy is their primary responsibility.

How can this group organize itself? One way is to specialize. Each person on the committee could seek to become a resource person for the budding ministry and for the whole church. For example, one member could become an "expert" at finding people emergency shelter, low-cost temporary housing, or hospitality. Another could head up ministries to the sick, another to the elderly or the disabled. One member could become skilled in financial counseling, and another could become aware of where to send an unemployed person to find jobs in the community. The opportunities are endless.

Second, this group or committee should learn to divide itself into "ministry teams." When there is a need to meet, it is a mistake to send just one person to assess or to meet it. One worker can often become drained by one needy family that identifies that person as their "lifeline." Learn to work in pairs for support and objectivity.

Developing Basic Structures for Meeting Needs

The most important way to develop momentum for mercy in a congregation is to begin to meet just a few diaconal needs within the church. Until some people see and experience the blessing of mercy, it will be hard to have the church really catch the vision. Therefore, the "friends" of mercy need to set up two basic structures: a mercy fund (money for meeting needs) and a service bank (an inventory of the skills of the members). Then you must watch carefully for needs and meet them well. Once that begins, momentum can build.

In one small church the pastor and his officers had been teaching about the need to minister in both word and deed. The people gave intellectual consent to the principle, but were skeptical about the church getting involved in "social work." One day a member of the church informed the pastor about the problem of an elderly widow member of the congregation. Mrs. Eastman lived on a pension of just three hundred dollars per month, and had little support from her children. Apparently her home was experiencing electrical problems. The pastor and a deacon visited her and, through loving firmness, persuaded her to reveal that her lights were "on the blink." A quick survey indicated that she needed a new fuse box. After hearing this report, the deacons appropriated the money for a new fuse box, and recruited a member of the church who could install it. Mrs. Eastman was stunned and elated; the church had never done such a thing. Soon she was spreading "positive gossip" all over about her wonderful church. People began to say, "Maybe our leaders are serious about becoming a caring church."

A Mercy Fund

The first structure necessary is a mercy fund. Any church, regardless of size, can establish a fund which can be drawn on to help people with physical and material needs. Ordinarily, it is best not to make this fund a line item in the operating expense budget of the church. *As much as possible, when beginning to establish mercy ministries, use existing resources.* Do not ask for money from the budget (just as you should not ask for more of your pastor's time)! That is a great way to provoke opposition to your vision.

The mercy fund should be a separate fund that can be expanded by designated giving in times of need. It will receive funds not being given to or used by other ministries in the church. Rather, the monies come from those sources motivated to give to mercy and previously untapped.

How can this resource be developed? It should be kept up through designated giving of individuals and by regular offerings. At first, just the "friends" may be those who pledge to it. John Calvin taught that an offering for the poor should be part of any worship supper where the Lord's Supper was observed (see the *Institutes* IV.17.44). Therefore we today have the tradition in many of the Reformed churches that an offering for the needy be taken up at any communion service. Other churches designate all offerings at special services for a mercy fund—New Year's, Lenten services, Good Friday, Thanksgiving, Christmas Eve. In other cases, one large offering is taken every Easter Sunday for the mercy fund.

A Service Bank

The second structure necessary is the "service bank." This is an effort to identify and to mobilize the skills and gifts of the congregation. Again, we must use existing resources. Many, many laypersons have time and talents to give to deed ministry. Why? Most of our evangelical churches are so "word-oriented" that virtually all the volunteer positions available are for teachers, counselors, evangelists. It takes a good measure of Christian maturity and experience to fill such slots. However, mercy ministry can use all Christians immediately! How does the service bank work?

Every member fills out a form indicating the services he can render, such as transportation, childcare, hospitality, yard work, carpentry, bookkeeping, caring for the convalescing, housecleaning, and so on. A file can then be arranged which keeps an orderly inventory of all the skills.

Suppose information comes that a single parent is having car trouble and cannot afford the repairs. A coordinator of the service bank pulls out the list of all the persons in the congregation who can do any basic auto work. He gives the list to a caller. The caller notices that one of the five people on the list was called last month. So the caller tries the others. One person volunteers to go to see the car; someone from the Mercy Committee accompanies the volunteer. There they discover the need for a new part. The Mercy Committee member, knowing that the woman has a very limited income, authorizes the volunteer to draw money from the mercy fund to purchase the part. The volunteer does so and installs it.

Establishing a Referral System

There is no use stockpiling money or material goods unless we can discover needs within our own congregation. And this is not easy! One problem is ignorance. Most church people have never learned that their physical, economic, and other practical needs are to be met through the local church. Another problem is the form of pride called shyness or self-consciousness. Many people are humble enough to serve others, but fewer people are humble enough to let others serve them! It is an important but difficult task—how can we find needs in our own congregation?

Let us recall a principle from a previous chapter. A person does not need to be destitute before we can offer aid in Christ's name. We are to love our neighbor as ourselves, and we do not wait until we are destitute to help ourselves! For example, even in the middle-class congregation, there may be elderly people who need at least practical help with transportation, home maintenance, and so on. Then there are single parents, the disabled, the chronically ill, the unemployed, students in college without strong family resources, and so on. Stop! Look! Listen! Needs are there. But how do we connect with them?

You must develop a referral network. At first, this network may not work well, because people are simply not sure how serious the church is about meeting needs. So the "friends" themselves must (at first, at least) take it upon themselves to keep their eyes and ears open for needs.

One part of the network for discovering needs is regular communication with the leaders in charge of mercy and every group leader in the church. Bible study leaders, Sunday school teachers and officers, youth group leaders, senior citizen group leaders, etc. are regularly contacted and asked about practical needs that they see in their group.

A second way to discover needs is through a comprehensive ministry of telephone care. Every three months, several people are recruited to call every member of the church. Each caller has a short list of questions that cover a lot of areas. Typical questions: "Do you have any prayer requests? Have you been ill or has there been illness in your family? How are your spouse and children doing? Have you any other needs?" Then the results of this phone survey are referred to the body that oversees mercy ministry.

Another help in locating needs is the "Need Card." In each pew, a church could put a small card or pamphlet briefly explaining the interest of the church to share time and resources with each other in time of need. There should be a space to describe the need/request and a place for the name of the person in need as well as a space for the name of the person filling out the card. The card can be placed in the offering plate or given to an officer or pastor.

Need cards will only work if the pastor at least once a month reminds people of their use. Very seldom will people fill out such a card for themselves. Rather, people will alert the leaders to the need of someone else they know.

The Need for Community Survey

To prepare a church for mercy ministry, there is no better means than a survey designed to assess community needs. Such a survey does a great deal of "digging up" both needs and potential ministries. This first survey is a largely educational and motivational experience for church people. Most members believe they know the hurts and needs of the community in which they live, but experience proves that this is not the case. Most suburban Americans live in isolation from the needy, so that many social needs are not visible to the casual observer.

Another purpose for a deliberate exploration of the community is *focus*. In some ways, trying to devise a program to help "the poor" is something like asking a doctor to prescribe medicine for "sickness." There is no cure for "sickness," because it is only a general term for many specific conditions. In the same way, *the poor* is really a vast heading for numerous specific conditions. A systematic assessment of the community helps us identify and pinpoint the characteristics of different target groups of people.

Act, Don't React

A community survey is pivotal for another reason. In the last chapter we said that a family should best meet the needs that it finds naturally. However, a local church must beware of only meeting the needs that "drop into its lap." Certain kinds of people may cry loudly for help, while much more significant crowds of people in distress lie hidden in the community or in your own congregation. A congregation should *act*, not *react* to needs. Therefore, a formal, well-planned survey of the community is usually necessary.

It is hard to emphasize this too much. Almost inevitably, any group of people who get involved with mercy ministry very soon become "burned out" through involvement with the families and individuals who approach the church for help. Soon the valiant mercy workers are tired and discouraged because of the many hours going into these hard cases, usually without much visible fruit. This is not to say that it is wrong to help people who seek aid, but it is often true that a higher percentage of those calling out for aid are people who have created a system of economic dependency, going from agency to agency and church to church. In many cases, the most needy and the most teachable are not the ones knocking on the church's door.

It is usually necessary for any church to go through a "reactive stage." Most middle-class churches are full of people who know little about the pain of the physically and economically needy. Concerned church members need to "get their hands dirty" and to even make some basic mistakes in trying to help hurting people. But it is important to build on this experience to mount positive ministries of outreach to needy *constituencies* in the community, not just to individuals who approach you. Unless a church gets beyond a "reactive mode" to an "active mode" a sense of discouragement and stagnation will set in. The only way to get into an active stance is to complete a community survey, to "network the city."[2] Following is a series of ten steps to take for this study.

1. Set Goals for the Survey

Goal 1 is to discover the (a) kinds, (b) degrees, (c) concentrations of, and (d) locations of basic felt needs. Keep a lookout for a specific list of kinds of people that the Bible tells us to care for.

How can we organize our findings? One way is to think in terms of people-groups. Here is a partial list (remembering that the categories overlap):

2. An extremely helpful book on "networking" is by Ray Bakke, *The Urban Christian* (Downers Grove, IL: InterVarsity Press, 1987). See chapter 6, "Into the Community." Though oriented to urban settings, most of the advice is directly relevant to studying any community.

- Poor (Gal. 2:10)
  - Homeless
  - Alcoholics
  - Drug addicts
  - Mentally disabled
  - Migrant workers
  - Working poor
  - Unemployed
  - Illiterate
- Disadvantaged Children (Ps. 68:5)
  - Abused and neglected
  - Juvenile delinquents
  - Learning disabled
  - Physically disabled
  - Mentally disabled
  - School dropouts
- Elderly (1 Tim. 5:9)
- Disabled (Lev. 19:14)
  - Blind
  - Deaf
  - Mentally disabled
  - Other disabilities
- Single Parent (James 1:27)
  - Widows
  - Divorced
  - Unwed mothers
- Prisoners (Heb. 13:3)
  - Inmates
  - Ex-convicts
- Sick (Matt. 25:36)
  - Chronically ill
  - Terminally ill
- Disaster victims (Acts 11:28–29)
- Aliens (Lev. 19:33–34)
  - Refugees

○ New immigrants
○ International students

This is not the only way to look for felt needs. It is helpful also to select another "grid" to define one's community. Craig W. Ellison proposes that we see five areas of felt needs, based on a "multidimensional view of human nature."[3] His divisions are along the following lines:

- Spiritual/moral needs
  ○ Child rearing
  ○ Forgiveness/freedom from guilt
  ○ Purpose in life/guidance and direction
- Social needs
  ○ Loneliness (elderly, etc.)
  ○ Marital difficulties
  ○ Sexual problems: homosexuality, prostitution, etc.
  ○ Divorce recovery
  ○ Parent/child tensions
  ○ Child abuse/neglect
  ○ Juvenile delinquency
  ○ Injustice/oppression of groups or communities
- Emotional needs
  ○ Depression
  ○ Internal and interpersonal conflict
  ○ Substance abuse
  ○ Suicide
  ○ Grief
  ○ Stress and anxiety
  ○ Problems of aging
- Cognitive needs
  ○ Basic literacy for adults: reading, writing
  ○ Education/tutoring for youth, children
  ○ Career guidance

3. Craig W. Ellison, "Addressing the Felt Needs of Urban Dwellers," *Urban Mission* 4, no. 4 (March 1987): 35–36.

- ○ Second language acquisition
- ○ Social skills/job-seeking skills
- ○ Nutrition/homemaking skills
- ○ Legal aid, advocacy
- Physical needs
  - ○ Food and nutrition
  - ○ Shelter/housing
  - ○ Clothing
  - ○ Childcare
  - ○ Elderly care
  - ○ Health care
  - ○ Safety
  - ○ Quality of life: economic self-development
  - ○ Disaster response

As we can see, each "grid" reveals certain felt needs that the other one hides, despite the great amount of overlap between the two. Use both grids as bases for asking questions.

Goal 2 is to discover the existing public and private agencies that are carrying on programs which meet mercy needs in your community. Your goal is not only to learn of their existence, but also of their degree of effectiveness.

Goal 3 is to discover the *gaps* between the needs of the community and the services provided. What needs are going unmet because there is no (or insufficient) action being taken to help? What needs are being neglected?

Goal 4 is to discover ways to meet and contact the people with the needs in question. How can you build bridges to them?

In summary, your questions are the following: What are the needs? What are the existing services? What are the gaps between needs and services? How can we find and meet these people?

2. Establish Your Procedure

The basic way that you will conduct your survey is through talking to people during interviews. These general procedural guidelines should be followed: (a) Make appointments. Don't just "drop in" on resource people. You will get more information and help if the person is not impatient to end your interview so he or she can return to scheduled duties; (b) explain your goals briefly; (c) always ask the person you are interviewing for a list of other resource people you should contact. Many of the persons you interview may ask for help from you or your church. There will be a tendency for you to respond positively to the first agencies you interview. As the survey proceeds, you will see that you cannot possibly meet all the needs. Beware of making any commitments, implied or otherwise, during your survey.

In general, ask the four questions: (a) What are the needs? (b) what are the existing services? (c) what is being neglected? (d) would you refer people to us or help us in any way?

3. Visit Social Service Agencies

Below are a set of representative service agencies and an example of helpful questions to ask each one.

Local welfare or social services department. Are there any geographical areas where there is a high concentration of a particular need (e.g., an area where there are many refugees, poor elderly persons, etc.)? How many people in this area receive assistance such as Medicaid, food stamps, Aid for Dependent Children (ADC) unemployment, supplementary security income (SSI)? How many people are unemployed whose benefits have run out? (Add this figure to the number of persons on unemployment.) What services or resources (beside the social services department) exist to give aid to the needy in the area? What private groups or voluntary organizations are there? Is there a community service directory available? What are the needs which are the most neglected by existing services? What are the needs which the church could respond to with financial and personal aid? Would your department be willing to refer needs to us and help us match our resources with the needs? Could you provide training for our volunteers?

Census records and/or city (or county) planner. Look up or ask for these statistics: income level by region; occupation and educational level of heads of households by region; size of families, size of house lots, real estate values by region; number of single-parent households and of one-person households; breakdown of population by race, age, nationality/language; population characteristics by age and race and nationality; projected changes in population.

Department of health and hospital social workers. What are the needs and in what geographical areas are they concentrated? Ask for figures on homebound elderly, disabled, infant care, nutrition problems, other chronic health problems. What other private agencies and voluntary organizations are meeting health care needs? Is a directory available? What health care needs are most neglected by existing services? What needs could our church meet with financial and personal aid? Would your agency refer needs to us and help us match our resources with needy people? Would you be willing to train our volunteers?

Department of mental health. Seek figures on mentally retarded, mentally ill, and any other categories the department records. Ask about the living conditions of each category. How many are in institutions? Homes with family? Independent housing? Specialized housing? What private agencies or voluntary organizations exist to meet mental health needs? Is a directory of such organizations available? What mental health needs are most neglected by existing services? What needs could our church meet? Would your agency be willing to refer needs to us and help us match our resources with needy people? Would you be willing to train our volunteers?

Public school officials. Ask for figures and location of the following needs: single-parent homes; truancy and delinquency; families who cannot nurture children; drug and alcohol abuse; child abuse; families not providing adequate nutrition and health care; teenage pregnancy; children and youth who need tutoring. Are there private agencies and voluntary organizations who are meeting these needs? Is there a directory of such organizations available? Which needs are the most neglected by existing services? Which needs can our church meet? Would your agency be willing to refer needs to us or help us match our resources with needy persons? Would you be willing to train our volunteers?

Other agencies. Also go to police departments, juvenile courts, veterans administration, other clergymen, job placement and vocational counseling offices, area realtors, and so on. Ask each of them: What are the needs? What are the existing services? What are the gaps between needs and services? Will you cooperate with us?

4. Visit Individuals Who Provide Services

Speak to doctors and lawyers, local policemen, mail carriers, beauticians, bartenders, pharmacists, pastors, and so on. They are not "social workers," but they may have more of a finger on the pulse of a community than anyone else. Look carefully. In a rural community, the key person may be the grain elevator operator. In an urban community, it may be an older "patriarch" of a particular neighborhood or ethnic group.

5. Visit Businesses

Often, local businesses and businessmen are more abreast of community concerns and personal needs than many others. Many of them must keep up-to-date with demographics and statistics (even more accurately than the service agencies) and long years of experience in the community provide them with valuable insights.

6. Speak to the Needy Themselves

Be sure to contact people who are actually in need and find out *from them* what are their needs, what are the existing services, and how well those services are doing. Attend community concern meetings, survey neighborhoods, ask kids questions.

7. Summarize Your Findings

Do so under the headings: Target Groups, Needs, Existing Services, and Gaps. Do not let this survey go on and on! You will never get *all* the information. Interminable research can eventually become an excuse for inaction.

8. Assess Your Findings

Determine the importance of each of the felt needs, and choose some priorities. Ellison proposes to look at: (a) the *intensity* (seriousness) of each need, and (b) the *extensiveness* (the number of persons involved) of each need. Isolate the most important needs. Now ask: Does your church have gifts, skills, or other resources that seem to match up with certain needs? If it does, elevate those needs on your priority list.

9. Sketch a "Spiritual Profile" of the Selected People Groups

Look at the groups of people with the felt needs you have identified. Do not let them remain simply abstract sets of statistics. Realize that these needs belong to real people. Now ask yourself: who are they? Are they a growing group of Southeast Asian immigrants? Institutionalized older people in your neighborhood? Apartment dwellers? Single mothers in public housing? Older, widowed black women living alone in row houses? Middle-aged businessmen struggling with alcoholism? Young white males dying of AIDS? Latchkey kids? Newly divorced people? Migrant Hispanic construction workers?

Visualize them. Seek to write a spiritual profile of the main groups. This will help you to look at them holistically, to see all the ways in which you must minister to them in word and in deed.

What are the elements in a spiritual profile?[4] Consider the following five items:

a. *Needs.* What are the felt needs of this group? What do they see as their own greatest needs and problems? Which needs appear to be the most neglected?

b. *Hopes.* What are the greatest hopes and interests? What do they aspire to (and thus, what are their greatest fears)?

4. For a helpful and detailed guide, see Edward Dayton and David Fraser, *Planning Strategies for World Evangelization* (Grand Rapids: Eerdmans, 1981). See especially chapters 12 and 13, which provide help in drawing a description of the needs and behavior of a people group.

c. *Values.* What common practices or values in this group seem the most unlike scriptural principles? Which ones seem the most similar?

d. *Worldview.* What is their religious perspective or worldview? How much basic Christian truth do they know?

e. *Ministry history.* What existing ministries are there to this group? Why are they effective or ineffective?

On the basis of this summary, imagine the kind of ministry that could reach this group of people. Many of these ideas will be "pipe dreams," perhaps, but do the dreaming now! In chapter 12 we will discuss more concrete ways of building ministry models on your findings.

10. Communicate Your Findings

How shall you use your survey? Share it with people, pray over it, use it to stimulate thinking. Perhaps you will use it right away as the basis for planning a new ministry program. Perhaps you could use it with the five invitational questions (see chapter 10) to stimulate the formation of some study/action groups who will look into beginning the program. Eventually it will help you to set priorities and to guide people who come to you seeking to reach out into the community.

CONCLUSION

We have discussed "fertilizing" and "spading" work. The congregation must be motivated by love for mercy, and the real felt needs of the community must be discovered. But a warning is appropriate here. Both motivating the congregation and surveying the community are *endless* tasks. Of course, it is true that you must not move ahead in mercy ministry too quickly, without first carrying out these important responsibilities. Yet you can also wait too long, excusing your inaction by reference to all the preliminary and preparatory work you still need to do. Only godly wisdom and prayerful dependence on the Spirit will enable you to discern when it is time to "move out."

FOR DISCUSSION

1. What can be done to stimulate mercy in your life? In your congregation?
2. What would be your goals for a survey?

3. This chapter has been intensely practical. Can you identify people who could begin these tasks:
   a. Establish a Mercy Committee
   b. Develop a needs survey
   c. Distribute a needs survey
   d. Visit social agencies
   e. Visit other service individuals
   f. Summarize/assess the findings

10

Mobilizing the Church

OVERVIEW: We can actually "plant" mercy ministries through church-wide projects, the organizing of grass-roots mission groups, and careful program planning.

In chapter 9 we outlined how to prepare the church for the ministry of mercy. We "fertilized" by nurturing the congregation with biblical truth and by identifying "friends" of mercy that God is enlightening and awakening to the opportunities. Next we "dug up the garden" by organizing a group of people who actually begin to meet needs within the congregation in a small way, at first. A community needs survey unearths many other potential ministries and (usually) provides contacts and prospects for immediate action. Now—how do we begin the task of earnestly ministering in mercy?

Now we "plant the garden" by starting both "top down" and "bottom up" ministries. These are two basic ways to begin ministries in the church. The first way ("top down") occurs when the leadership develops and establishes a program. Leaders seek to sell the congregation on the effort. They recruit volunteers, train them, and supervise them. The second way ("grass roots" or "bottom up") occurs when an individual or group of laypeople approaches the leadership with the idea for a ministry. The laypeople hammer out their own purposes, recruit other workers, and so on under the general guidance of the leadership.

To develop mercy ministries, a church will need to use both methods, but the emphasis in a congregation should always be on the "grass roots" way to multiply ministries. Acts 6 shows us that the pastors and elders of a church must concentrate on ministries of the word, and ministries of deed and mercy should be committed to those with wisdom and spiritual maturity. Also, unlike "word ministries," mercy ministries can deploy virtually all Christians, unseasoned and mature alike. Mercy succeeds best when it has strong grass-roots support.

Here are four steps for planting mercy ministries. They consist of both "top down" and "bottom up" methods. Although a creative mixture is important, they do not have to be done in any strict kind of order.

INITIATE CHURCH-WIDE PROJECTS

Now that you have developed some vision in the congregation and have set up a few basic structures for mercy ministry, it is time to involve the whole church in one or two mercy ministry projects. The projects to choose should (1) be focused on a highly specific mercy need that everyone can be united on, (2) be a short-term effort or at least one with a definite time span, (3) involve as many people as possible, (4) be a program that can be run by the laity not burdening the pastoral staff, and (5) be an effort relatively assured of visible results. This program should be designed on the basis of real need (your community needs survey could give you some ideas), but at the same time it should be a means of whetting the appetite of the congregation for mercy ministry. Thus long-term, slow-developing, difficult ministries should not be the first ones you attempt!

What are some examples? In some cases, the project could be an extension of the service bank. Perhaps a large number of volunteers from the church could repair/remodel the home of an elderly or needy family in the neighborhood or church. Perhaps the church could regularly do a support project for a local mercy ministry, such as a regular "Baby Shower," collecting maternity and children's clothes and articles for the crisis-pregnancy counseling center in your town.

George Grant, in *Bringing in the Sheaves*, suggests a regular "Brown Bag Project." Everyone in the congregation could receive a brown bag with a grocery list for canned and dry foodstuffs. One Sunday morning everyone brings the food to the church. The food can either go to a local food pantry or to one the church establishes. In either case, a church that routinely does such a project solves the food pantry's typical problems of stocking, storage, inventory, maintaining nutritional balance, and even staffing.[1]

Bernard Thompson suggests refugee resettlement as an early church-wide project.[2] By contacting World Relief (of the National Association of Evangelicals) or some other resettlement agency, the church could arrange to bring a family to your community. The mercy "friends" committee should not do this alone, but should recruit many others to find housing, locate jobs, provide English language training, collect furniture, appliances, clothing, and kitchen supplies, and provide medical and legal services.

The value of a church-wide project is that it establishes the identity and the purpose of the ministry of mercy in the minds of the congregation. These initial efforts should not be too ambitious or difficult. Nevertheless, the ministry of mercy can often be apparently disappointing. Thompson relates that just five weeks after his Colorado Springs church prepared living conditions for a Vietnamese family, the family decided to move to Denver to be with relatives. The church's hard work seemed to go for very little. Thompson said, however, that the experience taught them extremely valuable lessons for future work with the needy. There is no way to "prepare" for effective mercy ministry without getting started and learning through trial and error.

GROW MINISTRY UP THROUGH SPIRITUAL GIFTS

Understanding Every-Member Ministry

Apart from "top down" programs, we must very specifically begin to plant seeds for mercy ministry among the members of the congregation. This process starts by articulating clearly and regularly a theology of every-member ministry. Word ministries can flourish somewhat in

---

1. George Grant, *Bringing in the Sheaves* (Atlanta: American Vision Press, 1985), 191.
2. Bernard Thompson, *Good Samaritan Faith* (Ventura, CA: Regal, 1984), 114–17.

a church without this emphasis; deed ministries cannot grow without this theology sown like seed throughout the congregation.

From the pulpit, in classes, by word of mouth, it must be communicated that *every layperson is a minister*, and that *ministry is finding needs and meeting them with the goal of the spread of the kingship of Christ*. Here are the tenets that need to be affirmed and embraced by the members.

Every believer is a prophet, a priest, and a king. We are all prophets (Joel 2:28–29; Acts 2:14ff.). Every believer is to exhort (Heb. 3:13), counsel (Rom. 15:14), evangelize (Acts 8:4), and teach (Col. 3:16) with the word "dwelling richly" within. You must speak!

As a priest (1 Peter 2:9), you have access to the presence of God, as did the priests of old (Matt. 27:51; Heb. 4:14–16). You have the responsibility to offer spiritual sacrifices and deeds of mercy (Rom. 12:1–2; Heb. 13:12, 16). You must serve!

As a king (Rev. 1:5–6), you have authority over the world (1 John 5:4), the flesh (Rom. 6:14ff.), and the Devil (Luke 10:19). We all have divine weapons to demolish strongholds and obstacles to the kingdom of Christ (2 Cor. 10:4–5). You must take charge!

This doctrine is called the "universal office" of believer, and it is nothing short of revolutionary.[3] A layperson ministers in word (as a prophet) and deed (as a priest), and need not wait for the pastor to request it (because he is a king). Jesus himself said that the least in the kingdom of God is greater than John the Baptist (Matt. 11:9–11). Who can outrank an "ordinary" Christian? No one! So we see that every layperson has the responsibility to initiate, to plan, to guide and to manage ministries of both word and deed. Laypeople must not be passive.

Understanding Spiritual Gifts

Though every believer is prophet, priest, and king, each of us has received spiritual gifts that make us especially fruitful in particular areas of ministry.

First Corinthians 12:4–6 teaches, "There are different kinds of gifts, but the same Spirit. There are different kinds of service, but the

---

3. See R. B. Kuiper, "The Universal Office," in *The Glorious Body of Christ* (Edinburgh: Banner of Truth, 1983), 126–31.

same Lord. There are different kinds of working, but the same God works all of them in all men." This text can be expounded by asking three questions.

First, "what is a spiritual gift?" *A spiritual gift is an ability from the Holy Spirit to meet the needs of people* (1 Cor. 12:7). Gifts are given by the Holy Spirit to every believer; every Christian has one or more ("to each"). Verse 7 also calls it a "manifestation," which is something visible. (For example, though you may be angry, the anger is not manifest until you do something in anger.) Thus, while spiritual fruit (Gal. 5:22f.) is what you *are*, spiritual gifts are what you *do*. Each gift is an ability to "edify" another (1 Cor. 14:4), to spread the kingdom of Christ (Eph. 4:8), to build up the church (1 Cor. 12:7). Therefore, though God may adopt a natural "talent" to become a spiritual gift, he often edifies through performances that experts judge as substandard.[4] An excellent example of this is the two great contemporaries, D. L. Moody and C. H. Spurgeon. Spurgeon had such great natural gifts of oratory that, had he not been called to the ministry, he could have risen to be prime minister of Britain. Moody, by contrast, had very few gifts in the area of rhetoric or speech. But God used the preaching of each in mighty ways. Thus J. I. Packer writes, "*What constitutes and identifies a charisma is not the form of the action, but the blessing of God.*"[5]

Spiritual gifts generally break into three categories. There are *speaking* gifts (prophecy, teaching, exhorting, knowledge, evangelism, discernment, missions), *leading* gifts (government, administration, wisdom, faith), and *serving* gifts (giving, service, helps, mercy, hospitality).

Second, "what is a ministry"? Spiritual gifts are expressed through *ministries which are particular channels of service that focus on particular "people needs"* (v. 5). On the one hand, a particular gift can be fulfilled through many ministry channels. For example, the gift of exhortation is the ability to encourage and to build up another. A person with this gift could serve as the leader of a single parents' fellowship group, since such folk need lots of emotional support. Or the same person could be recruited by the pastor to nurture and

4. J. I. Packer, *Keep in Step with the Spirit* (Old Tappan, NJ: Revell, 1984), 84.
5. Ibid., 85.

to help a new believer/church member for a six-month period. Or the same person could be teamed with a good teacher to start an evangelistic home Bible study. Or this person might be recruited into a peer counselors' training program. Notice that each different ministry focuses on a somewhat different people need, but in each case the same gift can be brought to bear.

On the other hand, a particular ministry can be fulfilled through many different gifts. For example, consider what it takes to be a Sunday school teacher. A person with an evangelistic gift could be a good Sunday school teacher, and the class would probably have a good outreach. A person with the gift of mercy could be an excellent teacher for a senior adult class that would become a very supportive, caring fellowship. A person with a gift of teaching will do an excellent job and will probably put more emphasis on content and classroom work—the individual may not think as much about the social and outreach aspect of the class. We see, then, that (depending on the purpose and philosophy of your Sunday school), you may not want only people with a gift of teaching to be teaching!

Third, "what are 'workings' in verse 6?" Probably that refers to different levels of power and effectiveness granted sovereignly by God. All gifts of teaching are not alike; some teachers are more gifted than others. Considering the diversity of "energy levels," of ministry channels, and of gifts themselves, we see that the varieties of ministry possibilities are overwhelming. No one has been simply stuck into a single slot where he or she must labor. Rather, Christians must recognize their limitations and strengths and go about finding fruitful ministry channels within those areas.

Finding Our Callings

But how does one "discover" his or her gifts so they can be used? There are two basic approaches to this question—the inductive and deductive. The most popular approach at present appears to be the deductive method. A leading proponent, C. Peter Wagner, directs Christians (1) to study the definition of each spiritual gift, (2) to take inventory of their own self-perception and draw some tentative conclusions about their gifts, and then (3) to put the gifts to work in a ministry requiring them. Later, we must (4) continually reevaluate our spiritual gifts in the light of feedback about one's effectiveness.[6] This method holds sway in most settings. Questionnaires have been devised to help people discern their gifts. Some leading church growth experts advise churches to incorporate this process in new members' classes so that all new members can name their spiritual gifts.

The other approach is inductive. Gene A. Getz has concluded that Christians should not seek to isolate and identify spiritual gifts, a practice that in his view leads to confusion, rationalization, and deception. He sees people "cop out" of Christian duties (such as witnessing) by saying "that is not my gift." He also sees Christians deceiving themselves into believing they have certain desirable gifts and abilities. Instead of telling them to identify certain gifts, Getz believes in simply presenting Christians with the demands that they serve and work through the church in all kinds of capacities.[7]

We would here like to recommend a more balanced version of the inductive approach. This starts by helping members discover ministry channels, and later it helps them discover their gifts.

First, *expose members to lists of needs (not of gifts) inside and outside of the church.* Many churches introduce Christians to the idea of "every-member ministry" by giving them a list of gifts and asking them to identify theirs. That is a rather abstract way to do it! Instead, pastors and leaders should regularly brainstorm and make an up-to-date list of people needs which are going unmet (or undermet) inside the church and out in the community. The list may include new Christians needing discipling, disabled members needing support, certain children's ministries needing creation, couples needing premarital counseling. In chapter 9 we listed felt needs that may be acute inside the congregation or outside. Expose people to this list.

6. C. Peter Wagner, *Your Spiritual Gifts Can Help Your Church Grow* (Glendale, CA: Regal, 1979), 46–49, 249–57.
7. Gene A. Getz, *Building Up One Another* (Wheaton, IL: Victor, 1976), 9–16.

Second, *post the five invitational questions.*[8] These questions, spelled out in the next section, lead a member to consider whether there are any needs that he or she finds an interest in (see questions 1 and 2 below). If the church already has a ministry to the need, the person should "plug in." If the church does not have such a ministry, he should take steps to begin one (see questions 3–5 at the end of the chapter).

Third, *once involved in ministry for significant time, fill out a spiritual gifts inventory.* Once the member has been able to spend time in ministry, he or she will have feedback on effectiveness, and then a spiritual gifts inventory may be helpful in clarifying gifts.

Posing the Five Invitational Questions

The first question: *Is there a particular human need that you "vibrate" to?* A specific problem or hurt that you long to help with? One of the ways that people can discern God's gifts and calling to them is by noticing the kinds of needs to which they are most sensitive. For example, if you lift up the lid of a piano and sing a B-flat note, only the B-flat string will vibrate. Why? Because it has the "gift of B-flatness." It was built to pick up that wavelength; the other strings are deaf to B-flat. So too, there are some kinds of needs that we vibrate to. As a young pastor, I had some persons complain about the lack of evangelism by our church, some about its lack of organization, and some about our lack of care for the elderly. I began to realize that each person was a piano string who, because of specific gifts, was vibrating to one particular problem. So we should look at the various kinds of human needs and ask if God has laid a particular kind of need on our heart.

The second question: *What personal, emotional, and spiritual resources do you have to meet the need?* A desire to minister is not enough— we must also have the ability. Some persons have become involved in ministries too taxing for their level of spiritual maturity, or for their schedule, or for their other commitments. Do you really have what it

---

8. Based on the five questions in Kennon L. Calahan, *Twelve Keys to an Effective Church* (New York: Harper & Row, 1983), 6–8.

takes? We must be careful here. Everyone should approach ministry with a sense of helplessness before God and inadequacy without him. But we must also have an accurate self-understanding. We cannot press on into a ministry before God has equipped us or arranged our lives so we are prepared for it.

At this point, the person must determine whether the church already has a ministry to this people need which he or she can join. For example, a person who is called to children's ministry may discover that the church has already some channels to work through. But what if there is no such ministry? Then the individual should consider mounting an effort alone by working through the last three questions.

This brings us to the third question: *Are there at least two or three others in the congregation who share your burden or to whom you can readily communicate your vision?* How do you discover this? By asking the pastoral staff or other leaders to let the church know about your interest. A note in the bulletin could read:

> Sally Smith has a burden to see our church minister to the local home for mentally retarded women. After the evening service tonight, she would like to meet with anyone who would be interested in exploring this possibility through discussion, study, and prayer.

What if this invitation does not elicit positive response and support? Then the individual can either seek to do mercy just through his or her family or phone other members personally. Or, the person can conclude that God has not moved the church to begin the ministry. One thing the individual should *not* say is: "What's wrong with this church? Why doesn't it love people more?" The person should remember that God is the keeper of hearts. If you have a burden, then God put it there; it is not the result of your innate goodness and love. If he is not moving others in the same way, look at it as his guidance to you!

The fourth question: *Is there really an opening for your ministry?* For example, what if Sally Smith discovers that there are already a lot of (too many!) churches ministering to the residents and families of the home for retarded women? What if the administration of the home has put up numerous barriers to such a ministry? We must ask whether the ministry is timely and needed. Desire, ability, and *opportunity* are all determinants for God's calls. We may have much desire, manpower, and ability, but that does not mean God is calling.

The fifth question: *Before you begin, have you really "counted the cost"?* Have you carefully calculated what this ministry may require, and are you (and your family) committed to making that investment?

These questions may be raised in a new members' class or at the end of a study group or a class on every-member ministry. However, they should be posed at times to the entire church in a sermon, a talk at a conference, the church newsletter, and so on.

But the most important use of the questions is as a framework of procedure for the leaders of the church. As the pastor or officers enable laypeople to do ministry, none of the five steps must be omitted. People must be encouraged to explore their callings, but must also be carefully examined for maturity and resources. Then the congregation should be invited to study the subject closely. Ordinarily, the little group of ministry-visionaries would read books together, do field surveys, and pray together regularly. During all of this time, leaders must guide, help, and pray, but *they do not need to control or even be directly involved.*

The results of this approach should be the formation of numerous lay-led groups who take on a variety of ministries in discipleship, fellowship, evangelism, music, worship, education, as well as mercy ministry. Below we will refer to these as "mission groups" and consider them largely with regard to their use in the ministry of mercy.

ORGANIZE MISSION GROUPS

What will be the result of this process of planting "grass roots" ministries? Groups will begin to grow. Some will become large and no longer look like "small" groups at all, involving dozens or scores of volunteers and workers. Others will always stay small and tight-knit. Each will develop its own personality and character.

Churches who use this concept have developed rather different titles for this ministry form. Church of the Saviour in Washington, D.C., calls them "mission groups"; Bear Valley Baptist Church in Denver, Colorado, calls them "target ministries." For the sake of our discussion, let us call these "mission groups."

Patterns for Mission Groups

1. *A mission group differs from other small groups in that it meets mainly for outreach, rather than for nurture and support.* Each mission group chooses an outreach mission. It aims to meet an unfilled felt need with the word of the gospel and deeds of mercy. It targets the conscious and unconscious needs of a specific group of people to be loved, served, and reached for Christ.

2. *Members should be Christians who are committed to the purposes of the group.* Members should adhere to minimum disciplines, such as daily prayer and Bible study, regular meetings of members for prayer and edification, and duties of the ministry.

3. *A group develops through stages.* In the first stage, it is largely a *study* group that reads books and does field research to learn of the current condition of the group of people or the need being targeted. Information is pooled, discussed, prayed over. In the second stage, it becomes more of a planning group. An inventory of the members' skills and interests may be taken. Developmental resources are identified and a strategy for ministry is designed. Finally, the group becomes an *action* group, which carries out and oversees the ministry.

4. *A mission group is under the church's leadership, but it is not simply controlled by the pastors and board.* On the one hand, the mission group provides extensive information to the church's leadership about its work, and it regularly solicits the guidance and evaluation of pastors and officers. Usually some officer or official liaison to the officers

would be appointed. As it represents the local church, it must abide by the doctrinal standards and policies of the congregation. On the other hand, though it is under the ultimate doctrinal and moral authority of the officers, the group itself must have freedom and authority to set policies and make decisions (or else all the work will again fall on the pastors and elders who are already squeezed for time and attention). So too, a mission group will not ordinarily ask for budget money from the church as it begins. It should be self-financed by the members until its growth and effectiveness warrants expansion and the funding from the congregation.

5. *A mission group is not a standing committee.* It lasts as long as there are committed members who share the burden and purpose of the ministry. If interested members move away or are forced to withdraw, and if there are not sufficient replacements, a mission group is allowed to die with dignity. The leadership should not try to institutionalize the ministry, maintaining its membership with guilt-inducing pleas for volunteers, and so on. Mission groups live by God-given calling and desire.

Models for Mission Groups

What are some examples of mission group "missions"? The best models for mission groups exist in urban churches. The urban environment is extremely diverse, and within just a short radius from the church there are scores and scores of various ethnic, social, cultural, and felt-need groups. Thus active urban churches may have literally dozens of working mission groups. Suburban and rural churches live in more homogeneous regions and usually will develop fewer such groups.

The Church of the Saviour in Washington, D.C., has pioneered the concept of mission groups for the past twenty years. At one time they had mission groups that (1) recruited and trained families to be foster parents for children in Washington's dismal "Junior Village" foster-care center, (2) established a retreat center on a local farm for groups inside and outside of the church to use, (3) led Bible studies and ministry at a local prison, and (4) repaired and renovated crumbling homes in the inner city.[9]

The Bear Valley Baptist Church in Denver is becoming well known for multiplying "target ministries." These ministries come and go, and their number is always in some flux, but a recent count observed over two dozen. These mission groups include (1) "Jesus on Main Street," a ministry of evangelism and mercy to transients, runaways, mental outpatients, alcoholics, drug abusers, prostitutes, and homeless, (2) Care Company, a ministry to abused and disadvantaged children, (3) Denver Street School, which provides tutoring and education for the poor, especially high school dropouts, (4) Inner City Health Center, providing medical and health care for the needy, (5) a jail ministry, (6) Stepparenting Outreach, providing help and support to new "merged" families, (7) Turning Point, for alcoholics and their families, (8) Life Unlimited, a ministry to unwed mothers, and (9) Shield of Faith, an evangelistic outreach to cults.

Tenth Presbyterian Church in Philadelphia is a center-city congregation that began to develop "mission group" style ministries in the mid-1980s. Their outreach groups include (1) an adult literacy program, (2) a food and clothing closet, (3) a job placement and advocacy service, especially for those in the literacy program, (4) mercy dinners, a ministry to the homeless, (5) Harvest, an evangelistic outreach to the homosexual community, (6) a ministry to AIDS victims, (7) Ammi, an outreach ministry to the Jewish community, (8) International Students Fellowship, a ministry of word and deed to international students, and (9) Alpha Pregnancy services, a crisis pregnancy center for urban women.

Many churches become intimidated when they observe these models. They feel that they are terribly short on personnel, skill, know-how, and finances. The "average" church should realize that every congregation has started with small, halting steps, and has learned mainly through its failures and mistakes. A group of beginners in mercy ministry may wish to try to connect with a nationally recognized ministry with established

9. See Dan Baumann, *All Originality Makes a Dull Church* (Santa Ana, CA: Vision House, 1976), 81–85.

expertise and support services. Examples are World Relief, World Vision, Prison Fellowship, Christian Action Council, Bethany Christian Services, and Habitat for Humanity.

The author has seen other kinds of mission groups function very well in modest-sized churches with few or no financial resources. For example, one mission group consisted of just four persons who wanted to minister to a local federal prison. After meeting together for study, they learned that many churches held Bible studies and worship services at the prison. Finally, they developed a creative, multifaceted plan for action. First, they went weekly simply to meet and to develop relationships with some of the prisoners. Second, they each developed a correspondence with several men in the institution. Third, they participated in an existing program (not run by Christians) which helped ex-convicts readjust to society. This experience prepared the little group to help some of the men to find jobs and living quarters when they came out. Last, they developed a program whereby ten prisoners could come to Sunday church in the custody of a prison guard (who had to be paid overtime). After the service, the men were treated to a covered-dish dinner by volunteer families in the fellowship hall. Personal evangelism and relationship building took place.

Another small group of young couples met to begin to study what the Bible had to say about the fatherless, about orphans and neglected children. They each committed themselves to take in foster children or to adopt. First they read books together about the subject. Then, when some of the families began to get foster children, the group met for support, for troubleshooting (advising one another regarding discipline problems, etc.), and for planning outings for all the families and their kids.

Another mission group dubbed themselves the "Home Care Ministry." The group's purpose was to provide temporary in-home care for those in physical and emotional/spiritual need. These persons could include recuperating patients, elderly persons, unwed mothers, troubled teenagers, refugees, and others. The group made contact with hospitals, juvenile courts, and social service agencies to find people in need. A half-dozen homes in the church were equipped to take people in for a time period anywhere from several weeks to several months. A network of support families were recruited to support the hospitality families with meals, transportation, finances, childcare, and prayer.

Some mission groups have concentrated on service to the elderly, a fast-growing segment of the population. Options for ministry include nursing home ministries, friendly visiting, a telephone reassurance program, a housekeeper-helper program, variations of meals on wheels, retired persons volunteer program (finding useful outlets for the skills of the elderly in church or community service), a weekly transportation program, and so on.

Some mission groups have targeted youth and children through tutoring, becoming parent aides for those who have difficulty nurturing their children, operating playground programs, providing big brother/ sister relationships, working with juvenile offenders. Other groups reach out to single parents, various groups of physically and mentally disabled persons, and people dying of cancer.

The Importance of Mission Groups

In many branches of the modern church, the leaders are too immature to support and guide anything that did not originate in their own thinking. In the Reformed churches, for example, there is a high view of the office of the Minister of the Word. Unfortunately, a concomitant high view of "the universal office of believer" has not grown apace. Though we have seen clearly that Scripture teaches that every believer is a prophet, priest, and king, there is often an attitude of clericalism that misses the biblical doctrine of the priesthood of all believers.[10] It is usually more than merely a doctrinal error; it is also a manifestation of pride, fear, and a need to "lord it over" the flock (1 Peter 5:1–6).

A pastor or board locked into a mindset of clericalism will discover that it can get very little done in mercy ministry. Without the

10. In a recent critique of the church growth movement, a Reformed pastor writes, "People are continually being urged to do evangelism rather than recognizing and supporting the gospel proclaiming ministry of the church . . . by those gifted and called of God to do such" (R. Daniel Knox, "Evangelism, Church-Growth, and the Church," *Journey* [March–April 1987]: 13).

"decentralized" model of the mission group, the officers will find themselves burdened with greater and greater responsibilities. Soon officers will find that members bring pressure to bear to drop those ministries that reach the nonmember and especially the helpless and (often) "different" person.

Even in churches with two boards of officers, this can happen. Many churches have under the elders a board of deacons that does mercy and deed ministry. But deacons must not see themselves as the sole ministers of mercy in the congregation. The deacons will "burn out" if they alone visit the sick, care for the elderly, help the unemployed, operate the crisis pregnancy center, carry out the prison ministry, etc. The ministry of mercy must be of and by the people.

BEGIN A MINISTRY FROM THE TOP

Having now emphasized strongly the need for lay-led grass roots mercy ministries, we must now add some qualification. It would be easy for the pastors and officers of the congregation to stay detached and uninformed about mercy ministry. Pastors in particular (and the author is one) are workers in an information industry. We are used to talking, discussing, and writing papers about issues. We are given virtually no training in deed ministry; changing the diapers of an elderly person or cleaning up the vomit of a drug addict are experiences we find disorienting, to say the least. In most evangelical churches, the officers are from the professional class which is similarly "word-oriented" rather than "deed-oriented."

To see the congregation as a whole truly become committed to the ministry of mercy, the officers should undertake one carefully designed ministry of mercy in which significant church resources are used.

Preliminary Questions

In choosing a ministry, the church leadership should answer three questions.

1. *What are the biggest, most urgent needs here?* The community needs assessment should be the basis for this decision. Once a particu-

lar need has been isolated, the officers may want to undertake an even more thorough assessment of the extensiveness and intensiveness of the need before determining to make it the object of a ministry program.

2. *Who else has done anything in ministry to this need or problem?* It is absolutely crucial to learn about other churches or organizations that have begun ministries similar to the one you are now contemplating. Get printed materials, do phone interviews, or (best of all) go and visit the program on site. Gather all the data to see what parts of other programs are adaptable to your situation.

3. *Are there any laypeople whose gifts and calling appear to match the proposed program?* We have said that this is a "top down" program, and yet the officers should not proceed without finding some key lay leader who would be able to shoulder much of the program. Mature church leaders have learned that all the planning in the world will not make a ministry effective unless the "right" people can be found to lead it.

The program should not be considered feasible unless there are at least some prospective lay leaders.

Steps for Program Planning

Are "green lights" appearing? Is there some need in the community that most of the officers can see and agree upon? Are there at least some other ministry models from which some wisdom can be learned? Are there a couple of prospective lay leaders? Once these questions have been addressed, the officers can decide whether actual program planning should proceed.

The following approach is useful not only for church officers, but also for any mission group putting together a ministry program.[11]

11. The approach outlined here is adapted from John Guetter, *Program Planning and Evaluation for Deacons* (Grand Rapids: CRWRC, 1981). This is part of an excellent and distinctive set of training materials for deacons available from the Christian Reformed World Relief Committee, 2850 Kalamazoo, SE, Grand Rapids, MI 49506. Bernard Thompson offers a brief program-planning method based on the acronym POLE (Plan, Organize, Lead, Evaluate) in *Good Samaritan Faith,* 106–8.

1. *Write a careful problem/need statement.* This is a very specific description of an undesirable condition being experienced by someone. The statement should include: (a) the target group or population experiencing the problem or need, (b) a breakdown of the needs, (c) consequences or ill effects, and (d) the causes or conditions that bring about the problem. For example:

- It is estimated that in our neighborhood there are at least 1000 persons over the age of sixty-five.
- who are living alone but who are physically unable to care adequately for themselves or their homes.
- Loneliness, unsafe and depressing living quarters, chronic health problems, and poor nutrition are some of the results.
- One of the major causes of the problem appears to be American mobility; most of these people do not have children or relatives living nearby who can help them. Another problem seems to be the extremely poor pension afforded to them by X Corporation, the major employer in town for fifty years, for whom most of these people worked. Another cause of the problem evidently is that many of these senior adults are unaware of other benefits (Supplemental Security Income, etc.) that are available to them. The average educational level of this population is sixth grade.

2. *Establish a goal or vision statement.* This is a specific description of a future condition desired for the target people. It is virtually a reverse of the problem statement, and it should include: (a) the size of the group you hope to reach or work with, (b) the conditions you hope will exist in the group of people you minister to, and (c) a time frame. For example:

By the end of this year, because of our church's ministry, each of ten senior adults will be living in safe housing, eating a balanced, nutritional diet regularly, receiving regular health care, and involved in a weekly social group for persons over sixty-five.

3. *Brainstorm and choose strategies.* How will we reach the goal? What strategies or means will help us achieve this desired future condition?

Generate alternatives through research and brainstorming. Research first. Discover what any other church or program has done. Then hold a session or two of brainstorming. Brainstorming is a popular technique and the rules are now familiar: everyone should contribute every idea they can think of, all ideas should be recorded, no evaluation or criticism of ideas should be done initially, piggyback on the ideas of others.

Then, evaluate the feasibility of each alternative strategy you have generated. Ask whether it will accomplish the goal for the target group. Next ask whether it is in accord with the purposes and policies of your church. Finally, ask whether the church has what it will take to develop the strategy, and consider four kinds of resources: (a) *human* (how many people? what kind of people?); (b) *financial* (how much money at first? later?); (c) *physical* (what facilities? what equipment?); (d) *technical* (what kind of information or skill is needed? what kind of training and know-how is needed?); (e) *political* (what support is needed by key people, by the congregation?). Don't be too pessimistic! Don't simply ask "are these resources now available?" but also "how can we find or develop these resources?"

Then choose one or more strategies. For example:

Strategy 1. A system of support teams. Each senior adult in the program receives a team of two volunteers who visit for two hours weekly in order to provide (a) love, friendship, evangelistic conversation, (b) housekeeping and cooking, and (c) assessment of other needs which can be met through coordination with other groups.

Strategy 2. A group of volunteers who do repair and maintenance work to the homes and living quarters of senior adults in the program.

Strategy 3. Hold a monthly free clinic at the church providing blood pressure monitoring, diabetes testing, and other basic health checks.

Strategy 4. Establish a fellowship/social group for senior citizens to
meet at the church one weekday each week.

4. *Develop the program.* Identify all the activities that will be necessary to make each strategy operational. Do this by *thinking backward* from your strategy statement. Ask yourself what needs to happen for this program to get started. Having done that, ask what needs to be done for that activity to occur, and so on.

For each of these activities, ask these questions:

a. When do you want to arrive at this? What is your time frame
for this activity?
b. Who is responsible for this particular activity? Who is in charge?
What are his or her specific duties? To whom does this person
report? Where does this person go with a problem?
c. What resources will be needed for this particular activity: human?
financial? physical? technical? political? How will these resources
be assigned?

5. *Design the organization.* We should not be too specific in outlining this step here or in providing models and examples. Organizations do and should differ; room must be allowed for great creativity. However, the following questions should be addressed as you draw up an organizational flow chart or outline. Once the program is fully operational: (a) What will the basic areas of ministry be? (b) Who will be responsible for each area? (c) How will the areas be linked or interrelated? (d) To whom is each worker responsible? From whom will each worker receive support services? Keep it all very simple!

6. *Design evaluation.* This consists of four steps: (a) develop an information system so that specific facts about the ministry's work are regularly coming to supervisors, (b) establish the criteria for evaluating how you will know whether this ministry is being effective for the Lord, (c) determine time frames for evaluation, and (d) state who will evaluate the results.

Figure 3

Program Planning: An Outline.

Preliminary Questions
What are the primary unmet felt needs?
Who else has done anything to address these and what can we learn from them?
Are there any prospective lay leaders for such a program?

Steps for Program Planning
1. Write a problem or need statement
   a. Describe the target group
   b. List the needs
   c. Specify consequences of the problem
   d. Discern causes of the problem
2. Write a goal or vision statement
   a. Number of people you aim to serve
   b. Conditions you aim to effect
   c. Time frames and schedule
3. Choose strategies
   a. Generate/brainstorm alternatives
   b. Evaluate strategy proposals
      Will it accomplish the goal for the people?
      Will it fit the church purpose and policies?
      Do we have/can we develop resources needed?
         Human (personnel)
         Financial
         Physical (facilities, equipment)
         Technical (skills, training, expertise)
         Political (support)
   c. Select one or more strategies
4. Develop the program
   a. Identify activities needed to make strategies operational
   b. For each activity, identify:
      Who is responsible
      What his or her duties are
      What resources he or she will need
      Time frame for accomplishment
5. Design the organization
   a. What are the basic ministry areas?
   b. Who will be responsible for each area?
   c. How will areas be linked or interrelated?
   d. To whom is each worker responsible?
      From whom does each worker receive support?
6. Design the evaluation
   a. Information system
   b. Criteria for evaluation
   c. Time frame for evaluation
   d. Persons in charge of evaluation

CONCLUSION

Planting mercy ministries entails a combination of both "top down" and "grass roots" approaches. Initially, the church can stimulate mercy through some very specific, short-term projects that involve the whole church. The main way to create a merciful church, however, is to inculcate in the church a mindset that every member is a minister. Leaders must encourage members to propose and start ministries and to use their gifts. Leaders should help interested laypersons form mission groups that will carry out ministries to needs. Eventually, the officers should model mercy on a large scale by carefully designing and carrying out a significant ministry of mercy to a needy group of people in the church and/or the community.

Only if these measures are taken will we escape the middle-class captivity of most of our evangelical churches. A frightening proportion of our churches are trapped by what Frank Tillapaugh calls the "fortress church" mentality. That mentality is made up of attitudes that may be conscious or unconscious: "Let them come to us! Our doors are open." "We come to church to have our needs met, to escape the cold, cruel world." But there are biblical truths that knock flat the walls of our fortresses. Every member is a minister. Every member has kingdom power to destroy strongholds. Through us Jesus continues to immerse himself in the needs of the world.

FOR DISCUSSION

1. Explain how every believer is a prophet, priest, and king. How do these truths impact the ministry of mercy?
2. Look at figure 3 and discuss each of the preliminary questions. Are you as an individual or group ready to start planning a program? If so, take the steps so outlined in figure 3.

11

Expanding Your Vision

OVERVIEW: One of the main reasons that many churches do not develop effective mercy ministries is American individualism. We must see the social dimensions of the gospel and develop ministries of relief, social transformation, and justice.

WHY MERCY STALLS

This chapter assumes that your church has already been "fertilized," "dug up," and "planted" for mercy ministry. You see more and more people in your congregation understanding the ministry of mercy to be an integral part of the Christian's walk and the church's life. Many needs are being met both inside and outside of your church, and your congregation is beginning to get the reputation for being a church that cares.

At this point, how easy it would be to become smug! Certainly, if you compare your church with most others, you will appear to be an extremely vital, balanced institution. But instead, if you look at the impact that the church should have on its society, you will see you have only just scratched the surface.

Having planted for mercy ministry, it is important that you now "water" your church so that the seeds do not produce midget fruit and plants. There are four basic reasons why churches, who begin well in mercy ministry, soon discover that their development has become stunted in the seedling stage: (1) they do not build bridges to needy people, (2) they react to needs instead of setting positive plans, (3) they cannot recruit others to share the ministry, and (4) they do not have a "big vision" for community transformation. The first three of these causes we will discuss in the next chapter, but the last one we will take up here. Many churches stall in mercy because they are too individualistic in their perspective. They tend to look only for opportunities to do emergency relief, which is an urgent need, but which by itself will not be fruitful in the long run. It tends to treat symptoms rather than root causes. Strategies of development and reform must be undertaken, too, though perhaps not at first. A church must seek an impact on nothing less than the entire community and its social system.

THE SOCIAL DIMENSION OF THE GOSPEL

When we talk of mercy ministry we think of soup kitchens and clothing closets instead of changing the social conditions which bring about much of the ministry. Why do so many evangelical Christians become very nervous when discussing the responsibility for social reform?

Middle-Class Captivity

One reason is simply our "class captivity." Most evangelicals are middle class, and we cannot see our own involvement in social systems. Raymond Bakke tells of a meeting in which a member expressed his disapproval of Christians becoming involved in social action. "It sounds like a social gospel to me," he concluded. Bakke asked the man where he lived and why. He answered that he moved to his neighborhood because it was a safe environment with good schools and reasonable housing costs. In other words, he moved there because the social system of the community was *just!* Bakke pointed out that the believer was quite "socially involved"; he had committed his life and family to the place where his social values could be realized. How, then, could

> anybody who deliberately located in a community with good schools and employment really criticize those who work to rehabilitate social systems where they do not work? Those who say, "Let's just preach

the simple gospel," usually live where good working social systems are already in place.[1]

Systems of Evil

Another reason why American Christians are confused about social reform is that they cannot grasp the idea of systemic evil—underlying legal, administrative, and policy conditions and institutions which create and sustain needs among certain groups of people.

To become concrete, we may remember the example at the end of chapter 10: a church discovered that one of the reasons so many elderly in the community lived in or near poverty was that the main employer in town provided retirees with a dismally small pension. Should Christians discuss with the corporation its unfairly low benefits (Jer. 22:13)? The corporation may be full of well-meaning, good citizens, even Christians, and no individual there intends to gouge poor elderly people. Yet, can we say that the corporation is not guilty of evil? And can we tell individuals that they are, to some degree, involved in the guilt? The answers to both are yes.

"Corporate responsibility" or "structural evil" is a concept that middle-class Americans have largely failed to grasp. When we read the Bible, we see an entire army and family held responsible for the guilt of one member. A prime example is Achan (Josh. 7:10–11). Again and again in the Bible, God deals with persons in *units*, as families and nations, punishing entire groups because of the sin of one or some members. This confuses us because our own culture is infected with what John Murray calls "the fallacy of individualism and independentism." Murray shows us that the Bible teaches that organizations and institutions can be guilty of evil *in a higher degree than any one individual within it*, and individuals within it therefore participate in the guilt.[2]

---

1. Raymond J. Bakke, "The Challenge of World Urbanization to Mission Strategy: Perspective on Demographic Realities," *Urban Mission* (September 1986): 10.

2. John Murray, "Corporate Responsibility," in *Collected Writings,* vol. 1 (Edinburgh: Banner of Truth, 1976), 275. The Bible, says Murray, on the one hand teaches that "there are corporate entities which, as such, have responsibilities distinguishable from the strictly individual and personal responsibilities which belong to the persons comprised in these corporations." On the other hand, "the corporate entity does not exist apart from the individuals

What does this mean for Christians who want to minister to needy people? *It means that not only individuals must be changed, but legal, social, political systems must be changed as well.* There is a balance to strike here. Remember, on the one hand, that individuals within a guilty corporation are also guilty, for corporations are made up of persons. On the other hand, organizations give birth to systems and conditions that must be addressed directly, for no one individual is responsible for it. A system of economics or politics or justice can be selfish and oppressive, with many of the supporters of the system fairly unconscious of its effects.

So laws and policies must be changed *as well as* individuals. Personal evangelism to the individuals alone is insufficient to extend Christ's lordship over a society. "Lordship evangelism" seeks to be "as pervasive as sin itself"; it addresses both selfish individuals *and* selfish social systems with the gospel.[3] Christians, then, must not simply bandage the wounded. They must also pursue the attacker. Emergency relief is not always enough; social reform is also required.

Ideological Traps

A third reason why evangelical Christians tend to overlook the need for the transformation and reform dimensions of deed ministry is because they are captive to ideological biases. Most Christians lie somewhere along the political spectrum between "liberal" and "conservative," with most evangelicals clustered toward the conservative end. But neither ideology is the answer; "neither capitalism nor communism can bring justice to the poor."[4] Rather, God working through his people will bring that justice.

American liberalism tends to be hostile to the claim that the church should have public rights and public functions. Instead, the state is

composing or comprised in that entity. . . . the corporate credit or guilt cannot be conceived of as existing apart from the individuals who compose the entity." He concludes, "In any case the corporate responsibility must devolve upon the individuals and become individualized in a way distinguishable from strictly individual responsibility, but not in a way that relieves the individual of responsibility" (273). Murray does not (in this chapter) apply the concept of corporate responsibility to unfair social systems, but to church denominations.

3. Harvie Conn, *Evangelism: Doing Justice and Preaching Grace* (Grand Rapids: Zondervan, 1982), 50.

4. John Perkins, *With Justice for All* (Ventura, CA: Regal, 1982), 168.

seen as the panacea for society's ills; the state will order society in a just, fair, rational way. The roots of liberalism are in the eighteenth-century Enlightenment, which taught that reason alone can give all the knowledge needed to build a just society.[5] Liberalism is also highly individualistic, defending private, individual rights against institutions such as the family (children's rights against parents), and the church (homosexuals' rights to work for a church).

But American conservatism is no real alternative, for it is just as rationalistic and individualistic. For example, though conservatives expect the government to regulate "personal morality" (upholding traditional family values, and so on) it insists that "social morality" (giving to the poor) must be completely voluntary. There can be no accountability in this area. This is fundamentally inconsistent, and the exact reverse of the liberals' individualism.

Conservativism tends to be blind to the systemic, corporate structures of greed and selfishness that create poverty. Instead, it sees poverty as being eliminated strictly through individual initiative. And while liberalism puts much faith in big government, so the conservative has a similar blind faith in big business. The ideology of the Right insists that completely free enterprise, business unhampered by any constraints or limits, will bring prosperity to the country which will "trickle down" to the poor. But

free enterprise is handicapped by a serious flaw—man's greed. Both biblical history and American history remind us repeatedly that greedy men will use economic freedom to exploit—to profit at the expense of others. Employers pay employees as little as possible in order to maximize their own profits rather than treating their employee's economic interest as being as important as their own—or, to be thoroughly Christian—more important than their own. Advertisers create markets for products which no one needs, not from a motive of servanthood, but out of greed, pure and simple. Businesses measure their success primarily by their financial profits—not by

5. Peter L. Berger and Richard J. Neuhaus, *To Empower People: The Role of Mediating Structures in Public Policy* (Washington: American Enterprise Institute for Public Policy Research, 1977), 5.

how well they glorify God and serve people. What a far cry we are from a truly Christian economy![6]

Both big government and big business lead to exploitation and corruption because of man's sin, and because God's primary social structures for mercy—the family and the church—are not being recognized and supported in the public arena by either liberal or conservative governments. The Bible calls *both* government officials and businesspeople to exercise compassion and promote justice for those in need. But both government and business should recognize that neither of them can take the place of the church, the family, and voluntary associations in the fight against social problems.

Christians must not let their political biases lead them into passivity. Mercy ministry through the family, the church, and other voluntary associations is absolutely crucial.

What is the result of seeing and understanding the social dimensions of the gospel? Christians can expand their vision for community impact! Rather than simply providing handouts for the needy, Christians should be seeking to "make His blessings flow far as the curse is found,"[7] changing whole lives and the structures that break them. And to ignore transformation and reform is to be poor stewards of our time and resources. "If we ignore appropriate reform, we sentence ourselves to long-term and seemingly unending relief efforts toward a steady stream of needy persons."[8]

AFFECTING THE COMMUNITY

Now we are in a position to see that mercy ministry does not consist only of "relief," but of several levels of intervention. When we concentrate only on meeting emergency needs, we seldom see long-term effects.

The Case of Sophia

Sophia, a Philadelphia single mother of two children, receives $187 per month in benefits in addition to her food stamps. On that income,

6. Perkins, *With Justice for All*, 167.
7. From "Joy to the World," hymn by Isaac Watts.
8. Craig Ellison, *Urban Mission* (March 1987): 39.

Sophia's options are drastically reduced. The only place she can afford to live is in federally funded housing called the Projects. Sterile, boxlike structures in a state of disrepair are home to thousands of people in similar circumstances. The Projects are known to have more drug-related violence than anywhere in Philadelphia, which doesn't make it any easier for Sophia to raise her children. She spends hours each month walking in and out of businesses—everything from fast food chains to movie theaters. No jobs are available, because Sophia can neither read well enough nor add in her head fast enough. To solve her reading problems, she started school, and is tutored by a volunteer from a local church. Since she doesn't have the money for carfare, she walks to her tutoring site—several miles each way. Any unusual event will throw off Sophia's carefully planned budget. When her son's friend stole her food stamps for the month, she was forced to ask for help from the ACTS food closet. When her eight-year-old daughter wanted to invite friends to celebrate her birthday, Sophia had to borrow enough money to buy a cake mix and the invitations.

What does it mean to be poor? For Sophia, it means living where she doesn't choose to live. It means doing what others tell her to, when they tell her. It means having few options in her life. It means being stuck. Poverty: (n) 1. the condition of hopelessness 2. an inability to change one's life.[9]

This case study shows that need is multidimensional. Sophia needs more than a handout! She needs direct assistance. She needs to be helped to self-sufficiency. She needs help from those who can change the unsafe and destructive social system in which she lives.

Relief and Transformation

The Bible demonstrates that there are three dimensions of mercy ministry. First, there is what we can call *relief.* This is the alleviation of suffering caused by unmet basic needs. The Good Samaritan himself is a model of relief by offering physical protection, emergency medical treatment, and rent subsidy (Luke 10:30–35).

9. Priscilla Blair, "Poverty: One View," *ACTS Newsletter* (Tenth Presbyterian Church, Philadelphia, April 1987).

Second, there is what many call *transformation*. This is to build up, develop, and restore the person to self-sufficiency. Many have also called this "economic development," but more recently the word "transformation" has become the preferred terminology.

Relief programs alone can create patterns of dependency. When a slave's debt was erased and he was released, God directed that the former master send him out with grain, tools, and resources for a new life. (Deut. 15:13–14: "When you release him, do not send him away empty-handed. Supply him liberally from your flock, your threshing floor and your winepress. Give to him as the LORD your God has blessed you.")

John Perkins writes that simply putting welfare checks in the hands of poor blacks in small towns only ends up transferring capital into the accounts of the wealthy white bankers and storeowners. Government poverty programs provided "relief," but did not work toward community ownership, so blacks stayed dependent and poor. But when Perkins in rural Mississippi communities began organizing the poor into farming co-ops, housing co-ops, and credit unions, they were able to develop their neighborhoods, keeping money, jobs, and training there.[10]

Psalm 41:1 (RSV) pronounces "blessed" the man who "considers" the poor. The latter word means careful thinking toward a practical program of action. God is not interested in mere relief, but restoration. Education, job training, capital for beginning a business—all of these are necessary to develop the poor.

Reform: Doing Justice

Third, there is the level that many call *reform*. Social reform moves beyond relieving physical needs and seeks to change social conditions and structures that create those needs. It does not just patch up the wounded, but goes after the ones that have done the wounding. Job tells us that he not only clothed the naked, but he "broke the fangs of the wicked and snatched the victims from their teeth" (Job 29:17). Unfair wages (Jer. 22:13), corrupt business practices (Amos 8:2, 6), legal systems weighted in favor of the rich and influential (Deut. 24:17; Lev. 19:15),

10. Perkins, *With Justice for All*, 146–66.

a system of lending capital which gouges the little man (Lev. 19:35–37; 25:37; Ex. 22:25–27) were all denounced and opposed by the Bible. And not only was social reform an activity that permeated believing Israel, but the exiled Daniel calls the pagan government of Nebuchadnezzar to account for its lack of mercy to the poor (Dan. 4:27).

Historically, in times of revival, Christians have sought changes in social structures in the interest of justice and mercy. The fruit of the Great Awakening in eighteenth-century England came in many social reforms. Evangelical William Wilberforce abolished first the slave trade and then slavery itself. Zachary Macaulay helped put on its feet the infant colony Sierra Leone, a nation for freed slaves. Anthony A. Cooper, the Earl of Shaftesbury, led the battle for the child labor laws to protect children and youth from exploitation by industry. John Howard spent thousands of his own wealth and traveled extensively to reform prison conditions. Sir Thomas Bernard was an advocate of better educational institutions for the poor, and the establishment of better housing and community planning for industrial workers.[11] There is much to be done to proclaim the word through social reforms.

CIRCLES OF FELT-NEED INTERVENTION

In light of these biblical "levels," we can discern several "circles" of felt-need intervention that move along a spectrum from relief to reform. Here we will propose a model of seven concentric circles of intervention strategies.[12]

Relief Ministry

Circle 1: Direct assistance. This is the most basic way to help someone in need, and this is what most evangelicals think of when they think of the ministry of mercy. Direct assistance meets immediate needs of the most basic necessities—food, clothing, medical assistance, shelter, and finances for the same.

11. John Roach, *Social Reform in England 1780–1880* (New York: St. Martin's, 1978), 50–53.
12. Compare Ellison's different arrangement of the same basic categories in *Urban Mission* (March 1987): 35.

Examples of direct assistance ministries abound. A list of such services may include the traditional food closets or pantries, thrift stores (which sell or give away used clothing and other basic accessories), temporary emergency housing, repairs and renovation to unsafe housing for low-income families, free medical clinics and health care, home care services for the elderly and disabled, interaction and caring opportunities to the institutionalized and shut-in, crisis counseling, and some kinds of regular transportation services (such as for elderly people, to enable them to buy food and other necessities).

Figure 4

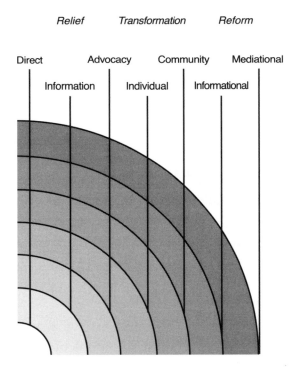

Circle 2: Informational and counseling. One form of this ministry is counseling. There is, of course, a great variety of counseling needs. And though someone may consider this "word" ministry rather than "deed" ministry, it is a service that is needed and closely related to those

with "social problems." People with physical and economic ills need counseling for dealing with stress, depression, marriage problems, child rearing, divorce recovery, drug and alcohol abuse, sexual addictions and dysfunctions, grief, sickness, and other life traumas.

Counseling may take the form of individual therapy or of accountability/support groups for those with various addictions, sexual problems, eating disorders, emotional disorders, and physical or terminal illnesses. Another kind of counseling is conflict mediation between family members, employee and employer, landlord and tenant, and so on. Financial counseling is also a critical service.

Another form of informational ministry is clearinghouse referral. Many people in need are lacking information about how to find jobs, how to locate decent housing, how to apply for various benefits, how to locate people who can be of help to them. Elderly persons, for example, may not know about the plethora of groups, agencies, and opportunities available to them, such as subsidized housing, volunteer programs, medical care, day care centers for the aged, housekeeper-helper programs, food and nutrition centers, and social groups. Persons with disabilities and chronic illnesses, single parents, substance abusers, people with legal problems—all need information about their situation and what resources are available to them. Evangelical churches should be clearinghouses of information on problems and needs of all kinds.

Christian churches often fall into one of two extremes with regard to informational ministry. Some churches procure community service directories and simply dispense information and referrals indiscriminately. But many government and private social agencies carry secular premises about human nature and morality into their services. Churches must be careful about referrals and networking with other groups. On the other hand, many churches refuse to cooperate with any other agency or even church which does not operate out of an identical statement of faith. Your church should be willing to work with agencies as long as the relationship does not compromise your own theological commitments.

Circle 3: Advocacy. Many people in need require more than just information. They need active assistance, people who will stand with them and even represent them. "Speak up for those who cannot speak for themselves, for the rights of all who are destitute. Speak up and judge fairly, defend the rights of the poor and needy" (Prov. 31:8–9). People need advocates who can help them find housing or deal with unresponsive landlords. In other situations, advocates are needed to arbitrate conflict management between husbands and wives, family members, employer and employees.

Another example is legal assistance. Many persons need lawyers or legal workers who can lead them through the maze of options, obligations, and regulations. Several types of Christian legal aid services aid needy people.

One excellent example is the Austin Christian Law Center (ACLC) in Chicago, which is part of Circle Urban Ministries (which also offers ministries of health care, counseling, emergency housing, and job skill training). Christian lawyers in ACLC have the advantage of being able to refer clients for help in many other areas besides the leGal. Thus the client is ministered to holistically. The ACLC director assigns many cases to Christian attorneys who are members of a pro bono panel. This allows ACLC to do far more work than its small staff would otherwise provide for. Other examples of such ministries are Emmanuel Legal Services in Boston and Christian Legal Aid and Referral Service in Albuquerque, New Mexico.[13]

Transformation Ministry

Circle 4: Individual transformation. How do we move beyond the handout to really develop the needy person into a condition of self-sufficiency? There are several kinds of ministries that do so. First, there is basic literacy and education. Millions of people in this country are functionally illiterate and lack basic math skills as well. Millions of new immigrants need English skills. Churches can begin adult education programs or ESL classes (English as a second language). A related service would be scholarships for education or the actual establishment of schools.

---

13. Ann Detierre and Mary Szto, "Missionary Lawyering," *Christian Legal Society Quarterly* (Fall 1987).

Second, there are housing ministries. Needy people need to own their own homes. Churches have begun to help build homes for the poor or do extensive renovation to dilapidated housing for the needy to live in. (Simply providing safe rental housing is good, but true transformation would help the poor to home ownership).

In Memphis, the Neighborhood Christian Center operates the Interim Housing Program. It allows low-income families to stay in a Center house for up to two years, paying only $50 a month for expenses. With the help of the Center, the families save money, usually about $3000 a year, to buy an inexpensive home of their own in the city.[14]

Third, there are job programs that provide vocational guidance, training, and placement services to people without the ability or means to find employment. Other forms of individual transformation would include training in basic financial management skills, and in basic social skills. One of the great advantages of transformation programs is the great ease at which evangelism can be woven into the very warp and woof of the ministry. In direct assistance, evangelism must be "tacked on" to the program, but in transformation it is a natural part.

Vocational Ministry Models

A small group Bible study in Atlanta, Georgia, began a "job bank" to help the unemployed. It enlisted Christian businesspeople in participating congregations and additional employers from the community to pass along job openings into the bank. Jobless people are referred by appointed leaders in the participating churches. In three years, the Christian Employment Cooperative grew to a network of 116 churches with 186 volunteers. It has placed more than 700 people in jobs. Training, follow-up, resume preparation, and counseling are all provided by volunteers.[15]

14. "Helping Poor Families Buy Homes," *World Vision USA* 3, no. 1 (March–April 1988): 6. For information on this ministry, write to Neighborhood Christian Centers, 735 North Parkway, Memphis, TN 38105.

15. "Citywide Employment Network Launched by Bible Study Group," *World Vision USA* 3, no. 1 (March–April 1988): 6. For more information on this ministry, write to Christian Employment Cooperative, 465 Boulevard SE, Suite 210, Atlanta, GA 30312.

St. Stephen's Episcopal in Sewickley, Pennsylvania, began the HOPE ministry (Help Offer People Employment). The ministry's tasks are to find laid-off workers temporary jobs, a seven-week course to train people in job seeking, and short-term provisions for food, housing, childcare, and money. The gospel is shared as part of the Job Seekers course, and fifteen to twenty persons have made professions of faith.[16]

Foothills Jobs is a Christian ministry begun under a World Vision grant in 1984, which has helped place over 500 people in jobs during its first two and a half years (the average starting hourly wage of the jobs was $6.04). An intensive job readiness training program gives the counselors an opportunity to measure applicants' motivation and assess skills. For three weeks, job candidates are given assignments that cultivate dependability, punctuality, and confidence. Once candidates pass through the organization's network of communication with area businesses, they are placed. New employees and employers are given follow-up visits to monitor worker progress.[17]

Job creation may be more important than job placement in many communities. Bethel New Life, in the West Garfield Park section of Chicago, operates five job creation programs. Stitches Unlimited employs twenty-five seamstresses, and there is also a "cash for trash" recycling program, a home care service, short order cook training, and real estate management. All of the programs are self-supporting, and they serve 2000 persons a year.[18]

In Great Britain unemployment is even a bigger problem than in the U.S. Christians in the U.K. have become highly resourceful in providing work for those without. In a recent book, Peter Elsom and David Porter list many strategies for churches to use, including the lending of "venture capital" to start new businesses, the formation of cooperatives, and the forming of "work agencies." The latter scheme creates new jobs. A new job is constructed by enlisting at most forty church members who could

16. "Melting Steel Hearts," *Christianity Today* (4 October 1985): 33.

17. "Stopping the March of Unemployment in California," *World Vision USA* (December 1986): 8–9. For information on Foothills Jobs, write to the director at 261 East Colorado Blvd., Pasadena, CA 91101.

18. "Job Placement or Job Creation? Let the Community Decide," *World Vision USA* (December 1986): 3.

provide pay for at least two hours of work once every two weeks. The work could range from relatively unskilled work to more skilled work.[19]

Circle 5: Community transformation. Community transformation empowers people. It does not simply bring wealth into the lives of the individuals. It brings ownership into neighborhoods to strengthen communities for self-determination.

A vivid picture of how community transformation is possible was presented in the sentimental yet poignant film *It's a Wonderful Life* (circa 1945) starring James Stewart. A compassionate but discouraged director of a small town loan association is given a vision of what the town would have been like without his work of helping the "little people" to buy decent homes and begin businesses. He sees a poor town, full of powerless people, broken families, and moral degeneration.

John Perkins writes:

> The oppressed among us know all too well that the oppressive forces which created their poverty in the first place keep them trapped in. The young black electrician, having never had an opportunity to establish a credit rating, finds it almost impossible to raise the capital to buy the tools and equipment to go into business for himself. The general rule is, "To get capital, you must have capital," and so the system perpetuates and widens the gap between rich and poor.[20]

Small Businesses

Since Wesley and Whitefield in the Great Awakening, churches have helped transform communities by developing small businesses. These enterprises not only create new jobs but build homes and commercial centers to help deteriorating neighborhoods. They keep capital and skills in the community. Many times small businesses are the key way to directly meet a neighborhood need uncovered by your community study. If the homes are in serious disrepair, begin a housing rehab

19. Peter Elsom and David Porter, *Four Million Reasons to Care: How Your Church Can Help the Unemployed* (Kent, England: MARC Europe, 1985).
20. Perkins, *With Justice for All,* 169.

and repair business. If single mothers are paying too much for clothing, food, and childcare, begin businesses that provide them.

Among the most effective community transformation projects are mutual savings and loan associations or investment corporations. Often noted as an excellent model of this is the Dwelling House Savings and Loan, a company that invests in poorer neighborhoods by making loans to low-income families.[21]

These businesses provide both individual and community transformation. For example, the trash and aluminum recycling center operated by Bethel New Life in Chicago earns $150,000 a year. They return the money to the 210 community residents who work with the project.[22]

But operating small businesses can be complicated! Even before the business takes off, serious organizational questions need to be answered. Will the business be owned cooperatively? Will it be operated by the church as a nonprofit ministry? Will it be an independent, for-profit enterprise owned by an agency/subsidiary? In what form will the ownership be established—by membership, shares, or contracts? These questions must be looked into carefully.[23]

Cooperatives

Many ministries have found the economic cooperative to be strategic to community transformation. A co-op differs from a corporation in a number of significant ways: (1) Corporations exist to serve the public for a profit; cooperatives exist to serve its members at cost. Those who use the co-op own it; (2) corporations are controlled by money, with each share getting one vote; cooperatives are controlled by people, with each member getting one vote; (3) in corporations, profits are paid to the stockholder in proportion to holding; in cooperatives, surplus earnings are distributed to members in proportion to patronage.

21. "Banker Invests in God's People," *Leadership 88 Letter* 1, no. 4.
22. Mary Nelson, "Lessons Learned from For-Profit Enterprise," *World Vision USA* 3, no. 1 (March–April 1988): 5.
23. See a very helpful issue of *World Vision USA* (March–April 1988), which is devoted wholly to these questions.

In poor communities, cooperatives can be enormously helpful for two reasons. First, the cooperative can provide goods and services at a far more reasonable price than most corporations will provide them. Second, the persons who own corporations do not live with the needy, so the profits of the corporation leave the communities of the consumers. The money of a co-op stays in the community to build personal income, savings, and capital, to create more jobs, and so on. Third, cooperatives owned by the needy themselves create the incentive to develop professional skills. Co-ops decrease the migration out of poor communities and can improve overall social and economic conditions.

What can churches do? Churches need to help co-ops get started by providing capital, technical assistance, training, and a supportive climate of opinion.[24] John Perkins provides a brief but specific chapter on how to begin several types of co-ops: marketing, purchasing (food stores, service stations), and service (electricity, insurance, housing, health care, credit, nursery schools, etc.).[25] Perkins himself saw many co-ops started through his ministry in Mendenhall and Jackson, Mississippi, now carried on largely through Voice of Calvary Ministries.

The operative word for community transformation is *creativity*. Bethel New Life Church in Chicago developed a self-help housing program which is having an impact on both the individual lives and the social system of its low-income neighborhood. In a square mile area around the church, a cooperative was created to build and renovate housing. The project was underwritten using creative financing from banks and "sweat equity," a commitment from the participants to donate a specific number of hours of labor. Applicants to the co-op gave a $500 down payment and contracted to work 750 hours building their home and the homes of others in the cooperative. The ministry has developed more than 350 units of low-income housing in nine years.[26] Clyde Johnson was one of the first participants in the co-op:

24. James A. Cogswell, *The Church and the Rural Poor* (Atlanta: John Knox, 1975), 84.
25. Perkins, *With Justice for All*, 170–77.
26. Nelson, "Lessons Learned from For-Profit Enterprise."

Two years ago, the 56-year-old plumber was struggling to make a living and sharing a run-down Chicago apartment with his wife and five children. He had to raid the coal bins of abandoned buildings to make sure his family had heat. Buying a home was out of the question. "It was hell," he recalls, "because I didn't have enough work to enable me to do the things I would have liked to have done and give my kids things I wanted them to have." What he did have, though, was a skill. And that made him an ideal candidate for the self-help housing project sponsored by Bethel New Life Church. . . . After more than a year's hard work, he and his family moved into their new home. It "has the best heat in Chicago," he says proudly. "I put all the plumbing in myself. I am an old man, but this is one of the best feelings I have ever had, to be able to build my own house. I feel a little bad, because everybody should have this chance to do for yourself."[27]

Reform

Circle 6: Information for justice. One of the key ways in which a church or a Christian can affect social systems is by speaking to and informing policy makers of important needs and social conditions. One of the ways to get better schools, better police protection, better sanitation services is simply to provide information to decision makers. This is no less than the church's God-given prophetic ministry. Theologian John Murray writes:

How is the church to proclaim the counsel of God as it bears upon civil affairs? It is obvious that there are two means . . . namely, the pulpit and the press. The church lives in the world and . . . if it is to be faithful to its commission it must make its voice heard and felt in reference to public questions.[28]

This means that a church must get to know the policy-making leaders of the community and must learn how to disseminate informa-

27. "People Power Winning Battles as War on Poverty Goes Local," *Insight,* Washington Times (15 June 1987): 21.
28. Murray, *Collected Writings,* 1:257.

tion to them. This is no less than social reform, and the church of Jesus Christ is bound to do it.

This "prophetic" ministry for justice may take very simple forms. Helping a neighborhood get better police protection and other services may mean a letter-writing campaign and lots of interviews with policy makers. But this service can also have far greater dimensions.

In the 1970s, the Presbyterian Church in Taiwan began to speak out against the Chinese ideology that holds Taiwan to be a province of China. Both Peking and the Nationalist Chinese government, run by the Mandarin refugees from the mainland, agree on this. But the majority of the people of the island, the native Taiwanese, have been there since the seventeenth century and do not think of themselves as Chinese citizens any more than Americans think of themselves as English.

The Presbyterian Church protested the government's forcing the Mandarin language on the nation (including the confiscation of Bibles in Taiwanese). It called for the election of a new government representing the people of Taiwan so that they could determine their own destiny. The church wrote an open letter to the president of the United States. The government responded severely. But how did this social concern affect church growth? One Taiwanese pastor said:

> The Presbyterian Church in Taiwan is no longer a foreign institution; it is now the church of the Taiwanese people. We are attracting many strangers. . . . A number of people I had not known before have come to me not only to express their solidarity but also to say, "Your God can now be our God."[29]

The same dynamic was operating in the New Testament when the people, seeing miracles heal their neighbors, confessed Jesus to be the Holy One of God.

Circle 7: Intervention for justice. The final form of social reform is legal or political intervention. It refers to starting initiatives, introducing

29. Harvie Conn, "Taiwan: Church Growth, Ethnicity, and Politics," *Exploring Church Growth*, ed. Wilbert Shenk (Grand Rapids: Eerdmans, 1983), 72.

legislation, sponsoring boycotts, and generally bringing pressure to bear to affect social structures and conditions.

Christians have differed over the role the church should play in political intervention. The black evangelical churches have been engaged in it for years, while the white evangelical churches have largely rejected it. Let's consider two guiding principles.

First, the church's work of transformation and even relief will certainly change social structures. It is not possible to draw a distinct line between relief and reform. They lead to one another. If a ministry lifts up the poor in a community, it will drastically alter the order of things. Therefore it is mistaken to say that the church should not be seeking to change the shape of society.

Second, the church cannot present unnecessary barriers to the inquirer after Christ. For an individual to join your church, he or she should be required simply to serve Jesus Christ. The person should not have to become a liberal Democrat or a conservative Republican to enter your fellowship, nor should the person be made to feel that it is a criterion for membership. Churches that are too heavily invested in the political agenda of a particular party or candidate can appear to be captive to an ideology instead of the lordship of Christ. The great danger in speaking officially, as the church of Christ, in favor of a particular candidate or party is that it cannot help but appear to lend the name of Christ to that political cause.

For this reason, except in the most clear, broad, and basic public issues (many churches believe abortion is one of these), it is best for interventional social reform to be carried out by voluntary associations, parachurch groups, which can use political power to change social structure.

THINKING BIG

The church must think big! "If God [this great God] is for us, who can be against us?"

A California Model

Craig Ellison suggests Allen Temple Baptist Church in Oakland, California, as a model of a full-service church. Allen Temple Church sponsors tutoring programs for youth, scholarship programs, adult literacy and education classes, and released time programs at the church in cooperation with a neighboring elementary school. In health care the church sponsors numerous clinics—dental work, blood bank, cancer screening, etc. The church has built a seventy-five-unit housing complex for the elderly and has helped neighboring homeowners to make repairs and renovations. A Job Fair Committee helps with job placement. A credit union begun at the church provides loans for members and investments in the community. Counseling and community recreational programs are also included in the ministry of the church. Interwoven is a very full and aggressive network of evangelistic ministries which has enabled the church of 1000 (in 1970) to more than double during the seventies, and it expects to double again by 1990.[30]

A New York Model

One of the most amazing examples of community transformation was accomplished by the East Brooklyn Churches (EBC), a coalition of churches in Brooklyn, New York, in the early 1980s.

The devastated Brownsville section of Brooklyn was full of abandoned buildings and rubble-strewn lots prowled by wild dogs and gangs. By 1975 there was nothing there but public housing; Boston mayor Kevin White saw it as "the beginning of the end of our civilization." The New York City housing commissioner announced plans to withdraw services and resettle even the public housing residents to a livable community.

But the EBC began to build an organization that confounded the urban experts. In hundreds of house meetings, it began studying the local power structures and began to use them. At first they tackled small goals—new street signs, crackdowns on local "smoke shops," and even cleanups of local food stores through courteous threats of boycott. The EBC registered 10,000 new voters, 70 percent of which were American and West Indian black; it doubled the voter turnout in the 1984 election. It stunned the local power establishment by demanding meetings with shadowy political bosses to talk about community services.

30. This church is studied in G. Willis Bennett, *Guidelines for Effective Urban Ministry* (Nashville: Broadman, 1983).

Finally it tackled the "Nehemiah" housing project, named after the rebuilder of Jerusalem's city walls. The EBC raised $9 million from denominations and foundations, and the city donated fifteen blocks on which 1000 new single-family homes were built. The state provided low-interest loans and half the buyers—nurses, paralegals, teachers' aides, transit workers—came from public housing, holding their little nest eggs and their dreams.[31]

CONCLUSION

The church exists just as much for the world as for its own members, because it exists ultimately for God. It is our Godward-reference that keeps us from making the needs of our own people and members primary. The more we look upward, the more we look outward.[32] The church is both the community of the kingdom and the agent for the spread of the kingdom of God.

We have looked at the many dimensions of mercy ministry and the broad circles of felt-need intervention through which the church can literally transform its community. The church is the light of the world (Matt. 5:14; Phil. 2:15), the new humanity (Eph. 4:24), a picture of the world to come, and a challenge to the world to submit to the King. The options are vast and the possibilities are overwhelming! Churches should not shrink from looking squarely at all the possibilities. Instead of feeling inadequate before them, the church must build a vision for the future, a vision of what impact it can have on its entire community.

FOR DISCUSSION

1. When is emergency relief inadequate? Provide an example.
2. Identify and describe the levels of intervention (circles of intervention) we can pursue in mercy ministries.
3. Which one of the community projects mentioned was most inspiring to you?
4. Is it feasible for your church to consider a similar community project? Explore your answer.

31. Jim Sleeper, "Boodling, Bigotry, and Cosmopolitanism: The Transformation of a Civic Culture," *Dissent* (Fall 1987): 418–19.
32. See C. John Miller, *Outgrowing the Ingrown Church* (Grand Rapids: Zondervan, 1986).

12

Managing Your Ministry

OVERVIEW: To maintain and to build a mercy ministry, we must learn to plan and to coordinate.

PROBLEMS ALONG THE WAY

At the beginning of the last chapter we mentioned several problems that keep churches stagnant in mercy ministry, despite many good intentions. We have only discussed one of those problems so far, namely, the preeminence of individual concerns over the social dimensions of the gospel. Now we turn our attention to the other three.

First, many churches stall in mercy ministry because they never learn to build bridges into the community beyond their own membership. They meet a few needs in their own midst, but they find that there are few "takers" for the resources they have. People begin to believe that there really aren't many needy people around anyway. But they are isolated from hurting persons.

Second, many churches stall in mercy ministry because they become absorbed and encumbered by needs of just a few people who come into the church and begin to drain everyone's energies. This is caused partly by a lack of skill in casework. (We will cover that subject in chapter 13.) However, this is due also to the church's natural tendency to react instead of act, to *fail to* *"set a vision."* A congregation must constantly restudy the community and renew its goals to build a vision of what can be done in its locale.

Third, the "friends of mercy" (whether they are officers or laity) often do not know how to broaden their base of operation through skillful recruitment and supervision of volunteers or through cooperation with other churches. Big visions take lots of help! It does not work to make bold plans unless you know how to win and encourage others to share the ministry with you. It is also crucial to reach out to like-minded churches in a spirit of cooperation. Many dedicated Christians, with a heart for mercy, become a desperately overworked little core group that cannot grow.

So we see that planting seedling mercy ministries is not enough. Our growth will be stunted if we do not continually "water" the church so that our seed can grow and the fruit can ripen. In this chapter we will look at each of these three problems and discuss some of the ways to "water" for growth in mercy.

BUILDING BRIDGES FOR OUTREACH

The first major reason that churches falter in the ministry of mercy is that they are not finding ways to reach out and really contact those in need. What good is it to have great dreams for community impact if you are not actually meeting people with needs?

Many churches have had the experience of stockpiling food for a community pantry or clothing for a public closet and then finding that no one makes use of their inventory. Why not? Most middle-class people have few or no contacts with the needy. Even when they are living nearby, long-time residents often have no idea that they are there. For example, most people believe that all poor people live in inner-city ghettos. However, while 36 percent of the poor do live in the cities, 39 percent live in rural areas, and 26 percent of all poor families live in the suburbs. Poverty is also rapidly growing in the suburbs. Between 1978 and 1983, 2.5 million white suburbanites were added to the population in poverty.[1] How can a church reach these people? Here are some suggestions.

1. Community Involvement

A church should be sure to identify each member who may be involved in any service agencies or helping organizations, either as pro-

1. William O'Hare, "The Eight Myths of Poverty," *American Demographics* (May 1986): 25.

fessionals or as volunteers. Nurses, doctors, social workers, childcare workers, nursing home employees—all of these people probably have valuable contacts with groups of needy people. If a church has few such people it may wish to encourage members to become involved as volunteers in various private and secular helping agencies, as a way of learning about the areas of need in your community. Use these members, then, as bridges to the needy.

2. STEP

STEP is both a concept and a national organization. The concept is this: an upper-middle-class church with many resources links up with a church in a neighborhood or community with many needy. The second church has many members with physical, economic, and personal needs, while the first church has a number of funds, skills, and gifts to meet the needs. Each church establishes a committee, and the two groups meet together as one body to coordinate the matching of needs with resources and gifts.

The advantages of this approach are many. The poor who are being helped are Christians, already under the care of a church and in fellowship with other Christians. There is far more accountability for those rendering the gifts and services and those receiving them. Another advantage is that it enables the middle-class church to build bridges to the needy neighborhoods through the Christian brothers and sisters who live there. It becomes possible for the two churches to strategize on ways to reach nonbelievers in the community. The second church has the bridges and knowledge, while the first church has the resources and a growing motivation to help.

There is a national organization that promotes this concept and helps churches into these relationships.

3. SOS Plan

In a previous chapter we outlined how to set up a service bank. This consists of two basic components: an inventory of the skills of volunteers and an information system of referral that reveals needs within the church. An "SOS" (Strategy of Service) Plan is the same basic structure, only based in the whole outside community. SOS is so named by June A. Williams in her helpful book that details how the program can be set up.[2]

Essentially, the program can be set up by following several steps.

a. *Set geographic boundaries for the ministry.*

b. *Set up a referral network within the boundaries.* This can be set up by (1) contact with any helping agencies, social workers, etc., inside your boundaries, (2) contact with individual service providers such as policemen, mail carriers, pharmacists, beauticians, etc., and (3) sending a letter to residents (especially target groups such as the elderly) or personally canvassing an area to publicize the ministry.

c. *Establish a volunteer system.* This system comprises (1) an ongoing recruitment effort, (2) a coordinator who can match needs to volunteers and keep records, and (3) a support system for the volunteers. The visits of volunteers may be assessment visiting (to determine needs, offer support, provide prayer and evangelism, and plan coordination for services to meet heeds), or "friendly visiting" (to offer love and caring to shut-ins, the lonely, the sick, the elderly). The work of the volunteers may consist of providing transportation, doing light chores, providing respites for those with the constant care of dependents, tutoring, or delivering emergency assistance such as food or funds for rent and utilities.

4. Public Visibility and Listing

Some churches by virtue of their size and/or their location, are highly visible to those in need, and each week (or even each day) people come to the doors asking for money, food, or other resources. Other churches, through their publicity or reputation, communicate to the community that they are serious about meeting physical and economic needs. Some congregations have even put ads in the paper or phone book inviting people to come and ask for these services.

2. June A. Williams, *Strategy of Service* (Grand Rapids: Zondervan, 1984).

This sort of "bridge" to the areas of need is the hardest to manage. There is no screening of people, as in a referral network. Accountability for services received is difficult to develop. Also, this bridge brings a higher percentage of insincere and dishonest recipients of aid than any other program or outreach method. A study of the poverty statistics will show that most of the poor are working, looking for work, or unable to work, but many of the small percentage who are not tend to appear at the door of churches.[3] Many Christians have been "burned" and disillusioned by episodes with people who come looking for help in this way. There are a number of ways to counteract this.

a. *Minimal screening can be done.* All calls or requests for aid should be logged to see if the person has been helped before. Some checking can be done to see if the person is "hitting up" all the churches in town.

b. *Meet the need personally.* Never simply hand out a resource, but sit down and talk with the person to explain the motivation of the gospel in the church's service and express concern.

c. *Nevertheless, make every effort to give aid through a body of people so that no one person appears to be the source of the assistance.* That one person (a secretary, a pastor, etc.), if seen as the decision maker and the dispenser, becomes open to harassment and manipulation and charges of corruption.

d. *Give help "in kind" rather than cash gifts.* Give food or clothing, not money for food and clothing. If the need is to have a utility bill paid, pay directly to the creditor. This is to protect the applicant from temptation.

e. *There should be few "strings attached" when first helping,* even though you wish to be sure that your aid is meeting a real (not a projected) need. If an applicant returns two or three times for aid, have a policy to require that he meet with two people from

3. O'Hare, *American Demographics.* Of the 19.5 million able-bodied adults in poverty, 9.1 worked, 1.4 million looked for work but could not find it, 2.3 were adolescents still in high school, 2.1 million were retired elderly, and 4.1 million were single parents at home raising children. Less than 1 million able-bodied poor are (unaccountably) not working.

the church to look into his financial problems for an overall assessment (see chapter 13). Some churches set up a work program, so that repeating applicants can do repairs and odd jobs around the church property to earn their money.

f. *Be sure to "close the loop."* Visit the recipient later and share the gospel. Have an efficient system for doing this, but do not make it appear that their acceptance of the gospel is the requirement for receiving aid. That will produce "rice Christians."

PLANNING AND GOAL-SETTING

The ministry of mercy is intensely personal, and those doing mercy work can easily become deeply absorbed in the personal problems of a few people. This can be deadly for the overall ministry of the church. We must constantly be reassessing our community and existing mercy ministries, setting goals for growth.

How can a church develop a vision, a picture of the church that it should be for its community? We propose here "the Y-Shaped Vision Building Model" (fig. 5). This is not necessarily a good planning method for a church just beginning in mercy ministry. Rather, for a church that has "planted" some mercy programs, and now wants to "water" the garden and expand and clarify the vision, this procedure should be carried out at least every three years.

Figure 5

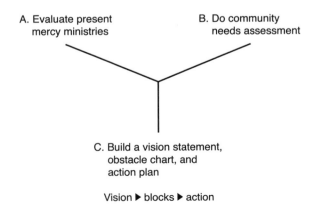

A. Evaluate present mercy ministries

B. Do community needs assessment

C. Build a vision statement, obstacle chart, and action plan

Vision ▶ blocks ▶ action

Evaluate Present Ministries

Using the seven circles of felt-need intervention, determine how many dimensions of mercy ministry your church is currently doing. Next, look at the ministries that are going on and evaluate them. Ask at least the following questions: (1) What target groups are being served by this ministry? (2) what needs are being addressed? (3) how many people are being served? (4) how much direct assistance (finances or other concrete resources) is being distributed? (5) how many volunteer hours of service are being rendered? (6) how effective is the ministry in reaching its goals?

Assess Community Needs

In an earlier chapter a detailed outline is provided for this kind of a survey. The survey should be repeated at set periods, not only because the community needs are in constant flux, but also because your own perception is maturing. This time, look for needs in terms of the seven circles of intervention. Do you see needs that can best be met through reform? advocacy? community transformation?

Build a Vision Statement

Now take both the evaluation of your present ministries and the evaluation of community needs. Both reports should be extensive and full of facts. Your planning group should have read both thoroughly. Now meet for brainstorming and strategizing. Do it in three steps.

1. *Vision statement.* Make a list of future conditions that you believe are important to bring to pass. Ask: (a) What untapped potentials do you have? (b) what situations need improvement? (c) what will those improvements look like (who would be doing what, when, how)?

Decide which of the items on the list are the most important; discard the less important ones. Ask: (a) What are the most important parts of your desired picture of the future? (b) who will benefit from each change and how? (c) what will happen if this change doesn't occur? (d) how feasible does it seem? (e) what leads you to believe this future condition is possible (Scripture, other congregations' experiences, other areas of life)?

Now make a final list of objectives, stating, "We want to bring about. . . ." This is your vision statement.

2. *Blocks and opportunities list.* In any situation there are driving forces pushing for change as well as blocking factors resisting it. Change amounts to moving the balance point, capitalizing on opportunities to increase driving forces, and/or removing blocks.

Discern the "blocks." Looking at each objective, complete the sentence: "This future condition is not happening mostly because. . . ." Ask: (a) How is the present situation today different from the situation you envision? (b) which resources are lacking: personnel, skills, space, funds, time? (c) are you lacking support from key people or groups, attention or interest from people, values and expectations of people? (d) are there structural factors lacking such as assigned responsibilities, explicit agreements, rules and traditions, decision-making procedures? (e) are there communication factors lacking such as clarity of the vision, frequency of communication?

Discern the opportunities. Looking at each objective, complete the sentence: "A force for positive change in this situation is. . . ." or "An opportunity for positive change is. . . ." Ask: (a) Which forces or pressures could push for change in the area you want to address? (b) what allies could I make in the situation?

Decide which blocks are the most likely to be removed by your action, and which opportunities are the greatest.

Then make a final list of blocks and opportunities under each objective.

3. *Action plan* (a list of goals or action steps). Look at each set of blocks and opportunities and answer the question, "What action(s) must I take to change the block or capitalize on the opportunity so the objective can be achieved?" Each answer is a solution or a *goal*. To find each solution, ask: (a) Which of these driving forces or blocks seems realistically beyond your ability to change? (b) what specific actions can eliminate or reduce this block? (c) what specific actions can increase the driving forces for change?

Make a list of the goals under each objective. Again, eliminate the less important ones if there are too many.

Now make a final list of goals, attaching to each a time frame and a person responsible.

SUPERVISING VOLUNTEERS

It is most important that in mercy, as in all ministry, the ministry is shared. Here we will discuss some principles for the motivating and oversight of ministry volunteers. Why include this in a book on mercy ministry? Many friends of mercy have ended their duties in frustration because of their inability in this area. They become disillusioned that "no one really cares or is committed," but much of the problem is due to their inability to handle people. Few laypeople know how to supervise volunteers. Even people who are professional managers do not understand the difference between supervising *volunteers* rather than *employees*. The following are some basic principles.[4]

1. Recruiting

Yes, a lack of spirituality and commitment is often the reason behind the proverb that "10 percent of the people do 90 percent of the work" in most churches. But poor recruitment is also a cause. *Volunteers tend to perform to the level at which they were recruited.* If a recruiter has done a last-minute, sloppy job of seeking someone's services, the volunteer will tend to take the responsibility just as lightly.

First, recruit to orientation, not to immediate performance. In other words, recruiting should go on far enough in advance so that the recruiter is not saying, "John, could you begin leading this group in two weeks?" but "John would you come to an orientation meeting for people considering group leading? Would you at least agree to think and pray about it?" If possible, the prospective worker should go and observe the activity on site. It is far easier to get a person to say "yes" to reflection than to say "yes" to immediate responsibility.

Second, recruit to a team, not to a job. Show the volunteer who else he or she will be working with, and identify immediately who will

---

4. Adapted from John Guetter, *Leading the Congregation in Diaconal Outreach and Effective Diaconal Outreach: Skills for Supervision* (Grand Rapids: Christian Reformed World Relief Committee, 1981).

provide support services. Support is essential: fears are calmed when a volunteer knows who will help with problems, substitute when necessary, provide training or expertise, and so on.

Third, recruit to a specific time frame, not to an indefinite duty. Tell the prospective volunteer exactly when the job will be over. When a volunteer takes any job without a stated terminus, it gives the burden of terminating to the worker. This is quite guilt-producing; the volunteer does not want to look like a "quitter" or become a burden to the recruiter. Therefore, the volunteer will ordinarily *not* ask to be relieved until he or she is to the point of weariness or frustration. Then that worker will be hard to recruit again!

Fourth, appeal to gifts and calling, not to guilt. Though all Christians have a responsibility to serve, you as the recruiter cannot be sure that God wants this person to work in your ministry. You must submit to God's sovereignty and realize that not all people will be given the calling and gifts to work with you. Rather than appealing simply to duty, the recruiter needs to point to the joy of service with infectious enthusiasm. That is an attractive approach.

2. Orienting

New volunteers should be given at the least an orientation interview or group session. Include (a) a clear delineation of the volunteer's tasks, on paper, in terms of hours and specific duties, (b) a list of resources, such as people to contact, in-service training, reading, and other supports, (c) a clear depiction of how the volunteer's work fits into the overall purpose and vision of the ministry, and (d) if possible, an opportunity to watch the ministry in action.

The best orientation includes formal training for the new volunteer. Effective training involves observing the actual ministry, a chance to actually experiment with the ministry tasks, and evaluating.

3. Assigning

The time comes for actually assigning the volunteer for the task. This should be done face to face with plenty of time for questions. Personalize the job description, allowing the volunteer to set as many variables as possible as to time, place, and ail the responsibilities. Clarify who the volunteer is responsible *to* and *for*. Set terminal dates. Clearly set the level of authority for each task. For example: does the volunteer simply wait to be told to act? Does the person recommend action and then wait for permission to act? Does the volunteer plan and then act and report immediately? Should the person plan, act, and only report when asked? Each of these is a higher level of authority. Be clear at what level the volunteer is operating. In different tasks the volunteer may be assigned different levels of authority.

Finally, get a direct verbal commitment from the volunteer. Be sure you understand and can articulate what each expects of the other.

4. Supervising

Set times for routine checking and communication through phone calls, personal contacts, and reports. *You* as the supervisor should initiate contact. Be swift to provide support services. Bestow credit and affirmation publicly; give criticism only in private. Beware of "upward delegation" (the volunteer giving back duties to you that you have given the volunteer). When the worker comes with a problem, press for a recommendation and try to get the person to figure it out with you, rather than solving it all yourself.

At certain set periods, the supervisor should sit down with the volunteer for a more extensive assessment. The extent will depend on how extensive the duties are. A conference with the volunteer can be very fruitful if six questions are considered: (a) What are your actual current duties, and do they match your original job description? (b) what do you need from me or the church to do your job? (c) what have been your achievements? (d) where are your greatest needs for improvement? (e) what are your goals for the next time period? (f) what resources will you need to meet the goals?

Three times a year, ask the volunteer to fill out the answers to these questions on three sheets of paper. Then spend one hour going over the sheets. You as the supervisor should help the volunteer revise or add to the sheets in any category. When the time is done, each of you can keep a copy of the sheets to be used as a basis for the next meeting. This practice will go a long way toward preventing the typical problems that create frustration and burnout on the part of so many church volunteers.

5. Terminating

This is the most neglected and abused step of all. Be sure to give some sort of recognition and expression of appreciation. Debrief the person who is leaving. Use the first three questions from the section above on supervisory conferences. It could be that you should spend time allowing the volunteer to express criticisms and frustration if necessary. If you must, apologize, reconcile, seek to help both of you learn from the experience. Finally, be sure that no jobs or people are "left hanging" by the volunteer's leaving.

NETWORKING WITH OTHER CONGREGATIONS

Most churches in our country are small—75 percent of all the congregations in North America have fewer than 200 persons in attendance. Many of the best models of mercy ministry are large churches, and so the average congregation becomes quite discouraged. "How can we make an impact on our community," goes the lament, "when we hardly have the money to make ends meet for our own operating expenses?" One answer to this concern is the concept of the mission group. Willing volunteers, rather than money, is all you need to begin significant ministries of mercy.

However, the other answer to this problem is cooperation and networking with other churches. Many of the exciting projects that we have presented in these chapters are beyond the abilities of single congregations, but they can certainly be accomplished by a cluster of churches. If your congregation is fortunate enough to be surrounded by other like-minded churches, it may be possible to "piggy back" mercy networks and structures on church associations or on other existing regional structures.

For example, Presbyterians are governed by "presbyteries," administrative bodies consisting of pastors and elders from each congregation who meet to conduct business. In each congregation, Presbyterians have under the elders a board of deacons who are to function as ministers of mercy. Some presbyteries have formed diaconal associations, consisting of representative deacons from each church. Through the deacons, churches can unite to undertake many, many programs. In Kalamazoo, Michigan, Christian Reformed churches have formed a vigorous Deacons Conference. During 1986, the conference employed three paid staff and utilized the abilities of 207 volunteers who donated 16,000 hours of service in mercy ministry. Over 5,500 families in the greater Kalamazoo area received direct aid and diaconal assistance.[5]

By no means must a church cooperate only with congregations from its own denomination or fellowship. In the Denver area, Evangelicals Concerned is an organization supported by evangelical churches of all sorts. The ministries it currently is operating or supporting include: Denver Habitat (assisting low-income residents to purchase single family homes), Native American Urban Transition Program (helping American Indians who leave the reservation to live in the city), Hope Communities (providing housing assistance for low-income people), F.R.I.E.N.D.S. (outreach to the mentally ill), COMPA Food Ministry (distributes food), Crisis Pregnancy Center, Tutoring Ministry (for inner-city children and youth), Vietnamese Resettlement Program (has resettled eighty refugee families), Sunrise Ministries (to the alcoholic and family), the King's Ministries (outreach to homosexuals).

How can cooperative ministries begin? Again, they should begin with a very detailed and accurate grasp of communities' needs, their extensiveness and intensiveness. Then call together the leaders of local churches that you believe you can work with. Share the needs, discuss how to meet them, pray and plan in a series of meetings. Patience is of the essence! It will take a number of meetings for reflection and relationship building even to come up with a viable plan. The possibilities are endless. In some cases, one church has a program that the other churches can build into and expand. In other cases, brand new projects must begin, with new personnel hired and put into place. Sometimes churches could hire a single staff person who could help each church reach out in its own neighborhood.

5. *Deacon Digest* (Grand Rapids: Christian Reformed World Relief Committee), March 1987.

CONCLUSION

A final reason that churches often stall in their development of mercy ministries is that they forget to continue to "fertilize" and "dig up" the garden. Once ministries get off the ground, it is easy to forget to continually be communicating, teaching, and motivating the members. We can never graduate beyond the strategies listed in chapter 9. Keep up the Sunday school electives, the public recognition of workers, the stress of mercy from the pulpit. Special emphasis should be given to motivating and enlisting new members. Be sure someone from the "friends of mercy" takes part in the new members' class. Remember, mercy ministry can make use of Christians at any stage of development. One does not need to be theologically sophisticated to change the bedpan of a disabled person, or to tutor a child who is struggling in school. That is part of the beauty of mercy ministry. It so easily mirrors the truth of the priesthood of *all* believers.

FOR DISCUSSION

1. Why do some mercy ministries stop functioning?
2. What are ways to remedy those problems?
3. Can you see the possibility for your church falling into any pitfall with mercy ministry? What could be done to prevent that?
4. Once a mercy ministry is started, what plans can you make for your church to continue to "dig up" and "fertilize" the garden?

13

Mercy Ministry and Church Growth

OVERVIEW: We must integrate evangelism with mercy ministries and provide follow-up strategies that will incorporate new believers from our mercy ministries into the church.

We have reached the point where we must catch our breath! Many Christians are not accustomed to thinking about the ministry of mercy as an essential duty of every Christian and every church. Consequently, this book places a new responsibility on them of which they previously had been only marginally aware. Not only that, but when most Americans *do* think of mercy ministry, they only think of clothing closets and food baskets at Christmas.

So when we begin to "expand our vision" by seeing the thicket of diverse needs all around us and by understanding the possibilities of economic transformation, we can easily become overwhelmed. Any sensible person will be asking at this point, "How can any poor church do all of this and have time, resources, or emotional energy to do anything else?" In particular, the question may be "Won't mercy ministry retard or impede evangelism and growth?"

The answer, of course, is that *no* church can do all the mercy ministry, evangelism, discipleship, missions, or fellowship that is possible. But we have no more cause to be overwhelmed by the ministry of mercy than by any other ministry!

We must never forget, however, that our mercy ministry is *kingdom endeavor*. Mercy ministry is not an end, but a means to an end—the spread of God's kingdom. The goal of mercy cannot be simply to feed as many people as we can, but to bring Christ's lordship over their whole lives and the social systems in which they live. Thus mercy ministry cannot "compete" with evangelism or the gifts, energy, or money of the church. Mercy and evangelism have the same goals.

CULTIVATING THE GARDEN

To return to our long-standing metaphor, we must "cultivate" the garden that we have fertilized, dug up, planted, and watered. We are out to see fruit, people won to Christ as well as whole communities transformed. Our goal is nothing less than the spreading of the kingdom, which requires that *all* of the ministries of the church be operating at full throttle and interdependently. So, as long as our church is not "ingrown," neither mercy nor evangelism, education, fellowship, and missions will be ends in themselves, but rather all means to the same end.

How easy it is to get "tunnel vision" regarding any one of these ministries! In some cases, a church can become obsessed with large numbers, and thus mercy becomes a means to the end of evangelism, mere "bait" to get a person to make a decision (see chapter 7 for more on this error). On the other hand, some people develop tunnel vision about mercy. They care only about getting the most resources to the most people, and they neglect (or even disdain) church growth, the building of the church through conversions. It is true that many churches that give mercy a priority do not grow and show no interest in it as well. In such a case, mercy has become an "end" instead of a means to an end. But, as we have seen in chapter 7, the kingdom is to be proclaimed in both word and deed. This leads Harvie Conn to subsume both verbal evangelism and social concern under one heading: "lordship evangelism."[1]

---

1. Harvie Conn, *Evangelism: Doing Justice and Preaching Grace* (Grand Rapids: Zondervan, 1982), 50.

LOOKING AT THE CHURCH HOLISTICALLY

Therefore, it is not only people that we must view holistically, but we must see the church that way as well. We must recognize that worship, fellowship, evangelism, teaching, and mercy live in a balance and grow together.

A holistic view of the church is not easy to achieve.[2] It is really very common for God to burden an individual's heart for one particular aspect of the church's life. For example, someone may be extremely bothered by how languid the worship and prayer life of the congregation is. Another may see so clearly how little evangelistic impact the church is having on the community. Now, along with the others, another person begins to tell the pastor and officers that, more than anything else, we need to begin ministries to the poor, the elderly, the disabled, and the refugees. Pity the poor pastor!

The problem is that the church is a living thing, and like all living things, its growth must be fully orbed, symmetrical. A child, for example, must grow in all parts of his body, in the head, the upper, and the lower body. If *all* the organs do not mature and grow, *none* of them can. In the same way, a local church must be growing in all aspects of its life. We have already shown how mercy and evangelism must go hand in hand, but we must also recognize that mercy interlocks with all other aspects of the church.

Individual and Corporate Growth

The church must grow in the spiritual maturity of its individuals. Members must be growing in grace and the knowledge of God (2 Peter 3:18), in Christian character and maturity (Gal. 5:22–24; Eph. 4:11–14). Christians must be filled with the Spirit, both for growth in holiness (Eph. 5:18–21) and for assurance and boldness in witness (Acts 4:23–31; Rom. 8:1–5). We have said repeatedly that Christians cannot be goaded into mercy ministry through guilt. Rather, believers must be exposed to biblical teaching on mercy by experiencing the grace

2. I am indebted in this section to the vision of Orlando Costas, "A Wholistic Concept of Church Growth," in *Exploring Church Growth*, ed. Wilbert Shenk (Grand Rapids: Eerdmans, 1983), 95–107.

and love of God daily in personal communion with him. *Then*, mercy ministry grows naturally.

A church must also grow "corporately." By this term we refer to the maturation of the internal structure, fellowship, and relationships within the body. A congregation is not simply a collection of people; it is a *corpus*, a body, with organic systems of relationships. "From him the whole body . . . builds itself up in love, as each part does its work" (Eph. 4:16). Corporate growth includes the maturity of the leadership (James 5:14; 1 Tim. 3; 1 Peter 5:1–5), the informal and formal pattern of church discipline (Matt. 5:23; 18:15), the mutual ministry to one another through spiritual gifts (1 Cor. 14:4–12), and the mutual accountability for our experience and service toward God (Heb. 3:13; 10:24–25; James 5:16). Mercy ministry within the body of Christ can only be done properly as an expression of this mutual ministry, this communion of saints. And mercy ministry toward the community by an individual is extremely difficult without the support and help of our brothers and sisters.

Numerical and Diaconal Growth

In addition, a church must grow "numerically." By this we mean the increase in membership resulting from a commitment to evangelism. It is clear that biblical evangelism is very church-centered. The goal is not individual "decisions," but active, functioning members of the body of Christ. "The Lord added [to the church] daily those who were being saved" (Acts 2:47). As individuals grow in Christlikeness, they will grow in Christ's passion for the lost, and a steady stream of new converts will enter the church. We have explored at some length how critical it is that our mercy ministry be carefully, inseparably wed to the proclamation of the gospel. It must *not* become simply an expression of humanitarian sentiment. It must be a deliberate effort to demonstrate the power of the kingdom of God even as we declare the way of entrance into the kingdom, namely, through repentance and faith (Mark 1:15).

Finally, each church must grow "diaconally" in its life of service. By our loving actions and deed ministry, the word of the kingdom becomes visible. The church must mature in *dikaioma* (the doing of justice, 1 Thess. 2:10; Titus 2:12), in *eleos* (the doing of mercy, Luke 10:37; James 2:14–17), and in *diakonia*. It must find scriptural ways to bring kingly justice and relief to the poor, the broken, the outcasts, and the oppressed. Diaconal ministry becomes "mature" as a church discerns the nature of the needs in the area, and the kinds of gifts and resources Christ has put within the congregation.

Growing Together

So we see how shortsighted it is simply to "paste" ambitious mercy programs onto a church that is not growing in these various dimensions. *Instead, mercy ministry must grow at the pace of the church.* A single effective mercy ministry, carried out by a few committed volunteers, can greatly stimulate spiritual, corporate, and evangelistic growth in the church. But then, be careful of running too far ahead of the congregation! Wait for them to catch up a bit, and then plow ahead with further ministries that can continue to stimulate the life of the church.

In other situations, mercy ministry can grow in the wake of the progress of one of the other dimensions. For example, your church may have developed an effective evangelistic visitation program that is encouraging everyone. But is anyone following up *diaconally* on those visited who seem to have economic, physical, and other basic human needs? Or perhaps the church is finding a program of small groups is blessing everyone spiritually. Propose to one of the most mature groups the possibility of doing mercy ministry as an outreach of the group. The spiritual "momentum" in that group of people can be both harnessed for and enhanced by mercy ministry.

Actually, it is quite difficult to mount mercy ministries that have staying power unless your church is evangelistically vital and growing. Why? First, new Christians are natural workers in mercy ministry. Mercy workers do not usually need years of training in the Bible. Young believers, with all of their enthusiasm, can pitch in immediately, and see their gifts and abilities used right away. Also, mercy ministry is difficult. Volunteers need periods of rest from the duties of mercy. If there are not enough workers so that responsibilities can be rotated, it is difficult to maintain mercy ministries over long periods of time. Service ministries function best in a vigorously evangelistic church.

THE INTERACTION OF MERCY AND EVANGELISM

We have been saying that mercy and evangelism are inseparable partners in kingdom endeavor, but we have not said much about the actual dynamic of their interaction. *Exactly how does mercy ministry promote the growth of the church through conversions?*

Mercy as Plausibility Structure for the Lost

Mercy ministry creates a positive image for the church in the community. This may not sound like much! Yet many churches spend thousands of dollars for visibility through advertising by newspaper, radio, television, and so on. Our good deeds "glorify God before men" (see Matthew 5:16).

But we must be careful here. Mercy ministry may not make us popular with everybody! Indeed, it may make us run afoul of those who disdain some of the people we want to reach, or think that the church should stick to "preaching the gospel." Jack Miller, pastor of the New Life Presbyterian Church in Jenkintown, Pennsylvania, explains that many members of a church or community may find mercy ministry threatening. Why? He writes that people with diaconal needs "are usually not attractive, and sometimes they have fallen into their problems through their own efforts." When we look for the "noble" pure, innocent poor man, we obviously find very few. Miller continues:

> We forget good doctrine when we think this way . . . when we go out to serve others, we will often find ourselves taken advantage of. It's unavoidable. Yet when we remember what a great pit *we* were pulled from by the Head of the Church, and what it cost the King in His self-sacrifice, we will be rebuked, humbled, and given persistence to pull others from the same pit. . . . This is the supreme cause of *diaconal blindness* in the local church. We have forgotten how great our own sins are, and feel, perhaps unconsciously, superior to the

"unwashed" sinners around us. . . . We commit our worst sin when we judge others in this way.[3]

Those with "diaconal blindness," especially non-Christian pillars of the community, may find your mercy ministry unpopular.

But generally, the ministry of mercy is a dynamic witness to those with whom you share the gospel, because it builds a "plausibility structure" for our message. Most Christians in evangelism seek only to make the gospel credible, to make it cogent and persuasive intellectually. But people believe in a message mostly for nonrational reasons. A belief appears convincing to the degree that it is supported by a consistent, loving group or community. The mercy ministry of Christians provides tremendous social and psychological support for the validity of the gospel.[4] Thus the economic sharing of the early church lent power to the apostles' preaching (Acts 4:32–33), and thus Jesus teaches that visible love among Christians will convince unbelievers of the truth (John 17:21).

The ministry of mercy, then, is the best advertising a church can have. It convinces a community that *this* church provides people with action for their problems, not only talk. It shows the community that *this* church is compassionate.

Mercy as Bridge Building to the Lost

The second way that mercy or "felt-need" ministries promote church growth is that they bring the church into contact with many non-Christians that it would not otherwise meet. Lots of churches have subscribed to excellent programs that train laypeople in visitation evangelism. But almost immediately after beginning this training, a problem appears—the church does not have enough prospects to visit. The church does not know many non-Christians. Felt-need ministries will change that.

Frank Tillapaugh in his teaching often divides all the non-Christians of the world into four groups. Each group has a particular

3. C. John Miller, *Outgrowing the Ingrown Church* (Grand Rapids: Zondervan, 1986), 156.
4. See Os Guinness, *The Gravedigger File* (Downers Grove, IL: Inter Varsity Press, 1983), 33–36. See also Peter Berger and Thomas Luckman, *The Social Construction of Reality* (Harmondsworth, UK: Penguin, 1967), 174ff.

relationship to your local church. First there are the "churchy" unbe-lievers. These are non-Christians who think they are Christians or who are at least religious and active in a church. How do you reach them? By advertising, by building a church building where they can see it, or by contacting new residents who will be shopping for a church. The second group is "webbed" unbelievers. These are unbelievers who are not church members or attenders, but who live in the neighbor-hoods, workplaces, family networks, or friendship networks of your church's members. Ordinarily this means they are people of the same race and economic standing. How do you reach this group? Through friendship and visitation evangelism, or through home Bible studies in the neighborhood or other similar outreach events such as prayer breakfasts, and so on. The third group of unbelievers are the "distant" non-Christians. These are people who live in other countries or areas of the country and world. How do you reach out to them? Through missions and church planting.

Finally, there are the "unwebbed" unbelievers. These are the *major-ity* of the non-Christians in your community; they are the people who are not in your members' webs of relationships. Who are these folk? They may be found among many kinds of people groups in your community: for example, international students, blue-collar ethnic Catholics, His-panic unwed mothers, black high school dropouts, Cambodians, fashion models, artists, professional musicians, homosexuals, Jewish people, the very rich, and prostitutes. In addition, the "unwebbed" include many people who are like your own members culturally but are alienated from the church. J. Russell Hale has identified many kinds of unchurched, including the "the locked out" (those like the divorce or alcoholic who feel condemned by the church), "the publicans" (those who see the church as full of hypocrites, uncaring and selfish), "the happy hedonists" (those who are only concerned with their own needs).[5] How do we reach the "unwebbed"? We reach them *through felt-need ministries*. There is no other point of contact for them. There is no other way to win the atten-tion of the locked out, the publicans.

5. J. Russell Hale, *Who Are the Unchurched? An Exploratory Study* (Washington: Glenmary Research Center, 1977).

When we stand back and look at these four groups of non-Christians as they relate to your church, we can quickly see that virtually all the evangelistic tools and effort we use ignores th "unwebbed" nonbeliever. Most churches make some effort to win groups 3 (missions) and 1 (the churchy non-Christians). Most traditional outreach programs are oriented to those two bodies of people. During the last few years, however, a great deal of new interest has been shown in "friendship" or "lifestyle" or *oikos* evangelism. Many books and training programs now urge Christians to identify non-Christians in their web of relationships and to begin to witness to them. This is a very positive development, for laypeople are being encouraged not to rely only on preaching evangelism and advertising for church growth, but also on every-member-witness to neighbors, friends, and family.

So we see that some churches reach out to groups 1 and 3, while a few churches reach out also to group 2. But how many churches truly go into "Jerusalem . . . Samaria, and unto the uttermost parts of the earth" (Acts 1:8 KJV)? How many churches include in their outreach our group 4, the "unwebbed" non-Christians, the *truly* unchurched majority in any town or community? How many models and books help us to do this kind of evangelism? Very few.

Our main point is this: the "unwebbed" are mainly reached through felt-need ministries. Such ministries become virtually the only "bridge" between your church and the lives of these people. For example, singles and divorced single parents are largely alienated from the church. How will you reach them? You could offer divorce recovery workshops, social groups, counseling, childcare, and diaconal services that find and help them. International students may be reached by English-as-a-second-language classes. Black high school dropouts could be reached through an adult literacy course or GED class. Many blue collar ethnics could be reached through a drug or alcohol abuse rehabilitation program, while Cambodians would be reached through a resettlement ministry.

Mercy as Communication Medium to the Lost

The third way mercy ministry promotes church growth is by serving as a highly effective communication channel for the gospel. Mercy is not simply a "bridge," a way to meet people with whom we can then proclaim the gospel. It actually is a communication of the gospel along with our words. It is a visual aid, a nonverbal medium message. A person communicates meaning most effectively when using verbal and nonverbal (tone of voice, facial expression, gestures) means. So, too, we communicate the gospel most effectively when we are both speaking and doing.

A key to effective communication is arresting a person's attention. Attention is "the psychological process of selecting only a portion of the available stimuli to focus on while ignoring, suppressing, or inhibiting reactions to a host of other stimuli."[6] That, of course, is our goal in evangelism. We want the person to focus on the gospel while ignoring the "host" of other opinions, worldviews, pastimes, and activities competing for his loyalty and attention.

Studies have shown that there are a number of factors that arrest a person's attention. Four of these factors are "vitality," "reality," "familiarity," and "novelty."[7] Evangelicals have used novelty in the past to gain attention, but these efforts have often degenerated into gimmickry. But the other three factors of attention should be looked at more closely.

By "vitality," communication experts mean that an audience "pays attention to those things which vitally, directly, and immediately affect their lives or health, their reputations, property, or employment."[8] The "familiar" holds a listener's attention when it is introduced in relation to something new or unfamiliar. For example, when teaching a church of farmers about a difficult theological doctrine, it is attention-holding to use illustrations about planting and harvesting. The "reality" factor simply means that attention is more sharply focused as more senses are engaged. For example, holding up a picture of a cat while describing it verbally will hold more attention than simply the verbal description. Holding up a real cat will rivet attention even more.

Therefore, deeds of mercy, the ministry to felt needs, is an absolutely critical component in our communication of the gospel. Deed ministry

6. Floyd L. Ruch and Philip G. Zimbardo, *Psychology and Life,* 8th ed. (Glenview, IL: Scott, Foresman, 1971), 267.

7. Douglas Ehninger, Alan H. Monroe, Bruce E. Gronbeck, *Principles and Types of Speech Communication* (Glenview, IL: Scott, Foresman, 1978), 132–35.

8. Ibid., 135.

gets attention. It relates to felt needs, so it has the "vitality" factor; it adapts in a focused way to the needs of a particular group of people, so it has the "familiarity" factor; and it is action, not just talk, so it has the "reality" factor. The need for the church to gain the attention of the world has never been more critical. Americans are bombarded with more mail, more commercials, more competing claims, more options than ever before.

The God of the Bible, not modern communication theory, is our paradigm. It was God who adapted his communication to the Israelites (Ex. 19:18ff.). Rather than speaking directly to them, he spoke through Moses. This was only a type of his ultimate communication to us. The Word became flesh so that we could not only hear but see the truth (John 1:14; 2 Peter 1:16–17). So too the ministry of mercy "fleshes out" the truth.

SIDE DOORS AND FRONT DOORS

We have said that modern evangelicalism has developed few models that help churches to reach out except to the "churchy" non-Christians. The "webbed" and especially the "unwebbed" non-Christian must be reached through felt-need ministries.

Centripetal and Centrifugal

R. Daniel Reeves recognizes two basic categories of outreach structure that a church can have.[9] A "front-door" church has centripetal force, drawing non-Christians in by attraction. In a front-door church, the main emphasis is on programs and methods of getting non-Christians to come to worship services. It is after they come that evangelism, follow-up, and nurture can occur.

A "side-door" church, however, has centrifugal force, sending its members out to contact the non-Christians in the community through various ministries. The unbeliever is ministered to and (often) evangelized outside the church services, and only later does the prospect come into the church services for further evangelism and/or nurture and follow-up.

9. R. Daniel Reeves and Don Jenson, *Always Advancing: Modern Strategies for Church Growth* (San Bernardino, CA: Here's Life, 1984), 67–88.

Side-door ministries are characterized by orientation to "felt needs," meeting physical, social, educational, and emotional needs, and by a focus on reaching a particular people group through communicating the gospel in word and deed. Many side-door ministries (such as outreach to Jewish people, homosexuals, and so on) are more strictly evangelistic, working to communicate and counsel with non-Christians. Others (such as support groups for cancer victims, tutoring poor people, crisis pregnancy counseling) blend social concern and evangelism, with many Christians being aided both inside and outside the church. Nevertheless, side doors focus on outreach. A singles' ministry and even a senior adult ministry can be considered side-door ministries.

Fishing Ponds

Reeves observes that front-door churches draw prospects largely through certain "fishing" methods. Front-door methods include the following:

"High-visibility events" are designed to interest target groups (concerts, well-known speakers, a highly publicized preacher, etc.). The location and appearance of a visible, attractive church building itself is important.

Church shopper outreach is done by advertising, telephone surveys, direct mail, and survey visitation.

Word-of-mouth outreach is critical as well. It occurs when "satisfied customers" talk up their church. General reputation attracts people, even out of curiosity. The larger a church gets, the more a "front door" (a reputation) develops.

"Andrew invitations" are the backbone of a front-door church's growth. The main source of church visitors comes as members bring friends and relatives to church. (This is not so much actual friendship ["Philip"] evangelism but invitation ["Andrew"] evangelism. These visitors, then are carefully followed up and evangelized by a well-trained visitation team or through some other such system.)

What, then, are side-door methods of "fishing"? There are basically three. Reeves considers felt-need programs to be a prominent side door. These activities meet specific conscious needs of a non-Christian target group. "Community-classics," large-group meetings outside of the church building, are another side door. While geared and contextualized to a particular type of person, these meetings do not meet felt needs directly, but instead there is a direct communication of the gospel. Examples are businessmen's breakfasts and luncheons, neighborhood evangelistic Bible studies, block parties with an evangelistic talk (or movie), retreats for singles, teens, etc. Finally, friendship evangelism is a side door. It can be planned (as when laypersons, trained in lifestyle evangelism lead people to Christ in their regular living patterns) or planned (as when a group of members identify and pray for a "web" of non-Christian friends, neighbors, and relatives).

Dangers

Reeves states that the majority of growing churches are front-door churches.[10] Why? Front-door churches work well where a community is growing rapidly and (therefore) is homogeneous, upwardly mobile, and full of new residents. Generally, front-door growth seems to go faster because it does not require a lot of skills on the part of laypeople. It tends to reach people who are close in background, thinking, and culture to the Christians within, and therefore programs can be more centralized and easier to control.

But there are great dangers with the front-door approach. It usually demands a "pastor superstar" model on the part of the minister; there is great pressure to be highly attractive and dynamic. In general, the church must promote itself, virtually "marketing" and manufacturing a glossy image. Along with the overdependence on image comes an underdependence on the ministry of the laity. It encourages lay passivity and even superficial Christian commitment. Often a closer examination of the growth of front-door churches reveals that (while rapid), it is comprised largely of transfer growth. In addition, Reeves notes that front-door churches are prone to traditionalism and slowness to change.

The most basic critique of the front-door church is that it tends to concentrate almost exclusively on just two groups of non-Christians, the

10. Ibid., 72.

"churchy" (group 1) and the "distant" (group 3). It does not deeply penetrate the non-churched culture. In urban settings, front-door churches tend mainly to attract suburbanites to come downtown, but they do not reach the highly diverse communities and cultures surrounding them. Most front-door churches do well in newer residential areas, but as the community ages and becomes more diverse, these churches have difficulty adapting.

A Multi-Entry Church

Up to now we have spoken of front- and side-door churches as if they are the only two options. We want to use this discussion to press home that churches must be "multi-entry" churches, with both front and side doors. Most pastors do not have the personal dynamism necessary for a front-door church. (But many are overwhelmed with guilt when they read about men who have grown a front-door church rapidly through their personal charisma!) Generally, multi-entry churches can reach out to *all* kinds of non-Christians, including group 4 (the "unwebbed"). Multi-entry churches put more responsibility on the laypeople to minister; they tend to be less culture-blind than front-door churches. While suburban churches may sponsor a few side-door ministries, urban churches should major in them.

What, though, are the difficulties of side-door ministries? Side doors reach a greater diversity of people, and thus the congregation becomes much less homogeneous and less easy to manage. There are different interests and needs and values being expressed. As a result, the internal structure of the church must be far more complex than in a front-door church. To assimilate and incorporate different types of people will take a variety of different small groups, classes, even subcongregations and separate worship services. Side-door ministries usually are harder to coordinate. They take place out in the community, usually outside of the church building, and they are less under the oversight of the pastoral staff. As a result, coordination and supervision can become quite a headache. The new Christians won through side-door ministries may take longer to shed old beliefs and problems. Nurture entails more counseling and instruction and thus consumes more time.

Now it becomes clear why some churches shy away from side doors and prefer the old standard front-door outreach methods. As Miller wrote, we prefer to win people without too many problems, who appear stable and happy and well-adjusted, who can immediately begin serving and giving to the church.

WORD AND DEED IN PRACTICE

We have seen that mercy supports and promotes church growth, and that mercy ministries are "side doors" that can reach new groups of people for Christ. How then can we methodologically set up our church so mercy and evangelism truly do work together and are partners in the church's mission?

Understanding the People

Begin your strategy planning by drawing up a "spiritual profile" of the people group you are trying to reach. In chapter 9 we provided a series of questions for this purpose. Discern their physical, social, emotional, cognitive, moral needs. Reflect on their hopes, values, worldview, and lifestyle. Be sure that you build a strategy that treats these folk as whole people, needing a variety of word and deed ministries.

When you begin to develop your outreach structure, you are setting up a "pathway" into your church, and each pathway must have four components: a "finding" strategy, a "deed" strategy, a "word" strategy, and an "incorporation" strategy.[11]

Finding Strategy

How will you actually meet and contact the people you are seeking to reach? How will you let them know you can serve them?

To find "webbed" nonbelievers, use your own people. Your members have basic web networks of relationships: biological (your family and

---

11. C. Peter Wagner has spoken of three of these strategies as "presence evangelism," "proclamation evangelism," and "persuasion evangelism." He tends to separate these three, and I do not agree with the term "persuasion" for the final type of evangelism. Nevertheless, this is a helpful set of categories. See his *Body Evangelism* (Pasadena, CA: Fuller Evangelistic Association, 1976).

relatives); geographical (your neighbors); vocational (your coworkers); and recreational (your friends met through the other networks). Different settings and people groups can be reached through different webs. For example, in an urban area, the geographical web can be used to find the needy, but this is not as true in the suburbs. At this point, we must not miss the challenge of John Perkins to "relocate." Many middle-class people must put forth great effort to find the hurting because we have chosen to live as far removed from human need as we can!

When it comes to reaching the "unwebbed," there are numerous ideas which we have offered earlier in the book for "building bridges." When surveying the community, you should have found quite a number of social workers, civic officials, businessmen, professionals, teachers, and others through whom you can contact the folk you are seeking.

Find the communication channel through which promotion can best reach them. Is it a newspaper? Word of mouth? A relationship? Another institution?

Deed strategy. This is the ministry to meet the felt needs. We have offered scores of examples throughout this book.

Word strategy. To every deed ministry, a church must affix a means by which the recipients of ministry will be exposed to a verbal presentation of the gospel. Persons contacted through diaconal and mercy ministries will generally be far more receptive to your church than people who have been contacted "cold" through advertising or visitation. You have already shown them compassion. Word strategies can include visitation by lay evangelists, evangelistic literature distribution, evangelistic public teaching or speaking at worship or at other sites, evangelistic meals where testimonies are shared, evangelistic Bible studies, and small groups.

There must be great sensitivity here, of course. It is not enough to stick gospel tracts in the food basket given at Thanksgiving! Nor should the recipients of aid feel that they must endure some "sales pitch" to get help. But, on the other hand, it is not right (in the name of sensitivity) to make no conscious, structured effort to share the gospel routinely with those who get aid.

For relief programs, it may be necessary to link up with existing evangelism programs. For example, a record of everyone who is given aid could be carefully kept, and each recipient would be visited by the evangelism visitation team from your church. With development programs, a presentation of gospel truth can be woven into the ministry itself in a much more organic, natural way. Those in a job training program, for example, would be exposed to the Christian understanding of work and to the gospel. No matter how it is done, *a word strategy must be affixed or woven into any deed strategy.*

It is not even enough to attach a gospel presentation to a ministry of mercy. On the basis of your understanding of a person's hopes, values, worldview, and lifestyle, the gospel message must be "contextualized," adapted to the language and capacities of the man or woman you are aiding.

Incorporation strategy. "Incorporation" is the means by which a new believer is made to feel part of a church family, developing friendship ties and becoming involved and active. It is extremely common for churches to set up side-door ministries without thinking: "How will we disciple and incorporate new Christians from this ministry into the church?" Side-door ministries face us with some interesting issues when it comes to assimilating converts into our church. On the one hand, persons won to Christ in side-door ministries already have friends in the church, and they are already "indebted" to the church (unlike the typical visitor through a front-door outreach). They even may already be part of a small group of your church before they begin coming to worship. That is a great aid in making the new believer feel like part of the church. General incorporation strategies can include assigning a member family to be a "sponsor," membership classes, involvement in a small group, involvement in a class or fellowship circle, and so on.

On the other hand, side-door ministries create major assimilation difficulties that front-door ministries do not. Many of the people reached through felt-need ministries are culturally different from the majority of your members. For example, a mercy ministry that reaches many poor black and Hispanic persons will discover that their new converts find the white, upper-middle-class worship services boring and the preaching incomprehensible. Or a ministry to drug abusers that wins some homosexuals and prostitutes will discover that their new converts feel extremely uncomfortable around such respectable looking "solid citizens." What does such a ministry do?

There are two choices. The first option is for the church to recognize that it must "make room" inside the congregation for the new people. It could be that special small groups, Sunday school classes, or other kinds of subcongregational life must be allowed for the people coming in. At Bear Valley Baptist, for example, they began a separate worship service for many of the "street people" they were reaching (runaways, alcoholics, prostitutes, homeless, etc.). This service is characterized by informality, contemporary music, and emotional spontaneity, very different from the traditional worship style, which reflects the American middle class's distaste for unpredictability and public displays of emotion. Most churches are quite unconscious about such matters. They say that "our doors are open to anyone," yet they fail to see that their style of communication, of worship, of education, of fellowship, and of leadership are rather focused to match one small cultural group. When a church begins to open "side-door" pathways into its congregation it will be forced to confront the need to make room structurally and culturally for a diversity of folk.

The other option is for the church to consciously, carefully, and constantly channel new converts into churches which *can* incorporate them into a body of believers. For example, if a church's outreach to unwed mothers is meeting the needs of many Spanish-speaking young women, what should it do? If it does not opt for the first basic assimilation method (e.g., to begin a Spanish-speaking worship service) then the church must be sure that there is a "word strategy" and an "incorporation strategy" designed to link the girls with a Spanish-speaking evangelical church. The link may be having the Hispanic pastor becoming involved as a part-time counselor at your church's crisis pregnancy center. Whatever the link, it must be well planned and intentional, not informal and unreliable.

When a church surveys all the felt needs and target groups of unreached people, it addresses a vast array that no single congregation can master. When choosing target groups to minister to, a church must strike a very difficult and subtle balance. On the one hand, it must beware of only reaching out to those groups that will be easy to assimilate ("people like us"). Selfishness and prejudice (and plain laziness!) may lurk behind that approach. On the other hand, it would be unwise not to reach out after some groups that could "fit" more easily in your church. It is true that it will be more difficult to win and then disciple people into another congregation.

Relating the Strategies

Be sure that all the various strategies "dovetail" to address the person holistically.

For example, you may wish to advertise publicly a "Divorce Recovery Workshop" as a felt-need ministry. But what happens if, through the effectiveness of this ministry, suddenly a large number of recently divorced single mothers begin to come to your church? Are you ready?

You should have ministries in each "need area." The women will need counseling for bitterness and depression by someone who understands the common emotional problems of women in the wake of divorce. The women will also probably need economic help, since most women keep their children but do not have the income-producing skills their husbands had. Financial help to return to school plus short-term emergency aid for the transition will be necessary.

It is also important to realize that the single mother will need support in her parenting. She may profit from another family "adopting" hers, giving her some welcome relief and encouragement and (perhaps) a male role model for her sons. Last, "flexible room" must be found within the church for these ladies. Some will not feel at home either in a married couples class or a group of younger, never-married singles. Other divorced women will not want to be in a group full of other divorced people. Your church must be prepared, in its infrastructure and group life, to provide live options to them to fold them into the body.

What a challenge! Perhaps there will be a need for a "task force" that ministers to all the economic, emotional, and social needs of this group of people. Most churches simply have a "they can come to us" fortress mentality, and so the exploding divorced population remains unreached. But if a church was to reach out in word and deed to them, based on a careful spiritual profile, the potential for harvest is enormous.

CONCLUSION

Now see the possibilities! There are thousands and thousands of unreached people groups all around the American churches. Yes, even in the suburbs. And each group requires careful strategy of outreach combining word and deed. When will we follow our Lord and make the word of the gospel *visible* through deeds of mercy and justice?

FOR DISCUSSION

1. In what ways does the recipient of mercy need to be seen holistically? How does the church need to be seen holistically?
2. What kind of spiritual growth do you need to see in yourself as you contemplate undertaking a mercy ministry? How can you also pray for growth in your church?
3. How can mercy ministries foster numerical growth of a congregation?
4. Describe a front-door church. A side-door church. Characterize your church according to these two types.
5. What are ways that you personally can meet needy people?

14

Meeting Needs

OVERVIEW: When helping a needy family, adjust your expectations by determining whether they are "broke" or poor. Identify all problems and dependencies and outline a ministry plan which addresses them. Let only mercy limit mercy.

It remains for us to lay down some basic guidelines for actually meeting needs in mercy ministry. Exactly how do we help a family that has physical, economic, emotional and social needs?

PRINCIPLES

When helping a needy family or person, several basic "rules of thumb" can guide us. Each of them grows out of the biblical principles covered in chapters 5–7.

Distinguish between Simple Poverty and Deeper Poverty

There is a difference between being "broke" and being poor. A need may come upon a family who has been somewhat self-sufficient. A physical disability, a marital breakup, natural disaster, or unexpected unemployment—any of these can bring sudden economic hardship. On the other hand, there are people and families who have lived in poverty for years. Some have spoken of a "culture" of poverty, in which poverty becomes a way of life that can even be passed from one generation to the next. The poor man may be poorly educated, cynical and distrustful of authority, preoccupied with the present, with no concept of "savings" or economic planning (in fact, no concept of planning or goals at all). There may be poverty-related habit patterns—addictions and crime, for example. Another way to distinguish between these two kinds of poverty is to remember the three causes of poverty that we examined earlier: oppression, calamity, and personal sin. The person who is "broke" usually has been brought into that condition by one of these causes. It is fairly easy to help him, therefore. For example:

> A young woman, age twenty-eight, had recently separated from her husband, who has fled to a state where he cannot be forced to support his wife and three children. The woman had recently had surgery and has sold her home to meet expenses, but she is still in need of funds.

But the person who is "poor" is usually in his condition because of a complicated, tangled interaction of all three conditions. An example:

> The husband is thirty-seven and the wife is thirty-six. They both work at minimum wage jobs to care for their six children (the oldest is nineteen and lives at home, unmarried, with her own baby). Both parents have only a fourth grade education. The mother and the oldest daughter have a drug habit, and the father abuses alcohol. Currently one of the children has a number of serious medical needs, but the family has no medical insurance.

Obviously, helping such a person will take far more time, wisdom, resources, and patience. The minister of mercy must understand the difference between the "broke" and the "poor" person, so expectations are in line with reality.

Begin with Few "Strings," but Add Conditions as Time Passes

In a previous chapter we discussed the biblical issues of "conditionally" of mercy. Should we say to a needy person, "we will help you *if*...."? Some churches insist that the needy person be a mature church member to be helped, while other churches give aid without any accountability at all. The best answer to this question is to recall the paradigm for all mercy ministry—the grace of God.

Grace is not *unconditional* acceptance, but it is *undeserved*. That is a very difficult balance to strike! God's grace comes to us *without prerequisites, finding us as we are*. God's grace does not come to the "deserving" (there is no such person), and it does not discriminate. Rather, initially it comes to us freely. But once it enters into our lives, God's grace demands changes; it holds us accountable. Why? Grace demands our holiness and growth *for our sake as well as for God's glory*. Grace intercepts destructive behavior, protects us from the ravages of sin, sanctifies us so we can be "holy and happy," two inseparable qualities.

In summary, grace is undeserved caring that intercepts destructive behavior. It is not unconditional acceptance, nor is it a legalism that says, "Shape up or I will stop loving you." Rather, it says, "Your sin cannot separate you from me," and then, in addition, says, "I won't let your sin destroy you." Grace comes to the unlovely person, but refuses to let him remain ugly. Grace begins as "justification," a free act of God alone, but it becomes "sanctification," a process by which the person cooperates with God in spiritual growth.[1]

This concept can be applied to many areas. In child-rearing books there is much talk about "striking a balance between love and discipline," as if the two were opposed. But this false tension is resolved with an understanding of grace. Grace means getting involved, protecting the child from destructive behavior, continuing to do that despite the child's lack of "deserving," and doing so consistently, not sloppily or haltingly.

It should be obvious how this applies to our work with the needy. Neither the "liberal" approach (no conditions on aid to the needy) nor the "conservative" approach (only help the deserving poor) understands *grace*. Instead, our mercy ministry must help people freely, yet aim to bring their whole lives under the healing lordship of Christ. Mercy is *kingdom endeavor*.

The "grace" principle works itself out in two helpful practices for dealing with a person in need.

---

1. Much of this material I owe to an unpublished sermon by David Powlison of the Christian Counseling and Educational Foundation, Laverock, Pennsylvania.

1. *Request entrance into the whole life.* In the very first contact with an applicant for aid, it is important to give aid with few conditions or "strings" as long as it is certain there is a legitimate need. Pay the rent or the utility bill; provide the food, shelter, or friendship. However, if the applicant returns, soon you must say, "If we are going to continue to help, you must be willing to *let us into your life.* You may have other needs that are keeping you in this economic fix. We want to look at your income, living expenses, and other problems. We are not doing this to be nosy, but we really want to help you for the long run. So we need to look at your whole life."

Many people will refuse to enter into such a ministry relationship, and so they remove themselves from consideration. But others will let you in. Then you can assess their financial management skills, family nurture skills, and so on. You may aid them provided they receive counseling, get vocational training, or do other developmental tasks. Accountability grows as responsibility grows.

2. *Let mercy limit mercy.* The second basic guideline has also been mentioned in a previous chapter: When, if ever, do you cut off aid to a needy person? There are many false motivations for terminating aid. Some Christians stop the flow of service out of revenge, after a needy person has acted irresponsibly or dishonestly. Or sometimes the flow may stop out of defensiveness; "I just can't take it! We can't afford it." But there is only one legitimate motivation. When the person in need is acting irresponsibly, and your continued aid would only shield him from the consequences of his own behavior, then it is no longer loving or merciful to continue support. Let mercy limit mercy. You will find, when this is your motive, the termination of aid can have some sobering effects on the recipient of aid. He or she may see your spirit is one of concern and compassion—tough compassion.

There is no way to draw an exact line where aid must end. If the individual has a family, you should probably not cut him or her off if it will hurt them. If there is more repentance and there has been some progress, be extremely patient. Take each case on its own and make the judgment. But in any case, if you must cut off aid temporarily, say:

"We are not *withdrawing* our mercy, only changing its form! Just like a doctor sometimes has to cut you to heal you, we are doing this out of concern for you."

Ask God to give you mercy so that you don't do this from a judgmental stance. We are all needy of God's mercy!

Set Priorities in Helping Both the Believer and the Unbeliever

We have also studied this question in some detail in a previous chapter. Galatians 6:10 indicates that we should set priorities. We should bring greater resources and energy to bear on the needs of Christians, fellow members of the covenant community. Mercy, after all, is one blessing and form of fellowship, the *koinonia* or sharing of life among believers. We are one body, and ultimately, we can call none of our possessions our own (Acts 4:32).

We are also to help "all people" (Gal. 6:10) as well. Mercy to the nonbeliever is a form of gospel communication. Mercy shall go as indiscriminately to the people of the world as does the verbal proclamation of the gospel. We are to aid the stranger and sojourner, even our enemy if he has a need (Luke 6:32ff.; 10:27–35).

But because of this priority scale, repeated denial and hostility to the gospel will affect our ministry to a needy person. We have seen that Jesus' miracles comprised his ministry of mercy as King, and we must remember that he called to repentance and faith those whom he healed (Mark 2:5; John 5:14). "Sin no more," he said, *after* he had given divine medical help to the crippled man. Notice, he did not make repentance a condition for giving his aid, yet he subsequently pressed his kingdom claims.

The ministry of mercy calls people to repent and to acknowledge the king—sometimes that message is explicit in our mercy, but it is always implicit. Ultimately, mercy is withdrawn from those who repeatedly reject the King. Jesus worked few miracles (not *no* miracles) in Nazareth because of their unbelief (Matt. 13:58). In the same way, the ministry of verbal proclamation should not be indefinitely prolonged (Matt. 7:6; 10:14).[2]

2. See "Biblical Guidelines for Mercy Ministry in the PCA," in *Minutes of the Fifteenth General Assembly* (General Assembly of the Presbyterian Church in America [1987]), 506ff.

This means that a recipient of aid who does not respond to the gospel will have less and less claim on the resources of the church. A steadfast rejection or expression of hostility to the gospel ordinarily means that the person will not give Christians the kind of access necessary to continue to develop the person economically and personally. In other words, they will not let us truly into their lives. At some point, rejection and hostility will mean that, in mercy (see above), we must terminate our mercy.

These are the basic principles. What follows is a suggested outline for actually sitting down with a family in need.

PRACTICE

Investigate the Need

First listen. Encourage the person to talk and share problems and pain. Then actively probe. Find out how long the problem has existed, what the person has done about it, what has helped it, what has aggravated it, what threat or pressure the person feels most in the situation.

What are the *basic causes* of the need? Remember, the basic causes of poverty are injustice (sinful, unjust treatment by an employer, a landlord, etc.), calamity (sickness, an accident, etc.), and sin (poor judgment, laziness, or a lack of self-control, etc.). Which ones are present?

What is the *exact extent* of the current financial need? To find that, evaluate total income and assets, and then the total expenses, liabilities, and debts.

What is the spiritual condition and church status of the family?

What *subproblems* are present?[3] When you first meet a needy person, the problem is often an inability to pay some major bill (rent, utilities) or inability to afford the expense of some basic need (food, shelter, medical treatment). The problem is an immediate lack of money—usually an easily determined specific dollar amount. However, it is quite shortsighted to look simply at this presenting problem. The problem usually can be broken down into one of several "subproblems" that are

---

3. Much of this material derives from the extremely helpful training guide: John Guetter, *Service to Families: Problem-Solving Skills in Diaconal Outreach* (Kalamazoo, Mich.: Christian Reformed World Relief Committee, 1981).

the immediate antecedents of financial crises. They are the patterns of living that often help create the financial shortfalls. Any one or combination of the following subproblems may be present.

Identify Dependencies

1. *Financial dependence.* That is, the person may be unemployed or underemployed. "Financial dependence" is defined as being in a condition in which income is simply insufficient to meet basic expenses. In most cases, the financial dependence is linked to one of the following subproblems. However, it is possible that people, without any other subproblem, can find themselves out of a job or suddenly in need due to some calamity.

2. *Physical dependence.* Due to age, chronic health problems, or other disability, the person may simply not be able to be self-sufficient physically *and* this may lead to a financial dependence—the inability to generate sufficient income for needs through employment.

3. *"Planning dependence."* Some people look superficially to be financially dependent, but investigation reveals that they have serious problems with economic planning—designing and staying on a budget, discipline at liquidating debts, savings, and so on. Many variables may be part of this subproblem, including inefficient shopping skills, unrealistic priorities for spending, and a simple lack of discipline. In some cases, a family's planning skills were sufficient until a major unexpected expense was introduced, and now their limited skills in money management are overmatched.

4. *Emotional dependence.* The person may have personal problems and inabilities to function independently. Addictions, depression, uncontrolled anger, or other serious problems of self-discipline are all sufficient to keep a person in economic straits. Another major form of emotional dependence is family problems. Spouses cannot solve conflicts or nurture children; many economic problems are aggravated or caused by severe breakdowns within the home. Sometimes emotional dependence does

not consist of a particular "bad habit," but is a general attitude of fear and low confidence that keeps a person looking to others for provisions of basic needs.

5. *Skill dependence.* Some people lack some indispensable, basic skills necessary for functioning in society, and this lack has severe economic consequences. The two more important are general literacy and marketable occupational skills. People also need basic job-seeking skills and general communication skills.

6. *Relational dependence.* Most of us do not realize how important supportive relationships have been to our successful social functioning. Some people in need have few relatives or friends who can provide support and encouragement to responsible behavior. If family or friends are unsympathetic and unhelpful, a person may need more than just money or skills or information. The person needs relationships.

7. *"Social dependence."* We mean by this an unfair lack of power. A person can be in a position where he or she is being victimized and needs legal or even political help and aid.

It should be obvious that these seven problems interrelate. It is most important to notice if one subproblem is the immediate or chief cause of another.

Outline a Ministry Plan

Now return from your interview and write out a ministry plan. Begin by stating the problem in words that are specific and which define the person's responsibility. For example: "You cannot resolve conflicts on the job without anger and this has cost you your last two jobs" and "Your rent has increased fifty percent in the last year while your salary has only increased five percent." Be sure to state which subproblems are present. You will want to discuss the problem statements with the person and seek to reach an agreement on each one. Remember to treat the other person with dignity. Under each problem statement, outline both goals and forms of help.

1. *Set a goal or goals for each problem.* The goal is a specific statement of what you wish the condition to be after the problem I "solved" and when you wish it to be solved. (This way, both you and the person in need know exactly where you are headed.) Here is an example: "By September to have all bills paid except *BLANK*, and by November to have no outstanding debts."

For the financially dependent, an example of a goal would be the following: "To enable the family to become self-supporting through income through employment, for a six-month period beginning in September." For a family lacking "economic planning" skills, a goal would be this: "To enable the family to maintain all payments without delinquency for six months." For a family having major internal problems, a goal could be as follows: "To see both children go one semester without tardiness, absenteeism, or other delinquency at school."

2. *What about the forms of the help?* Each subproblem requires a different array of services. Generally, the financially dependent need emergency aid to help them make ends meet. Be sure to discover what other resources are available—other family members, friends, other helping agencies. But also we need to identify vocational aptitudes, to aid in vocational retraining, if necessary, to teach job-seeking skills, and to help them find job opportunities.

For the physically dependent, we need to secure permanent income supplements sufficient for needs and to help them achieve a healthy acceptance of their condition. For the emotionally dependent, we need to confront them in love about their dependence, to eliminate attitudes and habits that obstruct them from keeping jobs, to get them counseling for their other problems. For those who lack economic planning skills, we must help them develop a financial planning and evaluation system. For the socially dependent we must act as or secure for them legal advocates. For the relationally dependent, we must create networks of support and friends.

Always explain the motivation behind the help as their experience of the grace of God. (Ask God to help you so that this is so!) The gospel must be shared with the person at some point during the helping relationship, if the person is not a Christian, or if his/her spiritual condition is unknown to you. If the person is a Christian, a plan should be drawn up to help the individual grow in grace during this helping period, to help him or her look at suffering from a biblical perspective, and to involve the person in the worship and fellowship of the church.

As you now look at all of your goals and forms of ministry, you will begin to hyperventilate. There are so many! You must prioritize the problems. Which problem seems to be more fundamental than others? Remember your look at root causes at the beginning of the investigation. Ask the person his opinion. Decide together. Brainstorm all possible alternatives to reach the goal. Add up the pros and cons of each. Allow the person to help in choosing an alternative unless the choice is dangerous or unbiblical.

FOR DISCUSSION

1. Why is it important to distinguish whether a person is "broke" or "poor"?
2. How is the fact that "grace is not unconditional acceptance, but it is undeserved" significant to mercy ministry?
3. Are you ready to sit down with someone to find if you need to start your mercy ministry?

Recommended Reading

Chester, Tim. *Good News to the Poor: Social Involvement and the Gospel.* Wheaton, IL: Crossway, 2013. [This book is very accessible and helpful on discussing how evangelism and social concern relate to one another in a church that wants to proclaim the gospel above all. It has a good biblical, theological foundation and is also good at describing the complexity of poverty, making it one of the best all-around books treating everything from theological foundations to practical instruction for church ministry.]

Conn, Harvie. *Evangelism: Doing Justice and Preaching Grace.* Grand Rapids: Zondervan, 1982. [Writing on a popular level, the author makes a case for the complete integration of word and deed ministry in the mission of the church. Evangelism is to be linked to deeds of mercy and justice, and the book provides some practical models for doing this. While a bit dated, this continues to be a classic.]

Corbett, Steve and Brian Fikkert. *When Helping Hurts: How to Alleviate Poverty without Hurting the Poor . . . and Yourself.* Chicago: Moody, 2012. [Both this book and Bryant Myers's (below) give important practical principles for working with the poor. They are oriented not as much to "relief" or "justice" as to what is called *development*, helping the poor to self-sufficiency. Corbett-Fikkert is a more popular treatment. They are the best Christian volumes available on this subject.]

Edwards, Jonathan. *Christian Charity: or, the Duty of Charity of the Poor, Explained and Enforced.* In vol. 2 of *The Works of Jonathan Edwards.* Edinburgh: Banner of Truth, 1974, pp. 163–73. [Though not easy reading, this work uses many powerful biblical arguments to eliminate common objections and excuses that Christians produce to minimize concern for the poor. The guidelines for distinguishing among the causes of poverty have many practical implications.]

Haugen, Gary. *Good News about Injustice: A Witness of Courage in a Hurting World*. Downers Grove, IL: InterVarsity Press, 1999. [Another classic, this book is more about the biblical nature of justice and advocacy for the marginalized than mercy ministry and the relief of suffering.]

Myers, Bryant. *Walking with the Poor: Principles and Practices of Transformational Development*. 2nd ed. Maryknoll, NY: Orbis, 2011. [Both this book and Corbett-Fikkert's (above) give important practical principles for working with the poor. They are oriented not as much to "relief" or "justice" as to what is called *development*, helping the poor to self-sufficiency. Myers is a more academic treatment. They are the best Christian volumes available on this subject.]

Perkins, John. *With Justice for All*. Ventura, CA: Regal, 1982. [Perkins lays down three principles of ministry: relocation, reconciliation, and redistribution. Around these he develops a very practical model of Christian community transformation. This is a classic on living out the theological principles of word and deed.]